The Strategy of Treaty Termination

# The Strategy of

# Treaty Termination

## Lawful Breaches and Retaliations

Arie E. David

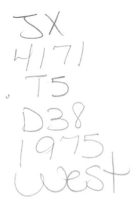
New Haven and London, Yale University Press

1975

Designed by John O. C. McCrillis
and set in Baskerville type.
Printed in the United States of America by
The Vail-Ballou Press, Inc., Binghamton, N.Y.

Published in Great Britain, Europe, and Africa by
Yale University Press, Ltd., London.
Distributed in Latin America by Kaiman & Polon,
Inc., New York City; in Australasia and Southeast
Asia by John Wiley & Sons Australasia Pty. Ltd.,
Sydney; in India by UBS Publishers' Distributors Pvt.,
Ltd., Delhi; in Japan by John Weatherhill, Inc., Tokyo.

For my friend Amos, who died in a termination conflict
we did not understand

# Contents

# Preface

Agreements between governments are always under some stress for change. Demands for change, which may be brought by parties to the agreement or by outsiders, may be for comparatively minor amendment or temporary suspension on through to total abrogation. Since treaties are among the principal instruments for making law and policy in the international arena, it should not be surprising that such demands often give rise to familiar arguments, with their concomitant differing emphases, about the necessity for continually changing laws while still maintaining their general authority. When a gap develops between the community's expectations and its formal policies, the latter, of course, must be terminated or revised, or expectations must be realigned. In national arenas, conflicts about the modification and termination of formerly authoritative arrangements are often dealt with and resolved in institutional contexts, and with a variety of constitutional guarantees. In relatively unstable and decentralized international relations, however, outmoded arrangements, when they cannot be adapted to new conditions by gradual adjustments through reinterpretation or other minor nonconforming conduct, are usually terminated or modified by the parties concerned through bargaining and similar modes of informal conflict behavior.

The most common technique of explicit treaty termination is the conclusion of a new agreement between the same parties. It is usually reached through the give-and-take of negotiations. There is no inherent difference in this respect between an agreement on termination and other types of negotiated agreements. Problems do arise, however, when the parties to an allegedly obsolete agreement cannot agree on the expediency of revising or terminating it.

In the vast number of cases in the relatively decentralized contemporary world, these claims and readjustments take place in an open arena, in which parties are constantly realigning themselves in patterns of reciprocal exchange through what often is— or seems to be—unilateral action in an atmosphere of crisis. Objecting parties usually reject the claim of "changing conditions" by invoking the presumably sacred factor of prior agreement or promise, and by exploiting the authoritative symbolic power of "treaty." Claimant parties seek to undermine the validity of the treaty by a variety of unilateral acts and faits accomplis, to which objecting parties respond by reprisals, and for which retaliations usually provide a further answer. The result of these actions is often a lateral expansion of conflict and the violation or termination of a host of prior agreements by both sides to the initial dispute.

President Grant remarked in his inaugural address after the American Civil War that he knew "no method to secure the repeal of bad or obnoxious laws so effective as their stringent execution."[1] Indeed, insistence upon outmoded laws is often fatal to the laws and may produce other harmful effects. So also, the adherence to the obligatory force of an outmoded international agreement does not secure its perpetuation. On the contrary, strict enforcement contributes to the termination of the agreement, but at the price of intervening damage. "If, though not fit to be perpetual, it has been imposed in perpetuity, the question when it becomes right to throw it off is but a question of time."[2] Where no reasonable duration is fixed in the treaty and a party continues to exact indefinite or prolonged performance, the claimant party will choose its own time for termination, and it will naturally choose the time and methods most convenient for itself. If the sole lawful means for terminating controversial international agreements were a new agreement by the parties, one party would be prevented from ever lawfully escaping a severely onerous obligation and the other party would always be encouraged to be recalcitrant. This obvious gap between law and political reality would inevitably lead to the weakening of the entire treaty institution.

These results stress the need to improve processes of treaty amendment and termination. Unfortunately, international law does not afford a well-tested body of principles designed to facilitate and

---

1. First Inaugural Address by Ulysses S. Grant, March 4, 1869, in *Inaugural Addresses of the Presidents of the United States*, H.R. Doc. No. 218, 87th Cong., 1st Sess. 129 (1961).

2. J. S. Mill, quoted in J. Brierly, *The Law of Nations* 334 (1963).

police the formally nonconsensual termination of the many types of agreements that currently govern relations among governments. To use Lauterpacht's words: "There are only a few problems of international law which have caused more embarrassment to international publicists, or which are more unsettled, than the doctrine [of changed circumstances]."[3] This embarrassment is reflected in the fact that, with the exception of a scant number of rather conventional law journal articles, no major work has been published on the subject since the 1930s.

The reasons for this neglect are numerous. To begin with, the problem of unilateral termination in modern times is monstrously complex. It involves fundamental questions of jurisprudence, policies, and empirical facts relating not only to the substantive international issues in each dispute, but also to the way governments bargain on these issues. The problem is not susceptible to traditionally neat, simple, yes-or-no legal answers. Thus, a great many writers in international law have crossed the problem of unilateral termination out of their books and marked it "no solution." They simply categorize the questions involved as being "political" rather than "legal."

Other answers to the problem of unilateral termination, especially those provided during the unstable period between the world wars, were just as ineffective. While legal theory during the 1930s gave a simple "no" answer to the question of unilateral termination, the general practice was that of considering treaties as scraps of paper. As we shall see in chapters 1 and 2, *all* the parties (not only Germany or Italy) bore the responsibility, and should have shared the blame, for this practice—scholars included. Modern writers, rather than face the problem and try to provide more effective answers, for the most part have professed disillusionment and have withdrawn to other subjects.

There are additional reasons for inattention to the subject of unilateral treaty termination. The optimism that immediately followed the end of World War II, and the harmony among the victors, produced some so-called permanent and temporary arrangements (for example, the division of Germany) that provided

3. H. Lauterpacht, *Private Law Sources and Analogies of International Law* 167 (1927).

for extensive changes. The latter, because of the great powers' accord, were believed to be capable in the near future of smooth termination or revision. The period after the war has also been marked by rapid growth in economic interdependence. International organizations, therefore, have been expected to provide for gradual changes and adjustments on the basis of perceived common interests and by means of voting schemes.

Furthermore, the cleavage between West and East tended in the early 1950s to discourage the facing of problems of termination. Mutually perceived external threats produced geographical organizations and agreements on political and military alignment. While conflicts within coalitions were settled by cooperation or were postponed to better times, conflicts arising between coalitions during the Cold War, instead of being resolved through pacific means, were only frozen and thus perpetuated by such means. Thus, the temporary arrangements that followed the Second World War seemed after a few skirmishes to have become permanent. And decolonization of areas occupied by Western European powers, which was one of the few fundamental issues on which the United States and the Soviet Union could agree, has for the greater part been achieved through the orderly procedures of the United Nations.

Lately there have been signs that many prior agreements and existing arrangements can no longer withstand the pressure of events. Demands for termination have mushroomed over the last decade. The atmosphere of disillusionment, which tended to hyperbolize external threats after following on hopes for reconciled harmony, has given way to a more realistic calculation of risks, costs, and benefits. Only a few of the more obvious examples of recent conflicts about termination can be cited here, indicating the general trend. The United States in 1971 abrogated a multilateral monetary-exchange accord and in 1973 it demanded revision of the NATO agreement. Earlier, the French government had withdrawn from NATO's military organization and unilaterally evicted the American forces from their bases in France. The United States and Britain, since they have not been able to reach a final and long-term agreement with West Germany on the reduction of the level of their troops in that country and their support costs, may have to make some unilateral decisions in that direction. Rumania put forward claims with regard to the Warsaw Pact Organization similar to those of France with regard to NATO. These disputes involve fundamental issues concerning the existence and role of geographical, political, and military organizations, and they have not been amenable to solution through the routine orderly procedures of these organizations.

Nor could these disputes be settled by international organizations of the universal type or by international adjudication. The Franco-American dispute, as is shown in chapters 3 and 8, involved some serious unilateral acts, reprisals, and retaliations. The Vietnam War exhibited, in part, the price that both sides to agreements of alignment may have to pay in the course of discharging their obligations. Its effect may be to accelerate demands for the termination of military commitments. Furthermore, the decreased tension between coalitions has generally not been preceded or followed by settlement of important and concrete issues. The talk among politicians about the current permanence of the originally intended temporary structures (provisional arrangements toward normalization following the end of the Second World War) may in themselves be indicative of people's expectations about their impermanence. Moreover, there is at present no lack of conflicts that originated in earlier times: Gibraltar, Guantanamo, Panama, hostilities following Iran's repudiation of Iraq's navigation rights under a 1936 treaty, and so on. In addition, there are other conflicts regarding decolonization that could not finally be settled by the United Nations, International Court, or brute force (for example, termination of the South West Africa Mandate, Sino-Soviet territorial disputes).

This is only a brief survey of present conflicts about termination, not the last word. We live in a period which, in retrospect, will undoubtedly appear to be one of the great revolutionary epochs in history. Thus it is that in our time the words "peaceful change," rarely spoken since the thirties, are being heard again. With each passing year of growth in both economic strain and technological sophistication for physical destruction, these words ring with more urgency.

Not only are old treaties currently in the process of being

terminated or modified but a great number of new agreements are being made, often on matters which hitherto have scarcely been dealt with successfully by explicit agreements (for example, arms control and other limitations upon nuclear weapons, economic diversification and integration). Some of these new agreements, though they are much needed and are in fact being extensively negotiated, are difficult to reach partly because the possibilities of future changes in conditions or future breaches entail high risks or costs, while the mechanism of remedial action has not been sufficiently worked out.

Current theories and doctrines about the termination of international agreements can be divided roughly into two main unrealistic groups. The first places primary emphasis on formal authority and hence focuses on the formal consent of the parties to the agreement, or on adjudication. The second group views the problem mainly as one of effective power, thus allowing unilateral termination as a routine exercise of state sovereignty. Although some writings combine these two opposing views, they still tend to separate formal rules from effective power. One popular suggestion, for example, is that the line be drawn between vital and nonvital disputes, that is, between disputes that threaten international peace and security and those that do not, on the ground that it is primarily the former which are "political" and therefore not amenable to substantial regulation. In regard to important disputes, then, conventional legal notions do not differ materially from theories of realpolitik.

Perhaps the only things more irritating and more naïve than purely legal works on international relations are critical texts on such works that stress only power. The problem of treaty termination in a decentralized arena necessarily involves examination of a large number of interrelated subjects. It concerns the empirical and conceptual analysis of both legitimacy and bargaining power, and the simultaneous feedback of international rules, claims, proposals, warnings, threats, and promises, including their gradual fulfillment. The following discussions, therefore, revolve around fundamental notions such as the conclusion of new agreements in a context of mutual mistrust, treaty breaches, deterrence, reprisal and retaliations, and reciprocal efforts to avoid—or at least to restrain—the damage from such activities to the economies of the parties and interested third parties. Appraisal and recommendation for conflict behavior under such conditions, of course, must also include inquiry of the longer range goals and policies of the emerging global community.

While I have integrated legal analysis and findings of the social sciences in building the main theory of this book, still, in terms of the cases chosen, and the range of problems and factors discussed, the study is intended to be merely selective. Where cases are used as illustration they are, in my opinion, representative; but I do not display a complete expatiation. Further, my choice of examples has been dictated primarily by the importance of agreements relating to power, security, and wealth and by the vividness and expectations of crisis that usually attend their termination. The analysis, of course, is equally applicable to important issues in other subject matters. With minor departures, chapters 3 through 9 preserve the sequence of events through which the more typical conflict about termination begins and is expected to develop before some sort of settlement is reached; the same cases are often regarded under different aspects at different points of the book. Nonetheless, for the sake of readers who are accustomed to skimming over contents and to reading only those portions pertaining to their specialized fields of interests, the book is divided into several parts. These parts are so arranged as to distinguish from the outset between four traditionally different perspectives.

The first part deals with the history of coping with problems of treaty termination, and—in view of the demonstrated fact that contemporary efforts amount to resurrecting past failures—it depicts the general model and alternative concepts upon which discussions in the following parts are based.

The purpose of part 2 is an increased understanding of the peculiar nature of the termination conflict and how it may be resolved by negotiation and new agreement. In order for theory to take full cognizance of conflict behavior, the starting point is descriptive rather than normative; that is to say, the competing predispositions and objectives of contending governments that try to win the disputes through assorted strategies and tactics, rather than the value positions of outsiders in disputes.[4] I have not set out to convince the National Security Council that holding onto Guantanamo does not make sense militarily, or the British government that political wisdom or respect for law dictates that it ought to relinquish Gibraltar. Nor have I tried to make a case for supplying the Sudan with more water from the Nile River, or for revitalizing NATO (though I recognize the desirability of such acts). Rather, I have tried to portray the contending positions as objectively as possible, to discern why parties do present their particular preferences regarding outcomes of disputes in certain ways, and to find out what follows on such a representation. The most important observation in part 2 is that the mechanics of the termination conflict are such that it tends to expand laterally—either through explicit negotiation or unilateral acts (or through a combination of both)—to eventually include the termination of other treaty arrangements between the parties, about which at the beginning of the initial dispute the parties had no quarrel. Obviously, the legal norms and procedures, which are discussed in part 3, should, among other things, be oriented toward solving this fundamental problem.

The practicing lawyer—who may be content with the task of notifying his client of his legal rights, formulating and advocating claims, forwarding them through required procedures, and retrospectively justifying his client's departures therefrom—may immediately turn to part 3. However, even there the discussion centers on the idea that in international relations governments communicate by deeds, not only by words, and that therefore the timing of procedural submission and of substantive argumentation, as well as their content and style, are of the utmost policy and tactical importance.

In a dynamic approach to conflict resolution, the expectations of parties, their competitive or collaborative spirit, and their

4. Compare with studies about lawful decision-making that before examining particular trends in decision postulate the value position or policy orientation of the observer relating to longer term goals of world public order. For such an approach see e.g., M. McDougal, H. Lasswell, and I. Vlasic, *Law and Public Order in Space* 58 (1963). For the one adopted here, see e.g. T. Schelling, *The Strategy of Conflict* 3 (1963).

value ordering cannot be assumed to be given. The way one views the more general processes by which human aspirations, expectations, relations, broad principles, or particular rules are formed, reinforced, and changed is determined largely by one's philosophy about the world, and consequently about law. An appraisal in terms of underlying jurisprudence, and a similar projection into future trends in decision, is undertaken in the fourth part.

This book originated in a doctoral dissertation awarded the Ambrose Geherini Prize by the Yale Law School in 1968. A grant from the Martha Garner Price Fellowships Fund enabled me to continue research and writing at the Rule of Law Research Center, Duke University. I am extremely grateful to the director of the Center, Arthur Larson, and to the staff for the hospitality and stimulating working environment extended to me.

Financial support for final preparation of the manuscript for publication was provided by the Yale Law School, primarily under a grant from the Mobil Foundation of New York City. I am indebted to the dean of the Yale Law School, Abraham S. Goldstein, whose understanding and encouragement I value as much as his material support. I would like also to record my appreciation to Dean Peter J. Liacouras of Temple University Law School for his early interest in my work and for according me other courtesies relating to this book while I was teaching intermittently at Temple during 1973 and 1974.

Special acknowledgement is due my associates at the Yale Law School who read the manuscript at various stages of preparation. Leon S. Lipson, through his insightful knowledge of international bargaining, added pertinent examples and helped broaden my theoretical approach. I profited directly from the enlightened jurisprudential outlook of Myres S. McDougal through conversations as well as through reading his great scholarly works. The manuscript also benefited from the observations and suggestions of W. Michael Reisman. Others who read an earlier version of the manuscript and provided perceptive comments were John Halderman of the Rule of Law Research Center, United States Ambassador Richard D. Kearney of the Department of State, and Egon Schwelb of the United Nations. My wife, Iris, went over various drafts and substantially contributed to the book's content and style. The manuscript gained much from the research assistance of Robert Davis of the Yale Law School class of 1974. Finally, I would like to thank Marian Neal Ash of the Yale University Press for her generous and extended attention.

A.E.D.

*New Haven, Connecticut*
*May 1974*

## PART 1

## The Problem in Historical and Modern Perspectives

# 1 "Rebus Sic Stantibus" in International Relations

> Things do not change; we change.
>
> Henry David Thoreau

Doctrines regarding the unilateral termination of international agreements on account of subsequent contextual changes have a long and troublesome history. Legal treatises dealing with this problem abound with a multitude of differing principles. Yet the very validity of a right of unilateral termination, let alone its precise nature and scope, continues to remain controversial.

Contemporary international lawyers primarily debate which of these various historic doctrines should be adopted as the authoritative pronouncement on the subject.[1] Unfortunately, the terminology employed in this controversy, rather than clarifying the substantive issues, often conceals them under the guise of assorted jurisprudential logics. Antiquated juridical concepts, normative directives, and legal institutions are advocated without sufficient reference to their political and historical contexts.

We begin by examining the various historic periods that gave rise to these formulations of contemporary doctrines of treaty termination on grounds of changing circumstances.

## THE CLASSICAL BALANCE OF POWER PERIOD

The so-called classical balance of power political system [2] of the nineteenth century was characterized by a minimum order orienta-

---

1. See Fitzmaurice, *(Sec.) Report on the Law of Treaties*, [1957] 2 Y.B. Int'l L. Comm'n 16, 58, U.N. Doc. A/CN.4/SER.A/1957/Add. 1; Int'l L. Comm'n, Report, 21 U.N. GAOR, Supp. 9, U.N. Doc. A/6309/Rev.1 at 86 (1966); Lissitzyn, "Treaties and Changed Circumstances *(Rebus Sic Stantibus)*," 61 *Am. J. Int'l L.* 895, 902 (1967).

2. The term "system" refers here merely to some kind of general arrangements for the operation of international relations in a world of many states, and as such it may be distinguished from a particular precept of policy or type of power configuration.

tion.[3] This was a period of mechanical and industrial revolutions, and the laissez-faire doctrines of England, though only partially realized there, provided a slogan for industrial elites throughout Europe and America. For the rising bourgeoisie the best law was a minimum law, which protected life and property but interfered as little as possible with the other affairs of individuals. Such a law enabled business to be free from alleged governmental suppression and from notions of morality and welfare that might obstruct the supposedly automatic adjustment of the free market.[4]

This was also a period of laissez-faire politics. The balance of power system was generally viewed as the political situation of perfect competition; "free bargain" or privity of contract was regarded as the touchstone of the international legal order.[5] International politics, like economic activity, was thought of in terms of Adam Smith's invisible hand theory:[6] the assertion that the political arena is supposed to stabilize itself by the involuntary operation of extraneous forces that lead to the formation and reformation of alliances and counter alliances on the basis of immediate interests.

The mechanical and technological revolution of the nineteenth century was a new thing in human experience, and it obviously had a strong impact on political and legal thinking.[7] Decisions

3. For the distinction between minimum and optimum public order goals, see McDougal, "Perspectives for an International Law of Human Dignity," in M. McDougal and Assoc., *Studies in World Public Order* 987 (1960); M. McDougal, H. Lasswell, and J. Miller, *The Interpretation of Agreements and World Public Order* 39–45 (1967). For similar differences between so-called three task systems— collective security, pacific settlement, and peaceful change—see Hanrieder, infra note 16. See also ch. 9 infra.

4. See M. Kaplan and N. Katzenbach, *The Political Foundations of International Law* 66 (1961).

5. See H. Kelsen, *Principles of International Law* 316 (1952).

6. A. Smith, *The Wealth of Nations* 423 (1937). For an analogy between market situations as developed in economic theory and the six international political systems as developed by M. Kaplan, *System and Process in International Politics* (1957), see K. Boulding, *Conflict and Defense* 274 (1963).

7. Theorists differ as to the nature of the equilibrating process in a balance of power system: "Very roughly, we might say that this process is conceived as automatic, semi-automatic, or manually operated" (I. Claude, *Power and International Relations* 43 [1962]). For an analysis of the automatic version of the balance of power system in which the equilibrating process is described in "terms reminiscent of the operation of physical laws," see id. at 43–47.

were supposed to be made in adjustment of uncontrolled, impersonal conditions that had to be appeased in order to maintain "equilibrium" and prevent "breakdown." Rules of law were not formulated in terms of policy choices, but rather in mechanical terms that narrowed the freedom of choice of decision makers. They were presumed to apply "automatically" whenever the conditions called for their application, however fair or unfair the decisions might be. The goal, either actual or verbal, was to return to *status quo ante,* in other words, normalcy, balance, and so on.

The political theorist or international lawyer of that relatively peaceful era could perhaps hardly be blamed for promoting such theories of peace and security. Like any human being who lacks insight into the relation between causes and effects, he advocated a behavior pattern that had often proven it could achieve its aim without danger. As Lorenz points out, "If one does not know which details of the whole performance are essential for its success as well as for its safety, it is best to cling to them all with slavish exactitude. The principle, 'You never know what might happen if you don't,' is fully expressed in such superstitions." [8] Automaticity—the mystery of the new technology—of course facilitated one's denial of his responsibility in making political choices. Unfortunately, some contemporary political scientists continue to try to build a political *perpetuum mobile* in which, it is said, the operation of certain rules or conditions by themselves enforces automatic obedience to certain others. They even claim to have proven such political systems to be self-maintaining.[9] All this, of

8. K. Lorenz, On Aggression 68–69 (1967). "[E]very superstitious custom that originated on the basis of some misinterpreted accident involves a tradition that it is moral to follow; for detaching oneself from it is dangerous, even more dangerous for the community than for the individual" (F. Nietzsche, On The Genealogy of Morals 170 [1969]).

9. Compare H. Morgenthau, Politics Among Nations 167–68 (1960), with H. Morgenthau, In Defense of the National Interest 51 (1951). For criticism of Morgenthau's views see Claude, supra note 7, at 29–37. The self-equilibrating version of the balance of power seems also to be adhered to in M. Kaplan, supra note 6, at 22. For criticism of Kaplan's theory, see W. Riker, The Theory of Political Coalitions 168–74 (1962). But see Kaplan, Burns, and Quandt, "Theoretical Analysis of the 'Balance of Power,'" 5 Behavioral Science 240 (1960). For a critical analysis see A. Levontin, The Myth of International Security 182–83 (1957).

course, is a myth: "system maintenance" includes a value allocation most favorable to the maintainers.

### Conditions for Stability

In reality, two main conditions seem to have contributed to the
general stability in the balance of power period. The first was the
tendency of parties in major conflicts to moderate their demands
and to be satisfied with relatively small changes in the status quo.
The second condition was the absence of radical changes in the
power relations of the major participants throughout this period.
These conditions were, of course, related to each other: an increase
in the aggressive capacity of a major power, as we shall see, posed
a potential threat to other nations' desire to remain big powers,
thereby increasing the stakes in each particular conflict.

The eighteenth and nineteenth centuries were periods of growth
in national identification throughout Europe. The focus of sentiments of solidarity and loyalty on the nation-state gave it strength
and coherence that other forms of political organization lacked.
The monarchy was the most common regime in Europe, but with
the growth of industrialization the demands of various pressure
groups for control and influence over governmental decisions were
intensified, democratic ideas were spreading, and participation in
politics was increasing. Though competitors in international relations, rulers were partners in internal relations and shared the fear
that the spread of republican ideas might bring devastating results
to all of them. Governments operated under a principle which
Riker conveniently terms "moral restraint." [10] The conservative
ideal of the status quo was so powerful that no essential national
participant was eliminated by conquest, division, or unilateral
disarmament. On the contrary, throughout this period the neu-
trals, and frequently the winners, helped to revive the losers.

There were also other reasons for this restraint, but here I wish
to stress only three factors: limits of national sentiment, limits of
military reach, and risk of intervention by third parties. First, the
existence of different national identities as focal points for sentiments of loyalty at home and outside made it difficult to conquer
and annex foreign territories other than border areas of mixed
cultural content. Thus nationalistic ideology had to distinguish

10. Riker, id. at 174.

between areas that could be unified, and areas that had to be conquered and held continuously by force.

Second, given the state of military technology and communications during the eighteenth and first half of the nineteenth century, it was difficult for an occupying power to control disturbances in remote areas. Even when one power could technically have established hegemony over another, the extension of communication lines, the dispersal of forces, and the economic strain that might have been caused by the high cost of transporting violence over long distances, would have weakened that power in its relations with other powers.[11]

Third, even when conquest of another power was possible and profitable, other powers could—and probably would—still intervene in the military conflict on behalf of the defeated nation. In the world of the eighteenth and nineteenth centuries, five or six great powers of roughly equal military strength were the essential members of the political system. Rules prohibiting radical changes in particular conflicts were regarded as self-enforcing because the other members could always unite against the transgressor. The major actors jockeyed for position by forming shifting coalitions, and occasionally by fighting limited wars.[12]

Some of these conditions were constantly changing during the nineteenth century. Mechanical innovations, technological improvements,[13] and industrial growth worked both to change the

11. For this and other factors, see Kaplan and Katzenbach, supra note 4, at 30ff. For a general discussion of military technology and means of transporting violence as they affect global spheres of influence, see Boulding, supra note 6, at 259ff.

12. The Napoleonic attempts to restore the Roman Empire were an exception to the generally accepted principle of moral restraint. It was, however, an exception that reinforced the rule. The success of French nationalism provoked similar national sentiments throughout Europe, and particularly in the German principalities. All the other big powers of Europe combined against France's imperial ambitions. The extension of lines of communication to Alexandria, Gibraltar, and Moscow resulted in a series of disastrous defeats. Yet, because they sought an enduring status quo, the victors did not dismember the loser. At the Congress of Vienna of 1815, the participants shared the conviction that moral restraint should be exercised in order to restore the balance of power to Europe. In order to increase the prestige of the newly restored monarchistic regime, the peace terms even allotted to France additional territories that had not belonged to it before the French Revolution.

13. The first steam engine was installed for industrial use in 1785, and the first railroad, between Stockton and Darlington, was opened to traffic in 1825.

power relations among the major participants and to increase the stakes in conflict situations. Germany, England, and France became industrially more developed than Russia, Italy, or Austria, while the gap between the Ottoman Empire and European powers continued to widen. At the same time, the concentration of industrial power and developments in the means of transportation, communications, and military technology made it possible to conquer, control, and administer larger areas. By the middle of the century the railroads alone had effectively reduced European distances to a fraction of what they had been before. Because of the slowly changing relative power of nations, the existing structure of boundaries became more and more obsolete and was subjected to greater and greater strain. The United States sprawled westward during this period, Russia expanded eastward, and western Europe controlled and administered larger parts of Africa and Asia. In Europe itself, to protect the boundaries drawn in the horse and buggy era, governments had to tighten their political alliances and to raise and maintain armies sufficient at least to repel possible aggression. Mutual deterrence became the keystone of international strategy.

### The Strategy of Mutual Deterrence

A particular strategy of deterrence may generally depend for its successful "operation" on a variety of factors, at least two of which are basic. First, in order to deter, prospective violence should be made as *frightening* as possible. Second, a deterrent threat should also be made as *credible* as possible. The first aspect of deterrence depends on the ability to punish or coerce. The second depends to a large extent on the ability to discern whether punishment or coercion is called for.

The two key variants of deterrence, however, pose a dilemma. In order to deter an opponent from performing an act, one has to hedge with highly destructive capacity. But if the threat fails and has to be carried out, the punitive action is usually painful or costly to both sides.[14] Credibility itself therefore depends on the

14. Compare R. Luce and H. Raiffa, *Games and Decisions* 110, 119, 143 (1957), with T. Schelling, *The Strategy of Conflict* 124–25 (1963); see also T. Schelling, *infra* note 15, at 37.

costs and risks associated with fulfillment by the party making the threat. Since to make a threat of "enormous punishment" may raise the suspicion in the mind of the adversary that the threatener might ultimately shrink from carrying it out, more than simply a communication of intention is usually required: one must maneuver oneself into a position where one surrenders one's judgment and no longer has any effective choice as to how one shall behave or respond. Therefore, a key concept in deterrence is automaticity: making retaliation depend solely on some specified impersonal and external event.

However, when things are believed to be either so safe or so completely predictable, there is no crisis. The conflict "is over as soon as it begins, there is no suspense." [15] There is usually another more dynamic dimension to conflicts which reflects what happens to the parties' calculations when moves and countermoves unfold over time. During the execution of a conflict the participants usually communicate intentions, make commitments to threats and promises, resort to unilateral acts, or take other similar steps that can raise or lower the danger of mutual damage or disaster. But however deliberate and calculated the parties' choices may be, however resolved each side may be to endure the test of nerve, the possibility is always there that once a crisis is initiated things will get out of hand. Uncertainty about subjective elements such as the parties' motives for certain moves, the strength of their convictions and resolve not to be pushed too far, their expectations as distinguished from their declared intentions (just how far is "too far"?), and their willingness to incur pain, damage, and sometimes voluntary, self-inflicted penalties, is what makes the outcome of a crisis, once initiated, so unpredictable.

If military conflicts in the eighteenth and the beginning of the nineteenth century had been confined only to the immediate parties, they would not generally have been considered crises in any real sense. Such bilateral conflicts would have involved neither particularly large losses nor a high degree of uncertainty. The capacity of a nation to incur and suffer quick and staggering destruction was relatively limited. Armies consisted mainly of professional soldiers, and populations were generally less committed to

15. T. Schelling, *Arms and Influence* 97 (1966).

the war effort. The fighting was brief, bloody, and, for the moment, decisive. Predictability was also relatively high: to win a local war one had to win a battle, the prediction of which depended on estimates of troop sizes, transportation facilities like the number of horses and the location of railroads, topographical conditions of the battlefield, food supplies, and other similar factors. Often, as in the conflicts between great and small nations, one side also held all the cards. What transformed such events into crises was, of course, the possibility that, because of the complexity of political alignments, other powers would become involved in the local conflict.

The fact that a deterrent threat comprises the fury of wide involvement and universal war, it may be recalled, does not in itself mean that it makes such a war inevitable. Since the fulfillment of a threat is costly to both sides, the parties may still ask the critical question whether a major war ought to be, or will be, fought. The more inexactly defined, vague, and obscure the event on which deterrence is made to depend, the easier it is to justify an escape from the commitment. Political alliances promise help in case of aggression, but the trigger of aggression, which ought to set the system in motion, is not amenable to precise legal definition, and consequentally is hard to establish in practice.[16] A proscribed act is most easily acertained when it involves a clear-cut instrumental event such as the external existence of certain rights, or a transgression that violates established territorial boundaries, as opposed to disputed intricacies of the merits of issues or the aspirations and domestic political predispositions of nations. For these and other reasons, physical transgression upon the legal boundary of a nation in the nineteenth century was the most recognizable final critical step in converting a situation from one in which participation in war was unnecessary to one in which it was called for.

In practice, however, an ally's resort to war cannot always be made to depend "automatically" on the mere use of proscribed means by an opponent. Many territories, especially those of small

16. See Hanrieder, "International Organizations and International Systems," 10 *J. Conflict Resolution* 297, 299–300 (1966). For discussions of the difficulties in defining aggression, see M. McDougal and F. Feliciano, *Law and Minimum World Public Order* 61–62 (1961); J. Stone, *Aggression and World Order* 17–19, 71, 93 (1958).

nations, are just not worth a war, and especially not a war that could get out of hand because of the possible involvement of all the participants. Throughout history, allies have been known to make alignments and change their minds when the chips were down. Indeed, "commitments" in the balance of power period often had a split meaning. Politics was an exercise in unscrambling intentional and unintentional puns. Politicians had a sufficiently Machiavellian instinct not only to share the risks with others by forming alliances but also to divide the gains when "conditions" or "circumstances" called for it. Despite the formalities of legal equality, the small nations were just as safe as an alligator strolling through a handbag factory (vide the partitions of Poland). As long as a major participant did not set particularly high stakes in its conflicts with other major participants, it could count on some loopholes in the opponents' commitments.[17] Most agreements of alignment lacked any real commitment, either because they were too informal and were concealed from the public and third-party officials, or because they were too formal and hence vulnerable to legal arguments. Termination of the former was not costly in terms of national prestige or the self-respect of national leaders. Termination of the latter also did not require much daring, initiative, or imagination; it was the domain of lawyers' craft.[18]

It was this flexibility of alignment, and consequent ease by

17. Prussia, for instance, was able to unify Germany by gobbling up a number of small states. Although in these conquests Prussia did not at first seem to violate the principle of moral restraint, it became involved in separate military conflicts with Austria and France. These great powers, however, did not join forces against Prussia, nor did other powers become militarily involved in these conflicts. Indeed, the flexibility of alliances on which maintenance of the peace was generally perceived to depend required the participation of a minimally large number of major nations in the system. The political support given to German unification was partly related to this desire of the great powers to guarantee a sufficient supply of future allies in case of disagreement with its present ones; see Kaplan and Katzenbach, supra note 4, at 32–34. For a discussion of the requirement for a minimal number of participants in the balance of power system, see Riker, supra note 9, at 166. Indeed, Russia in 1870 was quick to utilize the new major actor when it obtained from Prussia an informal consent to the unilateral termination of multilateral treaty provisions concerning the demilitarization of the Black Sea; see Hill, infra note 22, at note 15. Even so, Prussia's success somewhat contradicted the notion of "moral restraint" and, as discussed below, in the final analysis this principle was not effective in preventing hostilities and even general war in Europe.

18. See the following discussion of the legal doctrine of rebus sic stantibus.

which commitments could be evaded, that saved Europe in the nineteenth century from a global war. Paradoxically, while this flexibility enabled the participants to adjust short-term interests, it also imposed a straitjacket on their willingness to put forward radical demands in particular conflicts. The unknown arrangements, changing attitudes, deceit, and desertion of allies to satisfy immediate interests, increased the elements of chance and uncertainty in particular conflict situations. Typical of what Schelling calls deterrent threats that "leave something to chance," [19] the frightening event was not wholly dependent on the parties' will. Governments never knew just how committed others were until the commitment was challenged; even then they did not know how effectively a willing committed party could deliver on his commitment. Because of this uncertainty, every threat in support of a radical demand was perceived to involve some loss of control or some generation of crisis. And while penalties were contingent on the willingness of each major participant to fulfill obligations, the lowering of the shared risk of a penalty in particular conflicts was not wholly within its control.

There was, therefore, much empirical truth in the jurists' contention that, in the final analysis, law and order rested upon the objectified existence of agreements.[20] The frightening event that deterred the participants from breaking important rules resulted directly from the factual existence of the congeries of alignment agreements and not so much from the substantive content of specific agreements. The latter could be changed during the course of performance, yet the possibility that events would get out of hand was still present. Whatever the discerned combination of available power was at a particular moment, and no matter whether a particular participant was resolved to fulfill a former obligation to an ally or intended to renege on the bargain, the possibility of a general "breakdown" could not be brushed aside. Defection from a bargain and the desertion of an ally always

19. Schelling, supra note 14, at ch. 8.

20. See Kelsen, supra note 5. For this view as expressed in Article 62 of the Vienna Convention on the Law of Treaties, see the following discussion. Kelsen notes that the fundamental assumption of this theory "is exactly the same fiction as the social contract of the natural-law doctrine; and the states, subjected to international law, are, by their very nature, no more 'sovereign' than the individuals, subjected to the national legal order, are, by their very nature, 'free' " (id. at 316).

meant another bargain, as well as a new and perhaps equally temporary ally, and therefore did not detract from general deterrence.

Because of this element of chance, the deterring penalty for violating important rules could be perceived as part of the external environment and independent of the test of will or agreement between two or more adversaries in particular conflicts. Perhaps the matter could not have been better expressed than by the contemporary notion, discussed above, of the "invisible hand." This was also one of the greatest advantages of the system. The fact that a deterrent threat could be perceived as impersonal and exterior to the participants tied the hands of prospective violators of legal arrangements without imposing on them loss of face, humiliation, shame, or the disgrace that usually follows one's backing down from a demand because of the threat of one's opponent. Withdrawing from a risky situation, even if the adversary contributed to this situation, could be portrayed differently from submission to an opponent's superior capacity, resolve, and determination. It could be justified as wisdom rather than cowardice, as a reasonable acceptance of inherent facts, and as an adjustment to impersonal forces, conditions, and circumstances beyond both sides' control.[21] A similar effect was also the object of the particular principles of treaty termination.

### Executed Treaties as Legally Inviolable

Prima facie, the two most fundamental policies of the balance of power—stability and flexibility—seem to contradict each other.

21. In the case of the suspension by the United States in 1941 of the Load Line Convention, the attorney general concluded his recommendation to the president by stating that because the doctrine of rebus sic stantibus was clearly applicable, it was unnecessary to discuss "the well established international practice that violation of a treaty by one contracting party renders the treaty voidable at the option of another contracting party injured by the violation" (Biddle, "International Load Line Convention," 40 *Opinions of the Attorney General of the U.S.A.* 119, 124 [1940–48]). The invocation of general changes in circumstances avoided the question of responsibility and therefore decreased the embarrassment or tension that could result from accusing other governments of specific violations and illegal conduct. But see Briggs, "The Attorney General Invokes Rebus Sic Stantibus," 36 *Am. J. Int'l L.* 89, 96 (1942). See generally R. Fisher, "Enforcement of Disarmament: The Problem of the Response," 1962 *Proc. Am. Soc. Int'l L.* 1, 10; Schelling, supra note 15, at 121–22. Of course, this sort of thing does not really fool anyone but the more myopic lawyers.

Concern with stability militates against frequent termination of former arrangements, while flexibility, as the term was understood in the nineteenth century, favors frequent termination of former agreements in pursuance of short-term interests. One may reconcile the contradiction by pointing out that the application of these complementary policies can be a matter of degree. The question of just how flexible a decision maker should be may depend, of course, on a consideration of policies pertaining to particular contexts. That, however, was not the case with the rules of termination of the balance of power period, in which both stability and flexibility assumed static yes-or-no legal categories.

The legal distinction was between territorial or executed, and obligatory or executory rights. The former were totally excluded from the application of the rules, and it was unlawful to terminate them unilaterally.[22] These so-called executed, earned, absolute, real, acquired, or territorial rights are species of property law. It is not surprising that the right to property and possession was afforded absolute protection in the period of laissez-faire capitalism. But such a distinction between legal rights was equally important for the purposes of international mutual deterrence and political alliances.

First, it was noted earlier that successful deterrence required the identification of some clearly established external event or physical transgression by an adversary. The concept of inviolability of executed rights answered this requirement. Since the

22. "There is likewise general agreement that the effect of the change of circumstances is termination only of those provisions of a treaty which remain to be fulfilled and not of those provisions which have been completely executed" (C. Hill, *The Doctrine of "Rebus Sic Stantibus" in International Law* 16 [1934], also printed in 9 *The University of Missouri Studies* 3, 16 [1934]). See also 1 Oppenheim-Lauterpacht, *International Law* 939 n. 1 (8th ed.); Shaker, note 26 infra, at 128. The exclusion of executed rights from the application of the doctrine is explained by the circular argument that these rights do not constitute a treaty. It is commonly held that they are of the greatest legal strength and are protected against the world at large, including the grantor. "One of the consequences of this difference is that the treaties belonging to this category create, or transfer, or recognize the existence of, certain permanent rights, which thereupon acquire or retain an existence and validity *independent of the treaties which created or transferred them*" (A. McNair, *The Law of Treaties* 256 [1961]). Thus, it is said that such a right "cannot" suffer from any subsequent termination of the treaty which has originally created it. See also F. Vali, *Servitudes of International Law* 29–30 (1958).

value preponderance in executed treaties is in the hands of the objecting party, unilateral termination of the treaty usually cannot be made without a resort by the claimant party to an overt act of coercion. And when the subject matter of the treaty is a piece of territory or a physical *res,* unilateral termination must involve *physical seizure* by means of self-help.[23]

Second, the main characteristic of deterrence is that it is intended to prevent certain behavior on the part of an adversary by means of the ability to inflict injury upon him. There is a difference between a threat intended to keep an adversary from doing something and a threat intended to make him do something. It is usually easier to deter than to compel. To deter an opponent's action by threat one can usually remain passive, leaving the initiative and immediate responsibility for the damaging consequences to the other side. To compel an affirmative action by threat, one has in many contexts to commit oneself to a coercive overt act, and often to initiate that act.[24] A most important difference in this respect between executed and obligatory treaty provisions relates to the manner in which these provisions are respected and complied with. Generally speaking, compliance with the former is negative, in the sense that it consists of refraining from action. Because the agreement is already performed, it does not require continuous positive action by the grantor state. The continuous enforcement of executed rights, therefore, can be most conveniently pursued by a deterrent strategy. The enforcement of obligations, on the other hand, requires resort to compellent acts which may in themselves threaten the peace. Consequently, doctrinal formulations of the principle that treaties can be terminated following changes in conditions have generally been limited to executory treaty provisions.

Finally, the prevention of physical transgressions was all important, and the dreadful deterrent punishment, it may be recalled, would have been all but meaningless if it had to occur. Embodied in the principles of termination of international agreements was

---

23. For a more detailed discussion of this point, see ch. 7 infra.

24. Cf. Lieberman, "Threat and Assurance in the Conduct of Conflict," in *International Conflict and Behavioral Science* 110, 111 (R. Fisher ed. 1964).

this desire for flexibility of *obligations* in a world of shifting alignments.

## Obligations of a Terminable Legal Character

The policy of flexibility of obligations was not limited to treaty provisions, but was also applied with similar vigor to customary international law. Writers dwelt on the distinction between usage and custom, and generally denied the former the higher status of valid legal obligation. Thus, evidence of consent and an intention to be bound by the habitual practice, the argument went, was required for the establishment of a customary obligation. Governments took refuge in the right to define that to which they had "consented," and they maintained optimal freedom of action by refraining from acknowledging as obligatory, norms according to which they consistently acted.[25]

These fictions of the consent and the intention of the parties were also extended to the termination of explicit agreements. The most popular definition of the doctrine of rebus sic stantibus ("so long as conditions remain the same") until the mid-1930s had been based on the idea of a term (clausula) presumed to be found in every treaty. According to this view, the obligation of a treaty terminates when a change occurs in those circumstances that exist at the effective date of the agreement and whose continuance forms a tacit condition of the continuing validity of the treaty according to the implied intention or will of the parties. Any and all provisions might be absolute, but the treaty as a whole is always conditional. In other words, the function of the doctrine is to carry out the shared intention of the parties. When a change occurs in the circumstances that formed the cause, motive, or raison d'être of the consent of the parties, the condition of rebus sic stantibus becomes operative, and the treaty obligation ceases to be binding.[26]

25. Kaplan and Katzenbach, supra note 4, at 68; P. Corbett, *Law and Society in the Relations of States* 76 (1951).

26. The theory of the implied clausula has a long history, which goes back to St. Thomas Aquinas. See Baron de Taube, "Inviolabilité des Traités," 32 *Recueil des Cours* vol. 2, 291, 361, (1930). Hill, supra note 22, at 8 n.1, lists the writers who base the doctrine wholly or in part upon the intention of the parties. See also 1 L. Oppenheim, *International Law*, sec. 539 (4th ed. McNair 1928), but not

The net impact of this theory is to confirm the prevailing political edict and to make termination of international agreements to a large extent simply a matter of treaty interpretation. The idea that the application of the doctrine depends solely on the original intentions of the parties, however, is incorrect. In many cases, the parties have not envisaged the possibility of future changes in specific conditions. Sometimes the parties, although aware of such a possibility, preferred to keep silent at the time of the agreement, either because they feared protracted negotiation or opposition at home, and so on. Even if the possibility of termination had been considered, the parties would probably not have provided for complete nullity of the agreement, but rather for some other settlement that would not be inconsistent with the new conditions. The decision maker, confronted with such a case, should, of course, try to ascertain the genuine shared expectations of the parties by applying general principles of interpretation. Indeed, this policy seems to be reflected in the view that the distinct principle of rebus sic stantibus applies only when the alleged change in circumstances is *not* foreseen by the parties at the actual date of the agreement.

In reality, it is almost impossible to draw up a treaty that provides for a solution in the event that circumstances change unpredictably. The arrangements can provide only for changes that are foreseen. As for unforeseen changes, all that the parties can do at the effective date of the agreement (besides provide for adjudication, the unqualified right of withdrawal, or termination at any time) is to agree that the parties will have a right of withdrawal or termination only in case of a "fundamental" change of circumstances. But such an express clause is vague and general, and hardly helps a decision maker in a case of later controversy, since he will have to apply the same policies and principles as he would in a case in which the parties had remained silent. McNair, for

later editions. For the history of the doctrine, see E. van Bogaert, "Le sens de la clause 'rebus sic stantibus' dans le droit des gens actuel," 70 *Revue Générale de Droit International Public* 49 (1966). For a survey of the various doctrines, see Shaker, "Fundamental Change of Circumstances," 23 *Revue Egyptienne de Droit International* 109 (1967). He concludes, contrary to the ILC reports, that the "jurisprudence (national) and practice of States show a preference to the subjective concept of the doctrine" (id. at 121).

instance, suspects that the origin of the implied term doctrine is due to the fact that at one time it formed the subject matter of an express term in many treaties and that is why we speak of it as a clausula.[27] If this is the origin, it shows that the insertion of such a clause into a treaty is indeed little help to the decision maker, otherwise this practice would probably have been continued. In addition, since during the eighteenth and nineteenth centuries positivistic notions of treaty interpretation prevailed, by including an expressed clausula in the treaty itself, the parties ran the risk of losing to an argument based on *expressio unius*—that since the parties at the time of the agreement included in the treaty an expressed clause applying to events X or Y, they must have meant to exclude Z, and so on. An unwritten clause was more flexible in this respect and conformed with the general policy of continuous adjustment to unpredictable events in the balance of power period.[28]

Besides the general description given above, most writings on the implied term doctrine do not contain any real clarification of policies. This lack of policy clarification, of course, increases the possibility that each side to a conflict about termination will subjectively interpret the implied condition of the treaty by giving its own clarification of what is supposed to have been the "intention" of the parties. In formulating the doctrine, observers have introduced further subjectivities by the use of highly abstract and ambiguous terms (for example, "fundamental" change). And despite the alleged focus of the doctrine on the intention of the parties at the effective date of the agreement, the effect has been to make termination depend on the subsequent intentions and policy changes of the parties at the time of controversy.[29]

27. McNair, "The Functions and Differing Legal Character of Treaties," 11 *Brit. Yb. Int'l L.* 100, 109 (1930).

28. The inclusion of an explicit clausula in the distant past, however, may well have reflected a more sophisticated grasp of political-legal realities: symbolically, treaties were not made in perpetuity but as long as both parties wanted them or one party could enforce them. By the late eighteenth century, mechanistic conceptions of the physical universe infiltrated the law and continued to bedevil it. Thus the lawyers came to believe that a man-made law, like the law of nature, was not a real law unless it appeared to be made for perpetuity.

29. Compare with Williams, "The Permanence of Treaties," 22 *Am. J. Int'l L.* 89 (1928): "[T]he word 'conditions' in this statement including not only material,

Paradoxically, the more subjective a policy or principle is, the more objective or extrinsic it tends to become. A principle that authorizes unilateral termination, and whose application is perceived to depend on a one-sided interpretation of an "intention," is similar in effect to a principle stating that an agreement can be terminated on demand. Indeed, a minority group of writers in the nineteenth century rejected the implied term doctrine and propagated instead a doctrine based on an extrinsic right of unilateral termination. The theory developed by those writers had been strongly influenced by the growth of national sentiments in Europe. Following Hegelian ideas, they conceived of the state as a person in the process of development, and therefore opposed the notion that states are permanently bound by treaty obligations.

According to this view, a treaty obligation may be terminated unilaterally following changes in conditions that make performance of the treaty injurious to a list of fundamental rights—existence, self-preservation, independence, growth and development —all of which may be summarized under the title of "rights of necessity." [30] Writers do not define or clarify what is exactly meant by these rights, and since it is a matter of national survival, etc., states have traditionally insisted on determining for themselves what should be considered as such according to particular and temporary national interests. For all practical matters, therefore, the fundamental right theory of termination reaches the same conclusion as the implied term doctrine. This similarity of conclusions arising from diametrically opposed theories is sympto-

---

but also moral, facts . . . the essential 'things,' inanimate and animate, material, moral and mental, must remain in the condition in which they were when the treaty was concluded." The question whether a mere subjective change in the "attitude" of a party, or a bare change in a governmental policy, could be invoked as a ground for terminating a treaty, however, has since become a burning issue among both writers and members of the ILC. See, for example, Int'l L. Comm'n, Report, 21 U.N. GAOR, Supp. 9, U.N. Doc. A/6309/Rev. 1, at 87(10) (1966); Lissitzyn, supra note 1, at 899ff., and in particular his discussion of the 1895 conflict between the United States and Brazil.

30. See Hill, supra note 22, at 10. Garner, "The Doctrine of Rebus Sic Stantibus and the Termination of Treaties," 21 *Am. J. Int'l L.* 509, 511–13 (1927); 1 L. Oppenheim supra note 26; Woolsey, "The Unilateral Termination of Treaties," 20 *Am. J. Int'l L.* 346 (1926). For additional references see Harvard Research, "Law of Treaties," 29 *Am. J. Int'l L.* 666, 1100 (Supp. 1935).

matic of the policy of flexibility of treaty obligations and adjustment to "circumstances" and "conditions" on the basis of short-term interest, upon which peace in the classical balance of power was commonly perceived to depend.

### "Automatically" Terminated Obligations

The same policy is also reflected in the phrases generally used to describe the legal effects on treaties of the implied-term doctrine. The doctrine, it is said, need not even be applied by the parties in a particular conflict. Rather, the material change in circumstances itself "terminates" the binding force of the treaty. Immediately upon the occurrence of the relevant change the validity of the treaty "ends," a treaty becomes legally "void," the obligation has "ceased," or it is "no longer binding." The treaty is supposed to be terminated "automatically":

> If a *clausula* is presumed to exist in the treaty, then, if the essential change of circumstances occurs, termination takes place by reason of a term contained in the treaty itself, even if it is the law rather than the parties that placed it there. This must, therefore, involve an automatic termination of the treaty *ipso facto,* as soon as the circumstances that call the clause into play arise, for in that event it is a term of the treaty (even if implied by law) that says that the treaty is at an end, and termination on that basis cannot take place otherwise than automatically.[31]

What accounts for such a description are the following three factors, all of which are related to the strategic political notions of the balance of power period.

First, the assertion that the legal principle need not even be invoked by the parties in order to be operative seems to be a fairly accurate description of state practice. Indeed, of thirty-six recorded instances before 1934 in which a change of circumstances was adduced as a ground for the termination of an international agreement, only six expressly invoked the doctrine of rebus sic stanti-

31. Fitzmaurice, supra note 1. For these reasons he rejects the implied-term theory and adopts the one of objective rule.

bus.[32] The cause for this ratio was either that the doctrine itself stated it need not be invoked in order to be applied, or that in the power politics of the nineteenth century legal directives on termination were more useful in protecting the writer than in instructing the participants. The reader may decide according to his own taste. It is clear that the description of the operation of the doctrine in terms of automatic application is merely a formal statement of the obvious fact that the termination of obligations in the balance of power system could easily be affected.

Second, pushed too far, a policy of flexibility simply means the exclusion of all other relevant criteria for making decisions. Automaticity in application is a most suitable device for divorcing a principle from specific policies regarding the particular merits of disputes, and has the effect of decreasing objections and arguments about the substantive issues of termination. A concern with the merits of issues would necessarily entail an interest in the underlying grievances of disputes and in the internal conditions of participating states. However, as Kaplan and Katzenbach observe:

> However deplorable the principles espoused by a foreign government in domestic matters seemed, other nations did not regard it as their business. In a world political system in which peace depended upon flexibility of alignment, nations could scarcely afford to have their political judgment sub-

32. The statistic is Hill's and is quoted in Feinberg, "The Legal Validity of the Undertakings Concerning Minorities and the *Clausula Rebus Sic Stantibus*," 5 *Scripta Hierosolymitana* 95, 113 (1958). Moreover, the doctrine was not mentioned expressly in the most important conflicts of termination after World War II. According to Berger, id.: "the parties which sought to be released from the existing treaty obligations refrained from invoking by name the clause [the c.r.s.s.] of which they made use. On the other hand, those who defended the treaties expressly pointed to the fact that the c.r.s.s. had been relied on, as though this would level accusation against their opponents. This proves that the invocation of the c.r.s.s. in international law is still accompanied by some sort of disrepute." This is, of course, an extremely narrow conception of the process of treaty termination. Whether parties explicitly refer to c.r.s.s. or not, they regularly talk in terms of reasonable changes in objective circumstances for which the implied-term version of the doctrine is historically ill-suited (see note 78 infra). Another reason why it is usually objecting parties who prefer to invoke the doctrine by name is that, particularly since World War I, as the following discussion indicates, writers have expounded a narrow conception of the doctrine that rejects almost any claim to termination.

servient to moral criteria. The system assumed that politics would make strange bedfellows, as indeed it did. Lloyd George and Clemenceau never could comprehend Wilson's failure to understand this simple fact, or what they regarded as his reckless introduction of political morality into the affairs of Europe.[33]

Paradoxically, an international principle that declares treaties to be terminated ipso facto may have a direct influence on the states' internal structures of decision. The labeling of a treaty that is alleged to be terminated as void or voidable may enable domestic courts in a number of states to bypass the competent executive organs of their government in deciding for or against the continuous application of the treaty in regard to individuals. Formally speaking, a treaty that is conceived as void can be said not to require an additional official act of termination by the competent decision-making organ of government. If domestic courts, then, had been legally consistent, they would have held that particular international agreements claimed to be affected by changes in circumstances are either void or still binding. However they held such agreements to be voidable, maintaining that since the immediate parties had failed to exercise their right to terminate the treaties, the court must therefore regard the treaties as remaining in force.[34]

This obvious inconsistency in a positivistic doctrine that is claimed to form an essential part of a hierarchical body of doctrines, principles, and rules logically derived from one another is not surprising. The doctrine is mainly concerned with facilitating claims and decisions of termination when the policy of the contracting governments changes. Beyond this subjective element, the application of the principle is clearly intended to rest only with each individual government, with as few objections as possible

33. Kaplan and Katzenbach, supra note 4, at 69.

34. See H. Briggs, *The Law of Nations* 915 (1952). A similar decision in regard to general changes in circumstances was rendered by the Swiss Federal Court in Lepeschkin v. Gossweiler & Co., 71 *Journal des Tribunaux et Revue Judiciaire* 582 (1923). Similarly, writers do not carry the rule concerning the automatic termination any further, so as to suggest that third-party governments can regard a treaty as terminated even though the immediate parties themselves have not claimed termination.

from the other parties. That all promises and commitments to a specific policy could be repudiated at will, and that all domestic issues were perceived to be immune from international scrutiny further emphasizes, of course, the inviolable character of treaties relating to boundaries and other territorial rights.

Third, as was pointed out above, in the parlance of the balance of power period, stability did not include the modern notion that reasonable expectations resulting from the reliance on a treaty should not be defeated. Rather, it meant equilibrium of the conditions and forces over which the participants themselves supposedly had no control. The common belief was that, if a previous agreement of alliance did not accord with the political forces that truly operated in the world arena, an unstable situation would result. The political conditions of the arena were held, therefore, not only to justify the repudiation of old agreements but to force their termination in anticipation of a new alignment. Expectations that resulted from the overreliance on treaties could simply be brushed aside as unreasonable.

It is in connection with this metaphorical belief in the power of the "invisible hand" that one has to appreciate the difference between the implied term and the fundamental rights doctrines of rebus sic stantibus. The first doctrine is mechanical and instrumental. Devoid of explicit policies and assessment of issues, it minimizes the subjective responsibility of officials. Pushed too far, such an approach implies a surrender of all judgment on the part of decision makers, who supposedly are being forced to make the decision. On the other hand, the fundamental rights theory entitles the parties to invoke self-interest, growth, and development, and to effect unilateral termination on the basis of such claims. The application of this doctrine is therefore clearly perceived to depend on the initiative, will, superiority in power, and boldness of the claimant party. The difference is between decisions that are perceived as external to the parties and as part of the environment, and decisions that are perceived to depend on tests of nerve, will, and resolve between the adversaries. In repudiating treaties of alliance the distinction is between deliberately abandoning one's allies when challenged by a determined opponent, and being forced into a certain situation, along with one's adversary, by "events," "circumstances," or the activities of onlookers. When these events are perceived to terminate a party's obligations automatically, he does not have, perhaps, to swallow his pride and lose face. He can explain to others and also console himself with the claim that he is caught in a deterministic trap. The implied term doctrine of rebus sic stantibus, therefore, not only allowed for flexibility of obligations but also created some of the conditions necessary to facilitate this flexibility.[35]

## The Rigid Balance of Power

One of the most important events to make the balance of power system unstable was the annexation of Alsace-Lorraine after the

35. The arguments put forward by Austria-Hungary in 1908 concerning the withdrawal of its troops from Sanjak of Novibazar, and the declaration of the annexation of Bosnia-Herzegovina are instructive. By Article 25 of the multilateral Treaty of Berlin of 1878, Austria-Hungary was granted the right to maintain military forces in the former provinces and to occupy and administer the latter. Turkey, however, retained the formal sovereignty over these territories (Hill, supra note 22, at 56–58; Harvard Research, supra note 30, at 1121). In 1908 Germany and Austria-Hungary sought to extend their influence through Turkey to the East. Hence Austria-Hungary sought to return to Turkey the administration of the territory. The circular issued by Austria-Hungary on October 3, 1908 alleged that between 1878 and 1908 "the situation had undergone a radical change; Turkey was then weak in consequence of a bloody war and was powerless to maintain order and tranquillity in the Sanjak; during the thirty years that had elapsed she had recovered her strength and was able to maintain peace and order therein; there was therefore no longer any *raison d'être* for the maintenance by Austria-Hungary of military forces in the Sanjak" (Harvard Research, id. at 1121, quoting from 109 *Archives Diplomatiques* 279–280 [1909]). The withdrawal of the troops was a case in which the beneficiary of a territorial right sought to renounce benefits. As such it did not present particular difficulties. Nevertheless, Austria-Hungary felt obliged to justify before its former allies the abandonment of its former undertaking to control militarily this Turkish territory. It did so by using phrases identical to those developed by writers of the implied term doctrine of rebus sic stantibus.

The annexation of Bosnia-Herzegovina was a different matter. Termination of the treaty right to control and administer this territory would have required the restoration of the territory to Turkey. Austria-Hungary, on the other hand, sought to vest sovereignty over the territory in itself. A claim to termination such as this one was not authorized by the doctrine of rebus sic stantibus (supra note 22). Austria-Hungary, therefore, did not invoke in the circular note the doctrine by name, but in another portion of the same message it stated its belief that changes in Bosnia-Herzegovina had created an "imperious necessity" for itself to annex that territory (Harvard Research, id.). This language resembles the quarrelsome terminology of the fundamental rights of "necessity" doctrine of rebus sic stantibus. When an issue is considered by a government to be "vital," or of an "imperious

Franco-Prussian War of 1870. By annexing the French regions, Bismarck defied the balance's first principle concerning "moral restraint," thereby increasing the stakes between France and Germany. In addition, the inflammation of national sentiments produced by this event made France the inveterate enemy of Germany. Since neither nation was a potential ally of the other, the incentive of both nations to avoid war or to limit their objectives in war weakened.

The inability of France and Germany to align also limited the range of choices available to other governments. The hostility between the two nations produced strong alliances that were separately directed by each of them. France, being unable to recover the lost provinces, subscribed to the power of Russia. Austria-Hungary, whose interests in the Balkans clashed with those of Russia, allied itself with Germany. England was committed to neither of the two blocs, but it was committed to the defense of Belgium, whose neutrality Germany had to violate if it were to defeat France militarily. The trigger of "breakdown" came to depend on the will of only one of the immediate parties to a particular conflict. If either one of the adversaries decided to go to war, its allies had few alternatives to joining in the war, since to do otherwise meant they would be left without future allies. The alliances system acquired the inflexibility and rigidity necessary to make deterrence fairly automatic.

There were additional consequences of this rigidity. In the loose balance of power period the losers of the day continued to participate in the system because they could hope to become the winners of tomorrow. A nation could afford to lose a particular decision because it received from the adversary, or from third parties to the

---

necessity," it narrows the range of choice of that government (an effect similar to that of the so-called automatic termination of the implied term doctrine), and thus enhances the credibility of its willingness to go to war over the matter. Since Austria-Hungary had already had physical control over the contested territory, the dare and initiative had to be taken by the other parties. Russia, in the so-called Bruchlan bargain of Sept. 15, 1908, had consented to the annexation in advance, in return for some other concessions. Germany considered the Austrian decision "illegal" but supported its ally for "political" reasons. The other parties to the Treaty of Berlin considered the decision illegal but consented to recognize the annexation in order to avoid war (Hill, supra note 22, at 57–58).

conflict, some explicit or implicit promises about the content of future decisions or promises to change policies. Such settlements necessarily involved expectations of permanence and stability. Promises to change policies, however, are valuable only when they involve the satisfaction of one interest at the expense of another, and since the major participants became traditional enemies after 1870, the gains and losses in each conflict were perceived to alter their power relation in regard to future conflicts as well. A party could not afford to be the loser of today because that would also mean being the loser of tomorrow. The stakes were constantly mounting from one conflict to another, and with them the incentives to go to war.

Furthermore, because of the rigidity of the alliances, issues could not be separately dealt with as small matters, each to be considered and negotiated in terms of what was immediately relevant. The merits of particular issues were lost in the overall controversy. And since the alliance system had acquired the inflexibility necessary to make collective deterrence certain, states could only talk big and perform small. At the same time, democratic ideas were spreading within the nation-states and participation in domestic politics was increasing. A large number of political amateurs, equipped more with nationalistic enthusiasm than with profound knowledge, became political factors within the nation-state and, indirectly, in the international arena. This further limited the options of the elite strategists and contributed, with varying degrees of intensity, to rigidity and eventually to global war.

This process, in which the rigidity of alliances and the probability of a "breakdown" were constantly mounting, had started in 1870 and continued until the Second World War. It strongly influenced the rules of termination of international agreements too. Since general stability became more and more dependent upon the will of each party to a particular conflict, the rules were changed so as to limit the freedom of the individual members. The dangers to peace inherent in the unilateral solutions of particular disputes militated for a requirement that disputes be settled only by an agreement between all the contending parties. And realizing immediately after the conclusion of the Franco-Prussian War of 1870 that the "free factors" of the international arena could no longer be counted upon, the participants resorted to "legislation" to bring about this result. A seven-power conference held at London in 1871 issued the famous Declaration of London, which states that:

> It is an essential principle of the Law of Nations that no Power can liberate itself from the engagements of a treaty, or modify the stipulations thereof, unless with the consent of the contracting Powers by means of an amicable arrangement.[36]

The occasion for the issuance of this declaration was the denunciation by Russia of certain provisions of the Treaty of Paris of 1856 concerning the demilitarization of the Black Sea. The particular treaty provisions that barred vessels of war from the Black Sea lay in the gray area between obligations and territorial rights; they belong in the category of territorial rights whose violation did not involve any act of transgression on the territorial possessions of other states.[37] In denouncing the provisions of the treaty, Russia put forward an argument that closely followed both the implied term and fundamental rights doctrines of rebus sic stantibus.[38] Thus, the Declaration of London was intended to amend the traditional doctrine so as to bar the unilateral termination of territorial arrangements, whether or not they clearly fall within the inviolable category of executed treaty rights.

This interpretation is supported by an examination of the trend of decisions to terminate on grounds of changed conditions. Take,

36. Declaration as to Non-alteration of Treaties Without Consent of Contracting Parties, London, Jan. 17, 1871, H. Briggs, supra note 34, at 912–13. For further discussion see chs. 2 and 7 infra.

37. The treaty provisions concerning the demilitarization could not properly be regarded as executory ones, since the Black Sea had in fact been demilitarized since 1856. Nor could the provisions be regarded as executed, since they did not require a once-and-for-all act of implementation but rather a continuous performance of a mutual undertaking to avoid certain behavior.

38. "His Imperial Majesty cannot admit, *de facto*, that the security of Russia should depend on a fiction which has not stood the test of time . . . deems himself both *entitled and obliged* to denounce . . . Peace and *Balance of Power* will receive a fresh Guarantee if they are based upon a more just and solid foundation than one resulting from a state of things which no Great Power can accept as a normal condition of its existence" (Russian Circular note of Oct. 31, 1870, Briggs, note 34 supra, at 911 [emphasis added]).

for instance, the Harvard Research or Hill's study of the doctrine of rebus sic stantibus.[39] Most of the disputes cited by these authors occurred after 1871. There also seems to be a discernible strand running through these cases: the great bulk of them consisted of claims and counterclaims concerning the termination of territorial rights of the mixed executed-executory type.[40] In most of these cases there was no need for the claimant party to take any action to effect unilateral termination; the daring, initiative, and responsibility clearly rested upon the objecting sides, which declined to take them. The claimant parties therefore won these disputes by default.

The Declaration of London also marked the beginning of a new era in which legitimacy and controlling power concerning the termination of international agreements became divorced from one another. Despite the manifest unwillingness of objecting parties to enforce the treaties, they usually protested against their unilateral termination by invoking this declaration. Even parties which did not object to the claims for termination took pains to emphasize that they regarded the particular dispute as involving "questions of diplomacy," and specifically avoided "questions of international law." [41] This was a convenient way to facilitate particular terminations without undermining the validity of the general rule embodied in the Declaration of London. As events unfolded and the alliances system became more and more rigid, the declaration was also interpreted to proscribe the unilateral termination of all agreements, whether territorial or obligatory. The rules were perceived as static, while flexibility, adjustment,

39. Harvard Research, supra note 30, at 1113ff.; Hill, supra note 22, at 27ff. This is, of course, not the only factor in these cases, but it is believed to be the most important one.

40. In the *Free Zones* case, for instance, France did not expressly contest Switzerland's argument that the doctrine of rebus sic stantibus, whatever its definition and standing in international law, does not apply to treaties establishing territorial rights. France, rather, seemed to admit this contention tacitly by contesting the claim of Switzerland that the treaties in question had created territorial rights, see, e.g., Hill, id. at 44.

41. See, for example, the announcement of Russia in 1886 that Batum no longer constituted a free port. Germany consented in advance to the termination of article 59 of the Treaty of Berlin of 1877, on grounds of "policy" and regardless of the "legal" arguments involved, Hill, id. at 53. See also the annexation of Bosnia-Herzegovina by Austria-Hungary in 1908, supra note 35.

and change were regarded as political questions. Not only did they not take notice of the problems of peaceful change in the relevant social framework, but they also totally ignored the dynamic aspect of conflict situations discussed above.[42]

## THE COLLECTIVE SECURITY ERA

The interwar period, which was marked by economic break-downs and political failures, precipitated rapid growth in governmental functions and public law.[43] Emphasis shifted from the conflicting symbolic aspects of social living to cooperative ones—from the "free factors" of the international arena and the subjective consent of parties, to a new dominant credo of the "collective will" of the world arena. This quasi-mystical aberration should not, of course, be confused with the richer Grotian tradition that

42. Characteristically, when at long last mutual deterrence broke down and the global war started, it was done within the short range of a few days and as mechanically and automatically as the century-long operation of balancing and counterbalancing. "No one can quite say just when the war started. There was a great starting of engines, a clutching and gearing and releasing of brakes and gathering momentum until the machines were on collision course. There was no 'final' decision; every decision was partly forced by prior events and decisions. The range of choice narrowed until the alternatives were gone" (Schelling, supra note 15, at 221; and see his fascinating analysis of how the beginning of the war was affected by the technology, the military organization, and geography of Continental Europe in 1914). For a discussion of the reasons why the belligerents continued to fight the war for such a long period, see F. Iklé, *Every War Must End* 8 (1971).

43. Even the previously most sacred part of private law, the law of contract, was regarded as a subsidiary branch of public law. "The law of contract, then, through judges, sheriffs, or marshalls puts the sovereign power of the state at the disposal of one party to be exercised over the other party. It thus grants a limited sovereignty to the former. . . . From this point of view, the movement to standardize the forms of contract—even to the extent of prohibiting variations or the right to 'contract out'—is not to be viewed as a reaction to, but rather as the logical outcome of, a régime of real liberty of contract. It is a utilization of the lessons of experience to strengthen those forms which best serve as channels through which the life of the community can flow most freely" (M. Cohen, "The Basis of Contract," 46 *Harv. L. Rev.* 553, 586–88 [1933]). Subjective law was regarded as the characterization of the egoistic man who concentrates upon his private interests, and who is isolated from society. Objective law was regarded as the expression of the state as a whole, which proclaims its principle of universality and contrasts itself to its elements. For a discussion of this change in philosophy as it relates to contractual relations, see also Pashukanis, "The General Theory of Law and Marxism," in *Soviet Legal Philosophy* 111 (Babb and Hazard ed. 1951).

views international law as an instrument for the clarification of shared common interests.

Collective security was claimed to replace the insecurity of the previous political system of national alliances.[44] This theory concerns an international order in which not every state but all states are the guarantors of peace. "The scheme is collective in the fullest sense; it purports to provide security *for* all states, *by* the action of all states, *against* all states which might challenge the existing order by the arbitrary unleashing of their power." [45] Whereas the common defensive alliance envisages a collective response to a party external to the alliance, a collective security system seeks to prevent aggression from within the system. The latter scheme rests on the principle of "one for all and all for one" and promises security to any state that might be a victim of belligerency. While bilateral, localized wars are an acceptable and perhaps a necessary equilibrating instrument in the balance of power system, they are excluded from the collective security system except as a collectively authorized response to armed attack. And because a high degree of centralization is needed in order to manage the collective power of all or almost all the members, it requires an institutional body of at least close to universal membership within the relevant frame.

### Principle of Objective Law

The establishment of the League of Nations and other international organizations promised that international policy formulations and operations would go beyond the immediate concern with particular threats to or breaches of the peace. Much of the growth of governmental functions and public law in domestic arenas during that period was concerned with the individual welfare. A phenomenon common to many societies in the thirties was the

44. Collective security has not been effectively implemented as an operative system of international relations. But especially during the years immediately following the world wars, it has figured prominently in the theoretical and ideological debates concerning the management of international relations. See Claude, infra note 45, at 150.

45. I. Claude, *Power and International Relations* 110 (1962); see also Hanrieder, supra note 16, at 298; Haas, "Types of Collective Security: An Examination of Operational Concepts," 49 *Am. Pol. Sci. Rev.* 40 (1955); Levontin, supra note 9, at 184ff.

evaluation of legal doctrines in terms of underlying community policies with regard to the distribution of resources. The focus was on public policy rather than on the will of the parties in particular, more or less voluntary transactions. In American contract law, for instance, courts were not asked to examine the intention of the promisor, but rather to consider whether the defendant's words or actions were such that reasonable people would generally rely on them under the circumstances. Emphasis was put on the injury, directly proved and objectively measured, resulting from a breach, and not on the breach of the promise per se.

This change in contract law is worth special mention; a substantial number of writers allege that it has been transferred into the international arena. They have propagated a new version of the doctrine of rebus sic stantibus, by which the principle is seen as one of objective law operating not via the treaty but from outside it.[46] The former approach has been described as "a case of the Trojan horse, the enemy within the gates." [47] In emphasizing the objective character of the rule, the question of the continuous validity of the treaty obligation is allegedly integrated into the larger realm of the general and external authoritative order with which the maintenance of the obligation is inconsistent. This appeal to a general legal concept independent of the intention of the parties is claimed to place the issue in a proper perspective and to correct the danger of differing subjective interpretations. The new theory operates on grounds that reasonable parties would not have undertaken the obligation had they foreseen the essential

46. For criticism of the implied-clause doctrine and the adoption instead of the theory of objective rule see, e.g., Fitzmaurice, supra note 1, at 58–59; Waldock, *Report on the Law of Treaties* [1963] 2 Y.B. Int'l L. Comm'n 36, 83, U.N. Doc. A/CN.4/SER.A/1963/ADD.1 *Int'l L. Comm'n*, Report, supra note 1; Ting-Young Huang, *The Doctrine of Rebus Sic Stantibus in International Law* 10 (1935); 1 C. Rousseau, *Principes Généraux du Droit International Public* 584 (1944); C. Rousseau, *Droit International Public* 225 (1970).

47. Fitzmaurice, supra note 1, at 59(3). The theory of objective law gives the parties the right to claim termination upon the happening of a change in conditions and following *naturaliter* (Williams, supra note 29, at 91–93). He still maintains, however, that what occurs *naturaliter* is the automatic dissolution of the treaty; compare with Fitzmaurice, supra note 1, at 58. A careful examination of these writings reveals the gradual change from one theory to the other.

conditions that moved them to conclude the treaty would change so fundamentally.

This could, perhaps, be a useful doctrine of termination, provided that concepts like "reasonable parties," "fundamental change," and "essential conditions" were somehow defined in terms of policy and empirical facts. But even the reference to an "objective standard" or a "general and natural order" is not followed by further clarification of relevant policies. Quite to the contrary, practically all writers on this new theory of rebus sic stantibus take great pains to formulate the rule in the most neutral terms possible. The impression one gets from reading these works is that ambiguity is deliberately resorted to as a matter of purported strategy.

A variety of historical reasons may account for this overconcern with supposedly objective facts rather than with the merits of the issues, one of which was the great number of national economic crises. The Depression forced the movement in domestic arenas toward the welfare state. Economic remedies, however, were believed to lie in a system of national regulation without international restraints. Tariffs, quotas, exchange regulations, discriminatory exchange rates, and expropriation and subsidy to national enterprises marked the prewar period. Governments sought to solve their own domestic problems even if they exported them to other countries in the process. "Much that had been international in practice ceased to be so regarded. The eyes of politicians were turned inward to their own domestic problems, not outward to similar problems of their neighbors." [48] Thus, in contrast to internal laws, international principles stayed within the realm of minimum law.

Other reasons for the focus of policies of termination away from the substantive merits of disputes were closely related to the prevailing theory of collective security. Since the latter is similar to the balance of power system in that it is expected to deter rather than to act, much of the previous discussion concerning the extrinsic aspects of deterrence is equally relevant here. The balance of power doctrine of termination focuses on the intention of the

---

48. Kaplan and Katzenbach, supra note 4, at 72.

parties because prior identification of a friend—and sometimes of a foe—is essential for the operation of national alliances. On the other hand, the members of a collective security scheme must exhibit flexibility of policy and national sentiments and be willing to curb any aggressor, regardless of their attitudes toward particular issues. Such an abstention from judgment is necessary so that the participants can avoid "preconceived 'opinions' which would make it difficult to abjure neutrality once aggression has taken place." [49] Thus, while during the nineteenth century subjective changes in attitude or governmental policy had been understood to justify the termination of treaty obligations, during the interwar period such considerations were specifically excluded from the application of termination principles.[50]

Furthermore, collective security presupposes an almost universal agreement among the members regarding the appropriate collective course of action in specific conflict situations. However, the wider the participation in the decision-making process, the more positions the decision will have to accommodate in practice, and therefore the lower its strength, direction, and purpose will be. A settlement based on the merits of the issue is likely to be an enduring solution, but seeking it usually reduces the number of settlements that are acceptable to most of the members and so decreases the likelihood of reaching an agreeable solution.[51] So also, wide participation in the making of a decision usually means wide sharing of the benefits expected to result from that decision. An agreement is easier to reach in a system of national alliances because the number of parties is fewer (benefits are greater for each party), and because the agreement may involve greater changes in the status quo (increase opportunities for great gains).

49. Hanrieder, supra note 16, at 304; I. Claude, *Swords Into Plowshares* 233 (1964); Russell, "The Management of Power and Political Organization," 15 *Int'l Organization* 630, 633 (1961).

50. See note 29 supra; Fitzmaurice, supra note 1, at 61. However, since collective security by definition rejects national alignments, such treaties not concluded for a fixed period only have always been said to be terminable on demand. 1 L. Oppenheim–H. Lauterpacht, *International Law* 938 (1955); Waldock, supra note 46, at 68.

51. See generally Randolph, "A Suggested Model of International Negotiation," 10 *J. Conflict Resolution* 344, 346 (1966).

In collective security, on the other hand, because of the large number of participants, the number of those who believe they could be satisfied with the promised benefits is relatively small. These participants would thus be reluctant to commit substantial resources to the collective effort even though they might happen to agree with the collective political position. A collective security scheme, therefore, tends to focus on the relatively infrequent events that arise in extreme crises. In a crisis the urgency of the problem and the common threat are more easily perceived. The resulting collective agreement may thus also involve pledges of large resources.

For all of the above reasons, then, the collecive security scheme of the interwar period required an even greater degree of neutrality in regard to the merits of issues than the previous scheme of balance of power. It sought only to curb actual aggression and thus to intercede at the last and most serious stage of conflict situations. It did not seek to reconcile the conflicting interests at an earlier stage or to decrease disputes through peaceful change and harmonization at the incipient stage of growing aspirations.

### Treaty Termination Legally Banned

What accounted during the period between the world wars for this movement toward minimum order was the desire of the major participants to preserve the status quo. The coalition of the victors of the First World War was institutionalized in the League of Nations, which, incidentally, excluded the countries the Allies had defeated. After the war, two of the losers were thoroughly dismembered. The Allies appropriated Germany's colonies, its merchant fleet, its foreign assets, and some ten percent of its population. In addition, Germany was saddled with the obligations to continue paying its war "debts," to keep the Rhineland demilitarized, and to remain unilaterally disarmed—"temporarily," it was said, but these interim arrangements seemed to become permanent.[52] (As Leon Lipson has remarked, as soon as the

52. Riker, supra note 9, at 176. It was felt from the beginning that, following the German example, the Allies would also disarm. Point 4 of Wilson's Fourteen Points, which may be regarded as the basis upon which Germany surrendered, called for the universal reduction of all armaments "to the lowest point consistent with domestic safety." See also Treaty of Versailles, June 28, 1919, pt. 1, art. 8,

temporary endures for a while, we say shrewdly that the temporary has become permanent, and it is at that moment that the permanent begins to become only temporary.) The flexible legal norms that characterized the nineteenth century could hardly have been expected to survive unchanged after the First World War. Consequently, the rules of termination were geared toward curbing Germany's claims for change. Several legal devices were developed in this respect.

First, the tacit-clause doctrine of rebus sic stantibus was rejected on the main ground that it involved an immediate right of unilateral termination. The new theory of objective law, on the other hand, confers on the parties to the agreement only the right to invoke the principle and to claim termination. A substantial number of writers seem to be of the opinion that a party is not authorized to terminate the agreement unilaterally even if the request is refused or ignored.[53] This view can be considered as either puzzling or absurd, depending on the modesty of the critic. Since all the parties may agree to terminate an inconvenient obligation [54] for any reason or on any ground they deem sufficient,

---

*Treaties and Other International Agreements of the United States of America* 51 (1969). Similarly, the preamble to part 5 of the Treaty of Versailles stated that the objective of Germany's disarmament was "to render possible the initiation of general limitation of the armaments of all nations" (id. at 115). A collective security system functions best when coupled with at least partial disarmament. See Claude, note 49, at 266. The figures of the national defense expenditures during the period of 1926 through 1931 show, however, that with the slight exception of Great Britain, all the major powers not only did not reduce their armaments but even substantially raised them. See J. F. Kennedy, *Why England Slept* 18 (1961). Thus Germany put forward the claim that the Allies had assumed a legal obligation to disarm too, and that the fulfillment of the Allies' obligation was a condition for performing its own obligation to disarm. The British view was that "[t]o state what the object or aim of a stipulation is, is a very different thing from making the successful fulfillment of that object a condition of the stipulation" (British Statement of Policy, Sept. 18, 1932, in McNair, supra note 22, at 572; Kennedy, id. at 12. It was felt, however, that if these promises had not amounted to contractual obligations, there was at least a moral one for the Allies to disarm (Kennedy, id.).

53. See, e.g., Hill, supra note 22, at 15; Harvard Research, supra note 30, at 1124–1126; Fitzmaurice, supra note 1, at 61; Oppenheim-Lauterpacht, supra note 50, at 942–43; but see Garner, supra note 30, at 515–16.

54. Executed treaty provisions receive absolute immunity also under the doctrine of objective rebus sic stantibus.

a precise definition of grounds for termination is not needed for such cases. If, therefore, the principle of rebus sic stantibus has any distinct and separate occasion for application, it must be in those cases in which the parties do not agree. The absurdity of this principle, whose invocation confers upon the claimant only the "right to ask" the objecting side to agree to termination, should not obscure the fact that it reflects the political conditions that existed after the First World War. In the empty dreams of many international lawyers, Germany must have appeared to be the kind of mollycoddle who asked permission to ask permission.

Second, commentators have shifted the argument from what policies ought to govern the termination of international agreements to whether the doctrine of rebus sic stantibus is part of international law at all. Writers have dwelt on the distinction between legal and political disputes. The former are said to be concerned with sharing the existing distribution of values, while the latter are primarily concerned with changes in the laws that govern the acquisition of rights to values.[55] Some observers have concluded that the problem of termination is political, and that therefore the doctrine of rebus sic stantibus is not a rule of international law.[56] Past practice is also alleged to support this conclusion.[57] Thus, for example, Brierly, who treats the doctrine as a "pseudo-legal" principle, asserts:

55. F. Dunn, *Peaceful Change* 3 (1937). The example given for a political dispute is the demilitarization of the Rhineland. See also Claude, supra note 49, at 204: the distinction is between "disputes *within* the legal order" and "disputes *about* the legal order." L. Bloomfield, *Evolution or Revolution?* 60–63 (1957), reviews different definitions of "peaceful change" which generally correspond with legal definitions of political matters"; B. Wood, *Peaceful Change and the Colonial Problem* 26 (1940); Lauterpacht, "The Legal Aspect," in *Peaceful Change: An International Problem* 135, 141 (C. Manning ed. 1937); E. Carr, *The Twenty Years' Crisis, 1919–1939*, 245 (1940). See also C. de Visscher, *Theory and Reality in Public International Law* 308ff. (P. Corbett trans. 1957).

56. H. Kelsen, *Principles of International Law* 359 (1952). For other writers who reject the principle altogether, see Shaker, supra note 26, at 112.

57. Most writers on the subject stress verbal formulation and ignore operations when they claim the existence of customary international law against unilateral termination. The Harvard Research, supra note 30, at 1124, for instance, points out that in all the cited cases the other side protested to the unilateral termination of the treaty. The failure of the objecting parties to challenge the act is ignored. See also Hill, supra note 22, at 78. These arguments are absurd: "Unilateral termination" by definition means that it is accompanied by and made

There seems to be no recorded case in which its application has been admitted by both parties to a controversy or in which it has been applied by an international tribunal.[58]

To which Ting-Young Huang replies:

To say that there is no judicial organ or no decided cases to formulate and approve a sound and well-established principle in such a legal system as international law is simply to offer a serious criticism of the system itself.[59]

To put forward an argument such as Brierly's is, of course, to state the problem rather than to answer it. Other authors on the subject hesitate to recognize the doctrine as an inherent legal principle, but they seem to admit "reluctantly," to its desirability or necessity in exceptional cases. Some commentators are willing, therefore, to admit that the doctrine of rebus sic stantibus is a principle at least of international morals and public policy.[60] The doctrine is placed somewhere in between the realms of "ought" and "is," and the problem is solved by resorting to the ancient question-begger of the "quasi" or "imperfect" right.[61] It is said that the principle gives the obligated party merely a good moral case for having the treaty annulled by agreement. The result is

despite the protest of the objecting side. Without the protest—and sometimes even despite a protest, as demonstrated in ch. 2—it is a termination by agreement (tacit or express). Further, the same parties who made formal protests against unilateral termination in some of the cases cited themselves resorted to similar practices in others.

58. J. Brierly, *The Law of Nations* 335 (1963). To search for state practice pursuant to an overly demanding definition is, of course, to invite disappointment by definition.

59. Ting-Young Huang, supra note 46, at 19.

60. Garner, supra note 30, at 511. Cf. Briggs, supra note 21, at 90. For a discussion of the source of the doctrine, see H. Lauterpacht, *The Function of Law in the International Community* 270 (1933).

61. Westlake considers the right of denouncing a treaty on account of changed circumstances as an "imperfect" one, and thus insists that it should be exercised with a "grave sense of moral responsibility" (1 Westlake, *International Law* 296 [1910]). The Vienna Convention does not provide for a clear legal right of termination, but urges the parties to exercise "good faith." Its approach is, in the final analysis, the same. See ch. 6 infra. According to Vattel, the imperfect obligations do not give the right of enforcing them, but only the "right to ask" (E. de Vattel, *The Law of Nations; or, the Principles of Natural Law*, sec. 17 [Chitty ed. 1854]). See also P. Corbett, *Law and Society in the Relations of States* 31–32 (1951).

a legal system in which a void contract is said to be one kind of valid contract.

Third, some writers do not seem to be wholly satisfied with such political or moral solutions. The "political question" argument is indeed insincere. The principle of rebus sic stantibus, it is argued, cannot be part of international law because it has never been applied jointly by both sides to a conflict or by an international tribunal. But the result of this morally desirable and politically necessary principle not being a formal rule of law is precisely to preclude its application in future decisions of international tribunals. Certainly, this desire to have one's cake and eat it too cannot be gratified. A substantial number of observers, therefore, attempt to solve the inconsistency by making the application of the principle contingent upon a decision of a competent international decision-making organ.[62] Lauterpacht, for instance, states:

> [T]he existence of this judicial authority is such an essential condition for the working of the judicial principle of the clausula that in its absence the principle itself, however just and salutary, becomes inoperative, or, when operative, ceases to be a rule of law and becomes a maxim of politics.[63]

Thus the principle that was originally intended to maximize the freedom of action of parties, and that has always been applied by parties unilaterally, has suddenly become "inoperative" in the absence of a judicial authority.

In fact, this requirement of adjudication would mean that the principle of rebus sic stantibus is indeed inoperative. In most conflict situations international adjudication is but a phase in the diplomatic or negotiating process. The agreement to arbitrate (the *compromis*), if not the sole basis for arbitration, is a significant or vital element in the majority of cases in which the initiation of proceedings has not been institutionalized.[64] Thus a requirement for termination only by adjudication is similar to a

62. See, e.g,. Harvard Research, supra note 30, at 1125–26; Hill, supra note 22, at 83.

63. H. Lauterpacht, *Private Law Sources and Analogies of International Law* 169 (1927).

64. Compare W. Reisman, *Nullity and Revision* 84 (1971), with K. Carlson, *The Process of International Arbitration* 62 (1964).

requirement for termination by unanimous agreement. Scholars, of course, hastened to express doubts as to whether the termination of obsolete treaties falls within the compulsory jurisdiction of the Permanent Court.[65] Furthermore, the only case in which the Permanent Court was directly confronted with a claim based on the doctrine of rebus sic stantibus is the *Free Zones* case between France and Switzerland. There the claimant party (France) not only argued that the rule does not give a party the right to denounce or terminate a treaty unilaterally, but added that the court itself was not authorized to terminate an agreement without the mutual consent of the parties. The court, according to this view, could only direct the parties to the proceedings to reach an understanding, giving its affirmation only to one contention or the other.[66] The case involved a relatively trivial economic dispute with a friendly neighboring country, and it was, of course, overshadowed by the big issues with Germany. France could therefore afford to concentrate on the principle at stake rather than on winning the immediate physical issues involved in the case. Scholars, of course, have been quick to utilize the new "precedent," emphasizing that in the *Free Zones* case *both* sides to the controversy have agreed that——etc.[67]

65. See Williams, supra note 29, at 98–99.

66. *Case of the Free Zones of Upper Savoy and Gex* [1932] P.C.I.J., Ser. C, No. 58 at 406. The Swiss answer was that to direct the party who invokes the clausula to reach an understanding with the other is not to answer the question which in law is raised regarding the merits. The material question, of course, is whether the objecting party is obliged to acquiesce with the decision. France had to offer a convincing justification for its delay in invoking changes which had occurred more than seventy years before. The explanation offered was that in the nineteenth century the doctrine could be applied only with the agreement of the parties. International law at that time, according to the French explanation, supplied imperfect means for the realization of the right given by the change in circumstances. "[P]ractically, and during a long time, a State was without recourse against the bad will of another State" (Hill's trans., supra note 22, at 41). Upon the establishment of an international court, the argument went, France immediately appealed to it for an *affirmation* of its contention and for directions to reach a new agreement. Alas, what self-restraint! The French justification, however, may at best explain the failure to terminate the treaties unilaterally, but not the long delay in the invocation of the changes in question.

67. See, e.g., Harvard Research, supra note 30, at 1124. This is not the only controversial point upon which both parties in the *Free Zones* case agreed. See note 40 supra.

In addition, the theory about judicial decision making which prevailed at that period, guaranteed that the Permanent and International Courts would decline to assume the 'just and salutary" task that was conferred upon them. There have been only a few explicit judicial cases of termination, and they have, of course, held that the termination of international agreements is a legislative, not a judicial function.[68] The competent legislative organ of the League of Nations did not fare any better.[69] The objecting parties have thus been able to win the disputes, or at least to win

68. Judge Kellogg of the Permanent Court stated in the Franco-Swiss *Free Zones* case: "[T]hese questions of political or economic policy are within the sovereign jurisdiction of every independent state and should not and cannot be submitted to the International Court of Justice. There is also the League of Nations, which is a political conciliation body to which all the members may appeal. There is no need to impose upon the Court any such political questions destructive of its influence as a Court of justice" (P.C.I.J., Ser. A, No. 24, at 38, 42, 1930). The Court did not express an opinion relative to the arguments about the doctrine of rebus sic stantibus, but rejected the French claim on factual grounds (lack of proof). Other cases in which unsuccessful references were made to the doctrine were the *Nationality Decree Case* [1923] P.C.I.J., Sec. C, No. 2, at 187; and *Case Concerning the Denunciation of the Sino-Belgian Treaty of 1865* [1929] P.C.I.J. Sec. C. No. 16-I 22, 52. Similarly, the International Court in 1966 rejected on procedural grounds claims for the termination of the South West Africa Mandate Agreement. The Court directed the parties to the "international legislator," but did not indicate who that entity was. See Reisman, "Revision of the South West Africa Cases," 7 *Va. J. Int'l L.* 3, 76 (1966–67). For additional discussion see ch. 6 infra.

69. Article 19 of the League of Nations Covenant authorized the Assembly to "advise" "from time to time" the "reconsideration" of treaties which had become inapplicable. This article had been a dead letter from the beginning. The attempts periodically made to revive it merely watered it down. The explicit reference in Article 19 to the revision of treaties was used as a justification for restricting the authority of the Assembly. In 1921 the article was officially given a technical and restrictive interpretation based on a very limited notion of the doctrine of rebus sic stantibus. It was further decided in 1933 and 1936 that *absolute unanimity*, including the vote of the parties involved, was needed in order to confer on the Assembly's decision any legal effect (i.e. of "advising" the parties to "reconsider" the treaty). In the only two cases where Article 19 was invoked, a discussion in the Assembly of the substantive claims was procedurally evaded (Bloomfield, supra note 55, at 43ff.; see also Wright, "Article 19 of the League Covenant and the Doctrine of Rebus Sic Stantibus," 1936 *Proc. Am. Soc. Int'l L.* 55, 68). For references to other invocations of the doctrine during that period, see Schiffer, *Répertoire des Questions de Droit International General 1920–1940* 717–728 (1942). For a discussion of Charter Article 14 in practice, see Bloomfield, supra note 55, at 117ff.

the court-centered round of the match, by default of the "competent" external authority.

## Treaties Negotiated as Scraps of Paper

As World War II was approaching, the process of restricting the possible application of principles of termination was accelerating. The threat of unilateral terminations by Germany and other "have-not" nations was constantly growing. But the means employed were in utter conflict with the requirements of the political situation.

The collective security system placed emphasis on formal agreement among the participants. But in the absence of objectives relating to the common interests clearly delineated in advance, it was difficult to arrange effective action when crises occurred. There was no distinctive alliance upon which responsibility for action automatically fell. The equality in relative power of the major participants and the neutrality of principles of conduct prevented the focusing of responsibility on a single great nation. To some governments it was an advantage not to act at all, and to other governments it was an advantage still to look to others to act with them or for them.[70]

The chips were down in 1935 when Germany officially denounced part 5 of the Treaty of Versailles concerning its unilateral disarmament. When this occurred, the major participants even had to bargain on a mild joint reaffirmation of an accepted formula for the general principle of pacta sunt servanda. Furthermore, if all the breath the Great Powers expended on empty claims and reaffirmation of declarations against the unilateral termination of agreements could have been converted into power, it would have supplanted atomic energy. But despite protests and threats of all kinds, no action was taken against the German decision. Indeed, a detailed analysis of this conflict in the following chapter reveals that Germany's allegedly unilateral decision was in fact a shared outcome. The general feeling was that, at any rate, the rearmament of Germany would help restore the balance of power to Europe. Legitimacy in this and subsequent

70. Kaplan and Katzenbach, supra note 4, at 43.

termination conflicts with Germany was completely divorced from controlling power.

Nevertheless, Germany's rearmament following the unilateral denunciation of part 5 of the Treaty of Versailles created an ominous precedent, and thus threw doubt on the future validity of other burdensome provisions of this and other agreements. In a specially convened conference held at Stresa immediately after the German decision, Britain, France, and Italy joined in verbal opposition to the German fait accompli. The Declaration of Stresa reads as follows:

> The three powers, the object of whose policy is the collective maintenance of peace within the framework of the League of Nations, find themselves in complete agreement in opposing by all practicable means, any unilateral repudiation of treaties which may endanger the peace of Europe, and will act in close and cordial collaboration for this purpose.[71]

This declaration was followed by a resolution of an "Extraordinary Session" of the Council of the League of Nations, "considering" the wording of the Declaration of London, discussed here earlier, and considering further that "by this unilateral action the German government confers upon itself no right." The council "decided" to call into play sanctions regarding "future" violations of agreements that might endanger the "peace of Europe." [72] Another so-called authoritative pronouncement against the unilateral termination of international agreements was added to international law.

Several points demand brief observation in relation to the present discussion. The immediate lengthy conflict over the rearmament of Germany was ended with a solution favoring competition in armaments and regrouping of the participants in anticipation of bigger conflicts. Foreseeably, the effect was to endanger other treaty arrangements in Europe, so that France, Britain, and Italy appeared to commit themselves to close col-

---

71. Reprinted in 1 A. Toynbee, *Survey of International Affairs 1935*, at 161 (Royal Inst. Int'l Affairs, 1936); Churchill, infra note 73.

72. Reprinted in Toynbee, supra note 71, at 163.

laboration in opposing future repudiation of treaties by Germany. However, the price for the supposedly complete agreement between the three governments was the geographical limitation to which the principle of the sanctity of treaties had been subjected. And all of this was done at a time when preparations by Italy for military action against Ethiopia were visibly taking place.[73] Hence, the declaration and resolution, though supposedly condemning unilateral repudiation of treaties, in no way support the general principle on which they are allegedly based, since they consent to a violent repudiation of treaty obligations by one of its authors.

The idea is often advanced that, at least in regard to short-run effects, there is a narrow and practical point of view according to which the distinction between politics, morals, and law can be argued for.[74] But even from this extremely narrow viewpoint, the irony of the matter is that the expressions of amity between the three powers on the principle of unanimity in the termination of international agreements, if not hollow, were somewhat unsubstantial. At most they extracted from each other open-ended commitments which, in retrospect, and in regard to curbing future denunciations of agreements by Germany, were about as effective as trying to prevent a skunk from ejecting by holding him by the nose. What has come to be known since the late thirties as the practice of considering treaties as scraps of paper had clearly originated in the conduct of all major governments. The ending of the rearmament conflict had, in effect, been nothing but the beginning of treaty terminations in many other countries: Ethiopia, the Rhineland, Manchuria, Austria, Czechoslovakia, Albania, Finland, and so on.

## RECENT DEVELOPMENTS

Since the factors currently relevant to the formulation of principles of termination are dealt with throughout this book, there is

73. On the very day of the formal repudiation of Germany's obligations, the Ethiopian government appealed to the League of Nations for protection from the threatening demands of Italy (Toynbee, id. at 163). And at Stresa, Mussolini in his speech "stressed the words 'peace of Europe,' and paused after 'Europe' in a noticeable manner" (W. Churchill, *The Gathering Storm* 120 [1961]).

74. See generally L. Fuller, *The Morality of Law* 130–33 (1964).

no need to elaborate on them here. It suffices to note in the present context that the collective security scheme partly envisaged by the United Nations, and the alliance system of other international and supranational organizations, have generally moved not only in the direction of resolving conflicting interests of parties that threaten the peace, but also of according deference to material needs and lofty aspirations. Interdependence is constantly growing, and it becomes more and more difficult, both in economic and military situations, to draw a clear-cut distinction between domestic and international affairs. Despite this trend, recent writings and other authoritative pronouncements on the subject have continued to move toward minimum order. The stated policies of today are far more extrinsic, neutral, and hostile to change (any change) than was the case before.

### Article 62 of the Vienna Convention

The problem of termination, as stated by many observers, is how to maintain order and reasonable stability and at the same time permit or encourage continual progressive reformulation of policies to keep them in accord with the changing perspectives of the parties and the world community.[75] As things, conditions, or circumstances never remain the same, any principle of changing conditions, if taken literally, would mean that treaties would be binding for scarcely any length of time. Observers therefore speak of "important," "fundamental," "vital," "total," or "essential" changes. Such words are meaningless without empirical reference or connection to preferred goals and clarified policies. Parties to agreements, it may be recalled, can state the same ambiguous words in the agreement itself and still not avoid difficulties of interpretation which in effect require new decisions at the time of termination.

Consider, for example, the most recent and authoritative of these carefully defined principles. The relevant provisions of

75. See McDougal and Lans, "Treaties and Congressional-Executive or Presidential Agreements," in McDougal and Assoc., supra note 3, at 404, 601. For a discussion of the relationship between change, legitimacy, and treaties, see Levontin, supra note 9, at 141–54.

Article 62 of the Vienna Convention on the Law of Treaties read as follows:

1. A fundamental change of circumstances which has occurred with regard to those existing at the time of the conclusion of a treaty, and which was not foreseen by the parties, may not be invoked as a ground for terminating or withdrawing from the treaty unless:

(a) the existence of those circumstances constituted an essential basis of the consent of the parties to be bound by the treaty; and

(b) the effect of the change is radically to transform the extent of obligations still to be performed under the treaty.

2. A fundamental change of circumstances may not be invoked as a ground for terminating or withdrawing from a treaty:

(a) if the treaty establishes a boundary; or

(b) if the fundamental change is the result of a breach by the party invoking it either of an obligation under the treaty or of any other international obligation owed to any other party to the treaty.[76]

What is wrong with this article? Nothing is right![77]

From the Commentary to the International Law Commission (ILC) formulation of Article 62 we learn that "[t]he Commission gave the closest consideration to the formulation of these conditions," and that "[i]t attached great importance in [sic] expressing

76. U.N. Doc. A/Conf. 39/27 (1969) in 8 *Int'l Legal Mat.* 702 (1969); Rosenne, infra note 82, at 324 (subsection 3 is omitted).

77. It should be noted from the outset that with the growing interdependence in the modern world one can no longer think in terms of a single monolithic law of treaty termination. The origin of the conventional practice to encompass all agreements under a single rule, as done in Article 62, is also traceable to the eighteenth and nineteenth centuries. Because of the laissez-faire economic and political philosophy of the time, law was solely oriented toward minimum order. International agreements between the major actors were monolithic, dealing mainly with matters of power and security. But currently the NATO Treaty, the Geneva Accords, the Common Market Agreement, the U.N. Charter, or the Panama Canal Treaty, are too different in so many ways that they may require the application of diverse principles. See Bilder, "Breach of Treaty and Response Thereto," 1967 *Proc. Am. Soc. Int'l L.* at 193, 202.

them in objective terms." [78] A condition that "[t]he change must relate to a fact or situation which existed at the time when the treaty was entered into" [79] implies that circumstances existing at a certain moment do not necessarily exist at another, and that a subsequent change in circumstances may relate to some of these circumstances but not to others. Presumably, the commentator was trying to direct our attention to that change that frustrates ("importantly") the parties' expectations of continuity. This is, of course, a fundamental policy in the termination of international agreements. It received, however, inadequate treatment.

How can a change in circumstances not relate to circumstances that existed at a previously given moment? Presumably again, sometime between that moment and the moment at which the alleged changes occur, a new fact or situation comes into being. A change with regard to this latter type of circumstance, according to the article, is not a change related to the circumstances existing at the particular given moment, and therefore does not justify the invocation of the principle. Why this is so, or should be so, is unclear, and the question may still be asked, how new facts or situations may come into existence without the occurrence of some sort of change, i.e. without being somewhat related to previously existing circumstances. After all, a "fundamental change" may be composed of many interrelated—successive and simultaneous—changes. It is absurd to divide the world into a series of snapshots in terms of time (or space) and attempt to find or reject a relation between them on arbitrary grounds.[80] Whether the Commission likes it or not, any definition of change in terms of relation is necessarily a subjective definition, unless common criteria are given for such a relation in terms of experience and policy.

78. Int'l L. Comm'n Report [1963] 2 Y.B. Int'l L. Comm'n 210(10) U.N. Doc. A/CN.4/SER.A/1963/Add.1. The Commission "further decided that, in order to emphasize the objective character of the rule, it would be better not to use the term 'rebus sic stantibus' either in the text of the Article or even in the title, and so avoid the doctrinal implication [tacit clause] of that term" (id. at 209 [7]).

79. Id. at 210(10). This is the only interpretation given in the ILC Commentary to the similar words of the article itself.

80. For the practical differences following from this focus on single events see chs. 8 and 9 infra.

What is even more striking in this definition is the assumption on which it is based. The assumption is that reality is particular and concrete, so that a definition of a fundamental change must necessarily be in terms of actual facts which "exist" or do not "exist" at a certain moment (i.e. "at the time of the conclusion of the treaty"). That may not be precisely so, and in any case is subject to a great deal of conceptual and definitional argument. The world consists of events and relations, none of which can claim a superior grade of existence. The same holds true for any international agreement. A treaty, like any decision or rule of law, does not merely "exist" at a certain given moment containing rights and obligations, but is something more than this. It is the repeated occurrence of a certain kind of behavior, a certain kind of persuasive interaction in regard to the allocation of specific values. The understanding of any treaty, like the understanding of any decision-making process, involves not only an inquiry into the past but also a prophecy of the future. Our concern is with human behavior as it molds and is molded by the treaty.

This failure to conceive of treaties in terms of continuing patterns of communication and operation found its expression in another condition of Article 62: "the existence of those circumstances constituted an essential basis of the consent of the parties to be bound by the treaty." This condition is the product of two fallacies. The first is the notion that there is an absolute line of distinction between subjective consent and environmental facts. The second is that there is a one-way causal relationship between the two or that one is the "basis" or foundation for the other. Consent has no objectified existence distinct from social process and expectations.[81]

The absurdity of the conditions is even more striking when we realize that all we can learn from the commentary about the empirical reference of the concepts used in the article is that general changes of circumstances have been divided into changes occurring "inside" the treaty and "quite outside" the treaty, and that the latter may bring the article ino operation only if their "effect is to

---

81. The problem of the relation between consent and interaction can be compared with the philosophical or psychological problem of the relation between free will and environmental factors. See F. S. Cohen, *The Legal Conscience* 349 (1960).

alter a fact or situation constituting an essential basis of the parties' consent to the treaty." [82] Presumably, such changes are still related to the treaty even though they are somehow different from changes "inside" the treaty. But that is simply double-talk and a distorted picture of the world's interaction. It confirms Thomas Reed Powell's famous saying that "if you can think about something that is related to something else without thinking about the thing to which it is related, then you have the legal mind." [83]

It seems, however, that the failure of the Vienna Convention and observers to come to grips with the effects of social changes on treaties is even more fundamental. The prospect of determining the consequences of an infinite number of changes on many types of social interaction is indeed a monumental task unless approached with some discriminating criteria for judging which consequences are important. Unless a decision maker is able to concentrate on the important consequences of certain social factors, he is likely to be lost in an endless maze of trivialities. But to define a fundamental change in terms of a relation to facts (without any criterion) that constitute the essential basis of a consent, is to encourage decision makers to determine what is fundamental by referring to what is basically essential. The most logical of logical jurists would fail to indicate the difference between the three key words for the rendering of a decision. What should be decisive is not whether a fact that was fundamental to the foundation of the agreement has changed fundamentally, but the criteria for "fundamental" in terms of the effect on human behavior and preferred social order. To this, we do not find an answer other than the second requirement, which is that the effect of this combination of fundamental factors "is radically to transform the extent of the obligations."

Legal concepts that are not defined in terms of empirical facts or policy are necessarily circular, since these terms are themselves the creation of law. A criterion of importance necessarily pre-

---

82. Supra note 78, at 210(10). See also Int'l L. Comm'n, supra note 1, at 87[10]. For extensive references to the legislative history of Article 62, see S. Rosenne, *The Law of Treaties* 326 (1970).

83. Quoted from L. Fuller, note 74 supra, at 4. It was practically impossible, of course, to obtain agreements at the ILC and the Vienna Conference on legal concepts defined in terms of empirical facts. Cf. Rosenne, supra note 82, at 48ff.

supposes a criterion of values, and the distinction can be made only in similar terms. The question of what is an important change is senseless unless we attach significance to certain goals and come to grips with the social impact of these changes on the realization of such goals and policies.[84] Lacking any common criteria of what is fundamental, decision makers attach significance to certain changes through the screen of their own pursued and perceived values. After all, the very fact that parties are in conflict about the continuous enforcement of an agreement means that they attach degrees of importance to certain circumstances, and

84. The doctrine of rebus sic stantibus can make sense when it is functionally defined in accordance with modern economic theories and applied to treaties of economic transactions (which are not the subject of this book). An economic theory that may be most useful for this purpose is the theory of Second Best Optimum. This theory states that if changes in conditions are introduced into an optimal arrangement by a constraint which violates one or more of the optimum conditions, the other conditions, although still attainable, are no longer desirable. "In other words, given that one of the Paretian optimum conditions cannot be fulfilled, then an optimum situation can be achieved only by departing from all the other Paretian conditions. The optimum situation finally attained may be termed a second best optimum because it is achieved subject to a constraint which, by definition, prevents the attainment of a Paretian optimum" (Lipsey and Lancaster, "The General Theory of Second Best," 24 *Rev. Econ. Studies* 11 [1956–57]). "[T]here is no *a priori* way to judge as between various situations in which some of the Paretian optimum conditions are fulfilled while others are not. Specifically, it is *not* true that a situation in which more, but not all, of the optimum conditions are fulfilled is necessarily, or is even likely to be, superior to a situation in which fewer are fulfilled. It follows, therefore, that in a situation in which there exist many constraints which prevent the fulfillment of the Paretian optimum conditions, the removal of any one constraint may affect welfare or efficiency either by raising it, by lowering it, or by leaving it unchanged" (id. at 11–12). The most common example for the economic theory of second-best concerns trade barriers and customs unions. The theory shows, for example, that the removal of tariffs from some imports may cause a decrease, rather than an increase, in world productive efficiency and welfare. "[T]he adoption of a free trade policy by one country, in a multi-country tariff ridden world, may actually lower the real income of that country and of the world" (id. at 14). See also McManus, "Comments on the General Theory of Second Best," 26 *Rev. Econ. Studies* 209 (1958–59); Lancaster and Lipsey, "McManus on Second Best," id. at 225; Davis and Whinston, "Welfare Economics and the Theory of Second Best," 32 *Rev. Econ. Studies* 1 (1965). The latter distinguish between situations where peacemeal policy is all that is required to ameliorate a change in conditions (of which the corresponding legal technique is reinterpretation of the treaty), and situations where the policy-maker must consider all the functionally interconnected conditions in order to avoid undesirable consequences (corresponding to termination or revision because of changed conditions).

unless they are provided with a common criterion of importance, the claim and the counterclaim may seem to be equally founded. To call a norm such as Article 62 "objective" is indeed an offense against the ethics of linguistic propriety.

The question is how a decision maker who comes upon a peculiar fact and seeks to understand it should conduct his inquiry. A policy approach to decision making suggests that he should seek to discover the significance of the fact through its implications or effects in a given social context. A social fact has no real significance apart from the actual behavior of the participants. The legal differences that are supposed to follow from its arbitrary classification are meaningless for empirical decisions. Moreover, every legal problem, functionally viewed, involves a conflict of interests since the decision will affect the distribution of resources among the parties. The stability of any proposed or mandatory solution will depend largely upon a correct appraisal of the objectives of the parties in terms of those values which they pursue and those which will be effected or frustrated by the decision. Jurists and decision makers alike who shut their eyes to such "non-legal" evidence of factors as reveal the special significance of a claim, will soon find out that their nicely defined "impartial" or "objective" principles which are supposedly followed are in fact not followed.

### The Principle Brought to an End

Scholars have also advanced other definitions of the doctrine of rebus sic stantibus that are based neither on the original intention of the parties with regard to changes in existing circumstances nor on the very nature of the change, but which, rather, focus on the effects of the change on the agreement. Common-law lawyers usually tend to draw an analogy between the doctrine of frustration of contracts in domestic law and the doctrine of rebus sic stantibus. Continental jurists draw a similar analogy from the French public law theory of *imprevision*.[85] According to this view,

85. For such analogies see Williams, supra note 29, at 92; Cattand, *La Clause "Rebus Sic Stantibus" du Droit Privé en Droit International* 19ff. (1929); Alsing Trading Co., v. The Greek State, Arbitral Award of Dec. 22, 1954, [1956] *Int'l L. Rep.* at 633; van Bogaert, supra note 26, at 69. C. Rousseau, *Principes Généraux du Droit International Public* 544 (1944).

a change of circumstances that frustrates the objectives of the agreement should be a basis for termination. In its general lines this approach seems to have its merits, since the principle applies whenever specific, shared expectations with regard to the question of termination are lacking. Thus, it may evade the legal fiction of the intention of the parties and at the same time still be advantageous.

However, some writers see in the attainment of the objectives of a treaty a rigid condition of its obligatory basis.[86] Another school requires that, because of a change, performance becomes physically impossible (*force majeure*).[87] Others are satisfied with moral impossibility in the sense of unreasonable sacrifice.[88] Another school of thought, we have seen, brings up a definition of the doctrine requiring that fulfillment of a treaty would be injurious to a list of fundamental rights such as existence, self-development, independence, or some otherwise vital interest of a party to the treaty as a consequence of a change.[89] And some German writers—mainly of the last century—assert the right of termination on the mere basis of national interest and expediency.[90]

Most of the definitions that focus on the effects of the change on the agreement tend also to neglect to give criteria, in terms of policy and experience, for the relevancy of a specific change to the alleged effects. The definition of the doctrine in terms of fundamental rights or interests, in fact, broadens the doctrine as based upon the frustration of the objectives of the parties. Since, in a most general way, the parties in processes of agreement seek their self-development, this general objective is frustrated when changes

86. Williams, supra note 29, at 92. P. Fiore, *Nouveau Droit International Public* 412ff. (1885); 1 F. de Martens, *Précis du Droit Des Gens Moderne de L'Europe* §§52–53, 58 (ed. Vergé 1864).

87. See Hill, supra note 22, at 12.

88. See Garner, supra note 30, at 512.

89. W. Hall, *A Treatise on International Law* 368 (1917). Referring mainly to peace treaties, Hall adds a reservation: "provided that its injurious effects were not intended by the two contracting parties at the time of its conclusion." Garner, supra note 30, at 513; Oppenheim-Lauterpacht, supra note 22, at 940. Woolsey, supra note 30, at 349.

90. See Hill, supra note 22, at 12, for the views of numerous writers who have based the doctrine, wholly or partly, on the promotion of state interests.

occur that make performance injurious to this "right." prima facie, this theory seems to limit the doctrine of frustration, since the effects are required to be vitally injurious. But the words *vital*, or *existence* are not really as restrictive as they may seem to be. There is almost no agreement, either between governments or between commentators, as to what is meant by these rights, except perhaps that each state has a right to determine for itself what constitutes a matter of vital interest or existence.

The allegedly crucial doctrinal distinction between a definition in terms of "fundamental change" and a definition in terms of "vital interest" is even less clear, even though a majority of writers regard the first as an objective definition and the second as a subjective one. Since any change that may render performance of a treaty burdensome necessarily affects some interests of one party or another, the doctrinal definition in terms of vital interest cannot differ from that of fundamental change, unless—and even then it is doubtful—the latter is given common criteria based on the common interest as distinct from the special interests of the individual states.[91] This, as we have already seen, is not the case. To define the doctrine in terms of a fundamental change and then to proceed by attacking as anarchists the doctrinalists of the vital interest under the flag of order and stability, is to wage war on windmills.[92] The legal process must reconcile as best it can the real interests that are in conflict, rather than dismiss the existence of all of them as legally unsound.

Each of the above-mentioned definitions of the doctrine of rebus sic stantibus attempts to restrict in some way the relevancy of changes. In doing so, observers have also been aware of some cases or situations which, though excluded from the application

91. "Every assertion of a 'fact' about the social world touches the interests of some individual or group" Louis Wirth, quoted from H. Lasswell and M. Kaplan, *Power and Society* 118 [1951]). The assertion of an "important" fact merely touches an important or vital interest of some individual or group.

92. "Most writers, however, believe that it is impossible to base the obligatory force of treaties solely on the interests of the parties because this in fact substitutes mere utilitarianism for a normative principle and denies the judicial character of treaties. This definition . . . can be traced to Machiavelli" (Hill, supra note 22, at 12). A major goal of any principle must, of course, be the protection of overriding common interests (McDougal, Lasswell, and Miller, supra note 3, at 41).

of their theory, should not be so excluded, either because of additional considerations of justice or policy or because of actual state practice. Thus in *Lucern v. Aargau* (1882) for example, the Swiss Federal Court disjunctively combined two different versions of the doctrine when it formulated the precise grounds for termination:

> [T]here is no doubt that treaties may be denounced unilaterally by the party under obligation, if their continuance is incompatible with its vital interests as an independent commonwealth or with its fundamental purposes, or if there has taken place such a change of circumstances as, according to the apparent intention of the parties, constituted, at the time of its creation, an implied condition of its continued existence.[93]

Such a disjunctive combination allows decision makers and observers alike to benefit from the merits of more than one doctrine but suffer less from the disadvantages of any. It is strict with claimants and at the same time offers alternative criteria for cases where it seems improper to reject a claim on the basis of one criterion alone.

Article 62 of the Convention on the Law of Treaties is in a very novel way indeed a combination of various theories. All four types of theories—the very *nature* of the change, the *intention* of the parties or their consent, the *existence* of peculiar facts at the time of agreement, and the *effects* of the change on the agreement—are combined conjunctively and cumulatively in one and the same definition rather than distributively. This formula, then, is much stricter than any other particular theory that can be quoted in its support.[94] Thus, the article in its present form seems to suffer the disadvantages of all theories and to benefit from the particular merits of none, and is limited to the point where it may reject almost any claim for termination.

93. Quoted in Lauterpacht, supra note 63, at 169–70 n.2; McNair, supra note 22, at 690.

94. Article 62(1)(a) represents more or less the most popular theory developed by civil law jurists. Article 62(1)(b) represents the most popular common-law approach. Thus on its face the article appears to have the support of the majority of European and American opinions on the subject.

For better results, however, Article 62 has been further restricted. It applies only to executory treaty provisions,[95] and only when the alleged change in circumstances is not foreseen by the parties at the effective date of the agreement. Furthermore, it is possible to argue under the convention that even if a particular obligation satisfies all the conditions of the article (which is unlikely), the claimant party is still not authorized to effect a unilateral termination in the face of the other side's objection but only to invoke the article and to seek a mutually satisfactory solution.[96]

Never in its long history has the principle of rebus sic stantibus been so restricted and watered down as in our time. It does no good to suggest that perhaps the authors of the convention did not perceive all the implications of their formulation, for this is merely to substitute one discourtesy for another. Obviously, the limitation of the principle to the point where it rejects all claims to termination is the product of some policy considerations, and particularly the overemphasized goal of stability. The ILC, which had drafted the convention before it was deliberated upon and adopted at the Vienna Conference, has been overly concerned with the danger of abuse that the principle entails. The effect of this overdemanding formulation is, however, to divorce authority from effective control completely.[97] The principle supposedly embodied in Article 62 seems to have already shared the inevitable fate of all rules that require the impossible: it has been honored by breach from its very inception. At the very time when deliberations within the ILC on Article 62 were taking place, even states whose represen-

95. Article 62(1)(b): "obligations still to be performed under the treaty." Article 62(a): "if the treaty establishes a boundary." For a more detailed discussion of this point, see ch. 7 and app. B infra.

96. Briggs, "Unilateral Denunciation of Treaties, the Vienna Convention and the International Court of Justice" 68 *Am. J. Int'l L.* 51, 55–57 (1974). See the detailed discussion of this point in ch. 6 infra.

97. Thus, some critics express a sense of uselessness regarding the Convention. One suggestion, for example, is that Article 62 should be broadened on the ground that it does not matter much whether it is formulated one way or another: "The dangers for the stability of treaties and of the international community residing in the doctrine of *rebus sic stantibus* can be exaggerated. The idea that it can play a significant role in unleashing determined law-breakers and aggressors such as Hitler is fantastic. Great political issues are not decided by international law" (Lissitzyn, supra note 1, at 915–16).

tatives were the most vocal in demanding the restrictive formulation of the principle acted contrary to it.[98] Such conduct cannot but lend support to the suspicion that some governments operate on the basis of a conviction that the difference between having an unrealistically overdemanding law and having no law at all is small indeed.[99]

98. France, for instance; compare [1963] 1 Y.B. Int'l L. Comm'n 153–54 with the French conduct of the 1966 Franco-American dispute as discussed in the following chapters. For a discussion of the French decisions to withdraw from NATO's military organization and to terminate American and Canadian military bases in France in terms of Article 62 and other articles of the Convention, see Stein and Carreau, "Law and Peaceful Change in a Subsystem: Withdrawal of France from NATO," 62 *Am. J. Int'l L.* 577, 618 (1968).

99. Note an important change in the principle rebus sic stantibus since World War I. During the period immediately following the First World War, the Allies were overwhelmingly more powerful than Germany. Attention, therefore, generally shifted from the risks that are usually involved in bargaining on termination between parties of relative equal power to the imposition of restrictions on substantive legal or moral grounds that might give rise to claims to termination. Furthermore, termination by unilateral acts, we have seen, was generally said to be unlawful, which left little room for regulation of the bargaining process itself. As events unfolded it became even clearer that nothing short of war could settle Germany's claims. It is interesting to compare in this respect the outbreak of World War I (supra note 42) with the beginning of World War II. In the latter, several months elapsed from the time decisions to go to war had been made until the war was vigorously fought (hence this period was called the "phony war"). There was ample time to reverse the decision to go to war, but this could not be done because in the final analysis the claims and counterclaims were irreconcilable. This stands in contrast to the classical balance of power period, in which governments were flexible about their claims, and their main concern was how to prevent particular conflicts from ending in general war.

Currently, attention has been focusing again on both the clarification of policies regarding the events that may give rise to claims about termination (e.g. Vienna Convention Article 62), and the regulation of the dynamic development of conflicts once such a claim is put forward (Article 65 and the Annex). The authors of the Vienna Convention have failed to clarify in Article 62 the substantive grounds of termination following changed circumstances, and it is doubtful whether these grounds are capable of such doctrinal formulation at all. The following chapters will therefore be mainly concerned with the second task. It will be demonstrated that the regulation of the dynamic development of conflicts must necessarily also determine the content of substantive principles (app. A infra).

# 2 The Unilateral Termination of Modern Treaties

> You've got to be a model thief if I am to be a model judge. If
> you are a fake thief I become a fake judge.
>
> Jean Genet, *The Balcony*

This chapter explores some of the more general theoretical aspects
of bargaining on treaty termination as a way of gaining insight into
the dynamics of what have hitherto been characterized as unilateral, but are in fact reciprocal actions in the global arena. I shall
seek to demonstrate that the conventional legal concept of "unilateral termination" is currently not only meaningless as a criterion
of unlawfulness, but is also destructive of general international
law. Moreover, this either-or concept inhibits any comprehensive
discussion of the real problems of treaty termination. Indeed,
scholars who see the test for legality in "unilaterality" usually have
very little to say on the subject beyond giving a mere negative or
affirmative answer to whether or not such a practice is authorized.

A more promising approach is to be found in an empirical
breakdown of the choices made by parties during termination
controversies. Generally stated, our primary concern is the general
problem of governments reaching decisions when they are in conflict with other governments in regard to prior arrangements between them, and when there are risks and uncertainties involved
in the outcomes of their choices. In comparatively few cases will
the parties turn to any institutionalized form of third-party decision making.[1] For the most part they resort to strategic bargaining. Thus, the concept of strategy is a key to understanding the interdependence of the parties' moves during conflicts, and to
providing alternative criteria for lawful terminations.

## STRATEGIC SEQUENCES OF UNILATERAL ACTS

The concept of strategy refers to the sequences in which resources are manipulated in reaching a decision. Though strategies

1. Ch. 6 infra.

are ways by which parties affect the outcomes of disputes, they are also the function of all other variables in pre-outcome phases.[2] One cannot predict, for example, what a party may do in a given conflict if only the quality and amount of available resources are known. Since governments are continuously engaged in multiple relationships, risking their entire resources on a particular conflict could be fatal. Many strategies that are possible in a particular controversy may be rejected because they give rise to other consequences, undesirable in themselves.

In a most general sense, the choice of particular strategies is determined by the parties' predispositions and objectives in regard to the final outcome.[3] On a more detailed level of analysis, the concept of strategy is concerned with choices among alternative actions rather than directly with choices among alternative end-situations. There is, in short, a second order in the valuational process through which objectives are modified by considerations of strategy.[4] Since one participant does not usually have complete control over all the variables that may lead to his preferred outcome, his best course of action will depend in great part upon choices and decisions which the other participant or participants

2. McDougal, Lasswell, and Reisman, "The World Constitutive Process of Authoritative Decision," 19 *J. Legal Ed.* 253, 403 (1967).

3. This assumes that among alternate strategies that give rise to outcomes, a party will choose those which, in its estimation, yield the most preferred outcome. The maximization postulate, since it embraces whatever it is that people desire, is somewhat tautological, but is usually employed in the social sciences as a useful dynamic instrument of analysis. See, e.g., J. von Neumann and O. Morgenstern, *Theory of Games and Economic Behavior* ch. 1 (1944); R. Luce and H. Raiffa, *Games and Decisions* 50 (1957); A. Rapoport, *Fights, Games, and Debates* 107–08 (1960); M. McDougal, H. Lasswell, and I. Vlasic, *Law and Public Order in Space* 17 (1963); M. McDougal, H. Lasswell, and J. Miller, *Interpretation of Agreements and World Public Order* 16 (1967). I do not attempt in what follows to verify the postulate, but rather to describe particular choices in termination controversies, and to determine, from the perspective of an observer, the parties' objectives from these choices. Even retrospective examination of particular strategies and tactics may not always be successful in determining the more specific objectives of the parties. Often it is difficult to find out whether a particular choice was caused by a specific preference, a deficiency in skill, the lack of necessary information on the part of a participant or an observer, or a variety of other factors. Besides, for various tactical reasons or personal motives, the parties may have inconsistent preferences or may wish to conceal their true preferences, a fact that may be embodied in the strategy chosen.

4. M. Kaplan, *System and Process in International Politics* 170 (1957).

make. Hence the term "strategy" must always take into account the interdependence of the adversaries' decisions in solving conflicts and their expectations of each other's behavior.[5]

Each action, move, or step in the development of a given conflict is in itself a point of renewed decision for the participants. This decision is usually a particular choice made by a party from among a set of alternative courses of action. Each such specified move, in turn, provides the adversary with another set of alternative moves among which he must choose. The process of bargaining (tacit or direct) is, thus, a sequence of choices, made simultaneously or successively until resolution of the particular conflict is reached.

An empirically based concept of "termination of an agreement," then, does not denote a single act of participation in a conflict, but rather a flow of moves and countermoves, decisions and subdecisions, that have been made from those potentially available. In other words, the overall decision is partitioned into subsets of interdependent decisions which we may usefully try to distinguish from one another.[6] Some of the most obvious instances of such subdecisions in termination disputes are: an initial fait accompli; a claimant state's demand to enter into negotiation on the central claim to termination; an objecting side's total or partial rejection of proposals to enter into direct talks on the central demand; negotiations on the agenda for talks; varying degrees of warnings and commitments to threats and promises, which are tied to the central claim, related issues, or to the demand to negotiate; the gradual fulfillment of threats; reprisals to treaty violations; retaliations to reprisals; and so on.

## The Concept of "Unilateral Termination"

Central to the above model of the bargaining process is the idea, then, that it is not the arbitrary single act of one party, but rather

5. T. Schelling, *The Strategy of Conflict* 16, 83 (1963). The description in the text is modeled on the elementary variables that constitute games of strategy. The analysis of these games provides insight into the conduct of a variety of social conflicts. See also Rapoport, supra note 3, at 108. The limitations inherent in any limited factor-analysis, such as game theory and analytical jurisprudence, will be pointed out throughout the discussion.

6. Luce and Raiffa, supra note 3, at 39ff.

the chain of actions and reactions of *all* the parties to the dispute, that usually comprises a given decision to terminate a treaty (expressed simply: "it takes two to have an argument"). Hence such an analysis avoids falling into the pitfalls of conventional law writings, which, following the model of adversary judicial proceedings in domestic law, tend to fix sole legal responsibility for blameworthy decision outcomes on only one side or another.[7] This tendency both undermines the necessary objectivity of scholarship and obscures the fact that an adequate theory of international law must constantly take account of a reality in which issues are determined for the most part by the reciprocities of effective behavior, and not just by court wranglings.

In legal parlance, for instance, "unilateral termination" refers to a decision to terminate a former agreement objected to by the other side. Of course, objections can appear in many forms, ranging from violent enforcement to formal protests. In denouncing all unilateral termination as arbitrary and illegal, most jurists, however, do not distinguish between appearance and substance in the reactions of objecting parties.[8] As a matter of fact most, if not all, steps in the development of given conflicts are unilateral in the sense that they represent the choices that are made by each party. But each such choice, even when it is made despite the other party's objection, is usually made from among those alternatives which have been opened (or foreclosed) partly by the opponent's previous move; each such so-called unilateral act must take into account the past and probable future moves of others, which it usually invites and to which the same party will have to react in any way.

In this process of bargaining, therefore, the events that often are crudely referred to as "unilateral termination" are seen as a single move or sequence of moves, and not necessarily as outcomes; for they may represent only one among many other choices still available to the objecting party in the strategy sets of the particular conflict. The outcome of the conflict, on the other hand, is the point at which an observer may determine that the parties have settled for the time being. It is a solution to the dispute, except

7. Cf. R. Falk, *The Status of Law in International Society* 12, 335 (1970).
8. Supra, ch. 1, note 57.

perhaps in the ideal situation of total wars that end with the total annihilation of one side, or in situations of extreme coercion, not because there are no longer available options for a party or parties to choose from, but because they choose not to move any further on the same or related matters. If one regards failure to act as a choice in itself, it appears quite obvious that "unilateral" termination may occasionally be regarded as collaborative termination—as a kind of tacit agreement by which both sides chose to settle at that particular point of outcome from a set, or sets, of other possible choices.

Parties, however, do protest such "unilateral" outcomes of conflicts. Some protests are not to be dismissed lightly, since they suggest that the protesting party does not really consider the conflict terminated and the apparent solution permanent. But if a direct reaction is not forthcoming, or if the protesting party does not in retaliation initiate another conflict on a separate matter, then, for all practical purposes, the conflict may be regarded as settled. For various unrelated reasons, such as avoiding the establishment of a precedent and warning that similar decisions in the future will not be accepted, governments may still feel obliged—at least formally—to protest the unconsensual, formal character of a decision.[9] The very fact, however, that the focus in such protests is on the future, indicates that they consider the present dispute ended.

## The Berlin Crisis of 1961

There are additional reasons for formal protests against unilateral terminations. In some disputes, the objecting side must acquiesce in a solution but cannot publicly agree to it. Consider, for example, the recurring Soviet threats during the fifties and sixties to sign a separate peace treaty with East Germany—a unilateral repudiation of some treaty provisions. Such a treaty could not have done much more than formally legalize a situation that had long existed; yet its ideological value was obvious. A formal peace treaty between the Soviet Union and East Germany would

---

9. For a discussion of such reasons, see M. Kaplan and N. Katzenbach, *The Political Foundations of International Law* 22–23 (1961). For the role of protest in the formation or modification of customary international law, see A. D'Amato, *The Concept of Custom in International Law* 98ff. (1971).

have appeared to commit the former to the final division of Germany. Its immediate effect would have been to embarrass Western officials, nothing more. The West could not have publicly agreed to the final division of Germany, but in reality it lived with it. Some groups in Western Europe may even have preferred a permanently divided Germany to a Germany united and much more powerful. If the Soviet threats to sign a separate peace treaty had been carried out, however, there might have been pressure for evacuation of Soviet occupation forces from East Germany. In such an event, pressure for unification within Germany probably would have mounted. This may partly account for the fact that the threat, though frequently used, was not carried out.

A key concept in commitments to threats, i.e., credibility, depends not only on physical power but also on the reputation of the threatener. Past performance in fulfilling threats is an important, although equivocal, factor in credibility. Lieberman, for one, notes that "Russia's failure to carry out one threat to sign a separate peace treaty with East Germany might reduce credibility of a subsequent threat or might enhance it, since, because of the failure, self-respect or political reputation might be more significantly at stake the next time." [10] Had the West taken the view that past failures meant reduced credibility, it might have increased the chance that the threat would eventually be carried out.

So the West had to take the view that performance was more likely in the future. However, to take an official view that the chances of an adversary's threat being carried out are good, without committing oneself to some kind of material reaction, is politically difficult. Serious reaction was unthinkable in this case. Accordingly, Western governments have officially protested the possibility, regarding it as a "grave matter" of "great concern," and have tried to persuade the Soviets not to bring it about. Thus, the Soviet Union was able to continue to create "crises" (whenever the international situation seemed to call for them) by means of this threat, but without carrying it out. Of course, such crises have strengthened Soviet justifications for the continued stationing

10. Lieberman, "Threat and Assurance in the Conduct of Conflict," in *International Conflict and Behavioral Science,* 110, 112 (R. Fisher ed. 1964).

of their forces in East Germany, and their actual effect has been to make the possibility of a separate peace treaty with East Germany even more remote.

One way to create a crisis atmosphere and to appear to be enhancing credibility in regard to the fulfillment of threats, is to start performance on a smaller scale (as in promises). Such was the case in the erection of the Berlin Wall in 1961, again in defiance of some treaty provisions. The building of the wall to limit civilian travel to Berlin raised a huge outcry from the West. Apart from verbal protestations, however, no measures were taken against the unilateral decision. In this conflict, to react in the face of the Soviet fait accompli could have meant war—possibly nuclear war.

A government that does not react because the probable cost is war or great injury cannot be said to acquiesce lawfully in a unilateral act. If every acceptance of the realities of life were to be regarded as a shared outcome or a tacit consent, there would of course be no meaning to a lawful act apart from the power positions of the parties.

It is important, however, not to press this argument too far. Although, so stated, the dilemma seems to be a stark one, the decision whether to react or not is certainly more complicated. The difference in coercion between various forms of accepting "facts" is one of degree, not of kind. Before the extreme measure of blunt military force to effect unilateral termination or to enforce a treaty against an unwilling party, there usually is a jumbled middle ground of warnings, commitments to threats and promises, direct talks, various degrees of implementation, bluffs, backings out, and so on. In many cases it is difficult to find a clear-cut relation between "unilateral" decision and coercion.

Interesting points are raised in this respect when one examines the specific decision to build the Berlin Wall in relation to its broader context. The act of raising the wall was incidental to the main issues as they appeared in the claims, demands, proposals, threats, and warnings embraced within the 1961 crisis. The Soviet central claim was to conclude a permanent peace settlement in Germany, following the de facto division of the country. This claim was explicitly concerned with the elimination or diminution of the free access of Western powers to West Berlin rather than with the free movement of civilians within all of Berlin.[11]

In 1961, the Western governments differed on the choice of a strategy program for handling the dispute. The United States and Great Britain favored direct talks on the Soviet claims. France objected. The joint strategy chosen was a refusal to negotiate accompanied by a deterrent threat. The West has insisted that any interference with its access to Berlin would be serious enough to justify a war, including, perhaps, a nuclear war.[12] Chairman Khrushchev, however, vowed publicly that the deadline for settling the dispute would not be withdrawn in 1961 as it had been in 1959. Many observers agreed that the Soviet leader had gone much too far to back down. By August 12, 1961, everyone had begun to realize that the situation could not continue much longer and that something was sure to happen. The only question was whether it would involve war.

In such situations, if one side does not clearly concede and if the parties do not collide, it is because both sides tacitly collaborate in pressing the conflict into areas where gains and losses do not involve direct military confrontation. It takes perhaps only one side to start a conflict or enlarge it to the point of military engagement, but both sides are always needed to de-escalate the conflict or to narrow the issues and decisions made. The interdependence of the parties' decisions springs from their common interest in avoiding mutual damage.

Thus, in making some kind of "unilateral" act, the Soviet Union had still to explore the possibilities of collaborative reaction from the West. At least five points seemed to be logically inferable from the Western position: (a) unilateral satisfaction of the central demands would trigger war, perhaps nuclear war; (b) yet by favoring direct negotiations on the Soviet claims, the United States and Britain demonstrated a strong desire to avoid

---

11. The demand that initiated the Berlin crisis of 1961 was forwarded in a Russian *aide-memoir* of June 4, 1961, presented in a summit conference at Vienna. J. Smith, *The Defense of Berlin* 232 (1963). H. Speier, *Divided Berlin* 132 (1961). It repeated the original Soviet note of Nov. 27, 1958. For a more detailed discussion of the U.S. legal position, see chs. 4 and 5 infra.

12. Ch. 5 infra.

military confrontation; [13] (c) hence, some unilateral acts not in fulfillment of the central demands were likely to escape the threat of war, the West having been committed only to maintain the freedom of West Berlin and its people; [14] (d) even though, because of France's objection, direct talks were temporarily rejected, the central demands were, in the long run, negotiable; (e) therefore, if something had been done by way of mounting pressure, negotiations might have become acceptable to the West. An act that was only indirectly related to the central demand might even reduce the likelihood of war if, following that act, the West were indeed to accept direct talks. At any rate, were the West not to accept negotiations immediately, winning some important issue over Berlin would enable the Soviet Union to back down from its initial threat. This was another reason why the West would not resist such an act.

### Up Again Down Again: Lifting the Drawbridge to Berlin

On August 12, the East German army, equipped with tanks and armored trucks, began sealing off the East-West border in Berlin. Roads connecting the two parts of the city were damaged and barbed-wire fences were reeled out at various points. The act of sealing the border continued for the next few days, during which period (and also thereafter) no restrictions on travel were applied to Allied forces.[15] Despite seemingly hurried conferences, it took

13. Ch. 4 infra.

14. U.S. note of July 17, in *New York Times*, July 19, 1961, p. 4, col. 1 (late city ed.); text correction in *New York Times*, July 20, p. 10, col. 3 (late city ed.).

15. In the first six months of 1960, the number of Germans who had left East Germany via Berlin reached 88,500. The corresponding figure for 1961 was 103,000. In July 1961, there was a steep rise in the movement of refugees, which had probably been caused by the atmosphere of crisis with regard to Berlin. Between July 9 and August 13 approximately 1,500 refugees arrived in West Berlin each day. This increase in defections aggravated the problems of the East German economy at a time of severe crisis. Generally speaking, East Germany's borders had been closed to migration, but the special status of Berlin had made West Berlin an easy "escape hatch" for those who wished to cross the border. The flight of refugees could have been halted either by applying travel restrictions between East Germany and all of Berlin, or by applying restrictions to travel within all sections of Berlin. Restricting travel between East Germany and all of Berlin, though lawful, would have divided East Berlin from East Germany and, further, would have been interpreted as a concession to the West. Soviet claims in Berlin, on the other hand, stressed the need for changes in the status quo toward "nor-

three entire days for the Western commanders in Berlin to inform their Soviet counterpart that the border closure and the massing of the troops of East Germany within East Berlin were violations of the 1945 four-power agreements.[16] In any event, following closely upon the protest sent to the Soviet Zone Commander, the Western powers sent three identical notes of protest to the Soviet Union. The legal argument on which the notes were based suggested that the protests were for the record only.[17] In a letter reportedly sent to the president of the United States on the same day, the mayor of West Berlin urged "not merely words but political action." [18]

Finally action was taken. On August 18, the United States government announced that it was sending fifteen hundred additional troops to West Berlin. In terms of a military operation in Berlin, this number of troops was of course insignificant. The point is, however, that this token force was intended to move across the 110-mile route through East Germany. The convoy carried highly symbolic equipment—two bulldozers—and their declared purpose was to push their way through any Communist obstruction that might block the way.[19] Specifically, the movement of troops was aimed at confirming the Western powers' right of passage through East Germany and not at challenging the particular act in question, i.e., the division of Berlin. As it happened, the bulldozers did not find any obstruction to push away, and they reached Berlin the next day together with a scheduled British military train.

---

malization," i.e. equating the status of Berlin with that of East Germany. Barring travel between East Germany and Berlin would have reversed this alleged trend.

16. Reprinted in *New York Times*, Aug. 16, 1961, p. 10, cols. 3, 4 (late city ed.).

17. See Smith, supra note 11, at 286. On August 13, Secretary of State Dean Rusk stated that the East German action was a violation of the four-power status of Berlin. This violation, he added, would be "the subject of vigorous protest through appropriate channels" (id. at 272). There was no demand that the illegal East German measures be halted or that the right of free movement within the city be restored. As will be explained, criteria of unlawfulness should be based on the lack of reasonable alternatives to a paper protest.

18. *New York Times*, Aug. 17, 1961, p. 1, col. 8 (late city ed.).

19. The East German announcement of closing the border in Berlin went to great lengths to reassure the West that the right of transit between West Berlin and West Germany would not be interfered with. See the Announcement of the Council of Ministers of the German Democratic Republic, reprinted in *New York Times*, Aug. 14, 1961, p. 6, cols. 4–6 (late city ed.).

While dismissing Western protests against the closing of the border, an official Soviet note, issued on the day of the troops' arrival, more than implied that the objectives of the Soviet Union in the unilateral act were indeed limited. The "defensive" measure of closing the border, the note said, could only be ended with the conclusion of an East German peace treaty. Thus, the Berlin border issue was interjected into the proposed negotiations. Further, a new status quo had been established from which such negotiations could be evaluated in favor of making concessions to the Soviet central demands.[20] The following day, United States officials reiterated the old theme that the freedom of the "people of West Berlin" is not negotiable. The parties had evidently reached their modus vivendi and the crisis subsided. Some time later, when it became evident that Western concessions on the Soviet demand were indeed not forthcoming, the barbed wire along the border was replaced by concrete and cement, thus establishing an appearance of finality.

### UNILATERAL TERMINATION AS AN AGREED OUTCOME

The tacit collaboration in the outcome of the Berlin crisis of 1961 can be traced to the parties' common desire to avoid war. Although there were issues the parties were not willing to concede even at the price of war, the Berlin Wall was not such an issue. The Western Powers' bargaining position on the wall manifested a deep gap between legitimacy and effectiveness. In a press conference shortly after the closing of the border, President Kennedy justified the acquiescence to the Soviet decision by once again stating that American, British, and French guarantees in regard to Berlin clearly applied only to West Berlin. He also pointed out that, for many years (i.e. since the Soviet Union walkout from the Allied Control Council in 1948), the three powers had had no control over events in the Soviet zone of Germany or in the Soviet sector of Berlin.[21] However, in their paper protests the Western powers denied the authority of East Germany or the Soviet Union to make the decision.

How had it happened that the parties had reached a point

20. F. Iklé, *How Nations Negotiate* 168 (1964). Ch. 4 infra.
21. Reprinted in *New York Times*, Oct. 12, 1961, p. 20, col. 7 (late city ed.).

where they were prepared to oppose certain, but not all, of the decisions while at the same time maintaining that all these decisions were unauthorized, pursuant to the same agreements? The truism that some issues are more important to the participants than others hardly advances the discussion. It would only repeat the basic assumption that the parties have a scale of preferences regarding possible outcomes of conflict situations. Preferences are determined by expectations, and expectations change during interaction. The de facto process of dividing Germany into two separate states, of rearming and integrating forces into the military alliances of both sides, had started long before it had culminated in the building of the wall. What each side did in its "own zone," contrary to the expectations that had prevailed at the conclusion of the agreements in question, had never passed from the level of conflict of ideologies to that of hard bargaining. The West, while acquiescent in the division of Germany, could not agree to it officially. Thus, the gap between authority and control continued to widen resulting in an apparent loss of credibility to claims for maintaining political control as well as to claims for preserving legal rights.

It is unnecessary in this context to go further in the discussion of whether the decision to build the wall in Berlin was lawful or not. This would require an examination of the treaties in question and a more detailed survey of the parties' subsequent conduct, factors which would be tested against the major policies of the international community. All that need be stressed now is that a particular termination of an agreement cannot be determined to be lawful or unlawful simply by an arbitrary formal test of unilateralism. This formal principle, even if it has some value for some purposes, has none whatsoever in determining the true preferences of the parties regarding the outcome of a dispute. The principle has no more utility than the paper protests that invoke it. Frequently, this supposedly authoritative principle only helps state officials carry out their ideological maneuvers, with the net result of hiding the ball from those who are not familiar with the intricacies of a particular match.

Underlying scholarly support for this principle is an unwarranted assumption that at least the objecting side almost always has an interest in holding to the former treaty arrangement, if not in coming to a new and explicit agreement of some kind. Consent, however, is a matter of degree. It is always determined, as in the Berlin crises of 1961, by sequences of interrelated choices, exhibiting different degrees of collaboration and conflict (either tacit or explicit), and different degrees of satisfying the parties' contingent scales of preferences. The impression of unilateral decision, in what are obviously noncoercive outcomes, is created partly because the objecting side often feels a strategic obligation to express the less-than-whole truth about its expectations of the other party's choices. In the examination of concrete decisions, we even come upon cases where an objecting side has a concealed preference that, if an agreement is to be terminated, it should be done by the claimant unilaterally. Indeed, sometimes "unilateral" termination by the claimant party appears to be the strategic choice of both the claimant and the objecting sides.

### An Example: The Rearmament of Germany in 1935

Part 5 of the Treaty of Versailles was terminated in 1935 by a German official announcement of national conscription.[22] Prior to this, prolonged negotiations had been conducted on mutual arms reductions in Europe. During these negotiations France, unlike Britain, had taken an intractable position that excluded almost all possibilities of compromise. Further, France repeatedly threatened that it would forcibly oppose any unilateral denunciation of the treaty. The balance of power overwhelmingly favored France. Yet, even when the German defiance of the treaty provisions became official, France declined to react.

If one accounts only for the relative armaments of Germany and France, an optimum solution of the conflict would seem to have been a negotiated settlement. Germany's new conscription, as announced at the time of the decision, aimed at a "peace strength" of 600,000 men. This amounted to six times more than what had been permitted by the denounced treaty, and twice as much as the 300,000 men that Germany had requested and France had rejected a year before. The immediate outcome of Germany's unilateral decision with regard to war materials was also two- or threefold more than that which the revision of the treaty—to

22. Ch. 1 supra.

which Germany had previously acceded—could have provided.[23] For France to reach an agreement on the revision of the treaty was advantageous, since Germany's potential military capacity was greater. For Germany, one advantage in reaching a new agreement was to forego the risk of France's making good its threats of military force in defense of the old agreement.

In this case, however, as in many others, the outcome preferences of the parties were determined to a great extent by considerations extraneous to the immediate issues at stake. Some useful insights can be gained in this respect by testing the psychology of political decision making against the highly simplified and artificial parameters of parlor games. Even the latter—and poker is a good example—are not always played on a strictly competitive basis, for often a player will incur an almost certain loss in order to take an exciting risk or to impress other players with his audacity at bluffing.[24] Similarly, for 1935 Germany the way in which the conflict was to be conducted was as important as the material gains in armaments directly involved, if not more so. In Germany, the Treaty of Versailles in general, and the unilateral and total disarmament of part 5 in particular, were regarded as the everlasting humiliation following defeat in World War I, and Nazi Germany was nourished and inflamed by these feelings. The government promised the country that it would strongly reassert its national sovereignty, and establish for it a "place in the sun." Termination of the old arrangements by the formal consent of France and Britain would have fallen short of satisfying those who were haunted by such feelings of national disgrace and humiliation. To demonstrate the "revival" of the country, the government

23. 1 A. Toynbee, *Survey of International Affairs 1935* 144 (Royal Inst. Int'l Affairs, 1936).

24. Luce and Raiffa, supra note 3, at 60. For discussions of how the serious affairs of life might be investigated through a study of the play of games, see also Riker, *The Theory of Political Coalitions* 13ff. (1962); Rapoport, supra note 3, at 107ff. The frequent statement that international relations are like a parlor game or a round of poker is, of course, simply incorrect. The psychology of a game can hardly be compared to the psychology of decision making in crisis situations. Nor does a reasonable man seriously equate the stakes in penny-ante poker with the stakes in nuclear war. Nonetheless, with appropriate caution, we may use game theory to isolate and study at close range limited features in interaction, and thereafter set our conclusions in a comprehensive contextual model.

needed something more assertive and spectacular. Hence, unilateral denunciation of the treaty provisions, without the consent of other powers, really suited Germany's objectives. Indeed, the German government, at least in the short term, stood to gain from the decision in direct proportion to the strength of the Allies' protests against the unilateral fashion in which the decision was made. In short, in March 1935 Germany gained not only in armament, but the decision also signified the first international conflict in two decades a German government had won, and won "unilaterally."

Of course, much was dependent upon the Allies' choice of strategy. However, they had always been at odds as to the kind of future peace and security that was desirable in Europe.[25] This disagreement was already reflected in the preamble to part 5 and in the related exchange of notes [26] in which two objectives for the disarmament of Germany were clearly stated. The first (France's) was to keep a potential aggressor disarmed. The second (England's) was to provide for the beginning of a new era in which collective security and general reduction in armaments would replace the old balance of power and competitive armament system. The two objectives were, in effect, contradictory. The severe economic, political, and military restrictions left the Germans with unappeased grievances. Indeed, as a result of the peace settlement Germany became a potential aggressor. To be consistent with the Versailles settlement, the Allies, particularly France, had to preserve an overwhelming military power as a deterrent against

25. At Versailles the French had taken the view that the war was caused by Germany's aggression. Future wars, according to that view, could be prevented by imposing economic sanctions and political and military restrictions on Germany. Another view, supported by Britain, claimed that it was the miscalculated breakdown of the Concert of Europe that had led to the war. This theory sought to prevent future wars by replacing the old scheme of balance of power with the system of collective security. In order to give true meaning to the latter, and to guarantee effectiveness to the League of Nations, it was necessary, according to this view, to accept Germany's participation on an equal basis. Neither theory wholly prevailed at Versailles, the result being that the peace treaty reflected irreconcilable contradictions (L. Yates, *United States and French Security, 1917–1921*, chs. 2 and 7 (1957); Rosecrance, *Action and Reaction in World Politics* [1963]). For the impact of these arrangements on legal principles of treaty termination see ch. 1 supra.

26. Supra ch. 1, note 52.

Germany's outward desires for change. In the post-Versailles years, therefore, France wrecked all attempts at revising part 5 while diplomatically pursuing a policy of balance of power. British diplomatic efforts, on the other hand, supported a new agreement on armaments with Germany while favoring no particular military alliance except for collective security.[27]

This difference in policy orientation between France and England reflected many factors and conflicts of interest. Most importantly, at that particular period (1921–35), Germany, though a potential aggressor because of the grievances of Versailles, did not yet have the military capacity to embark on an aggressive policy. Britain, because of its geographical location and other factors,[28] had no need to be overly concerned with aggressive capacity. Throughout its history, Britain had actively intervened in European conflicts only when one side had actively pursued an offensive policy. The contrary was true for France, whose great bogey had always been the potential strength of Germany. Germany had a larger population, a higher birth rate, and richer material resources. Hence, France's preference was to have strong allies on its side, which meant specific military and political guarantees especially from England (balance of power), rather than to be politically and militarily "equal" to Germany under the umbrella of a vague and noncommittal world-embracing guarantee of collective security.[29]

27. For similar practice at present, see I. Claude, *Power and International Relations* 115 (1962). Claude suggests that because the ideal requisites of collective security have not been met faithfully either in international practice or in the norms and procedures of the Covenant and the Charter, there has not been a real collective security but simply a rechristened balance of power system (id. at ch. 8). Collective security, in contrast to the balance of power theory, lays stress on aggressive policy rather than aggressive capacity. "[O]ne asks, 'Who is too strong?' while the other asks, 'Who commits aggression?'" (id. at 124). Germany's rearmament as such, therefore, did not make Germany the focus of general mistrust. Other differences between the two schemes are noted in ch. 1 supra.

28. The security and policies of England were tied up and dependent upon its overseas dominions. For this and other factors see J. F. Kennedy, *Why England Slept* 14 (1961).

29. Although equality of armaments in the balance of power theory is tantamount to equilibrium and peace, in reality each participant strives for arms accumulations at least equal to, and hopefully greater than its opponent's (Claude, supra note 27, at 126). In collective security it is the preponderant collective power

Of the various outcomes possible, either by a new formal agreement or through continuous and informal bargaining, France preferred the latter. Enforcement of the old agreement by military action, though physically possible, was politically difficult, partly because of Britain's objection. The most likely and preferred outcome under the circumstances was competition in armament. France had to choose a strategy that would inevitably draw Britain and other potential allies into a political, and possibly military, coalition with France. The best tactical maneuver with regard to the abandonment of part 5 of the Treaty of Versailles was a seemingly "unilateral" termination by Germany, amid an atmosphere of highly tensed crisis. If one recalls the German government's stated reason of national revival for participating in the "game" in the first place, it becomes easier to see those aspects of tacit and second-order collaboration in the situation which, together with the conflicting interests, formed the resulting outcome.

In parlor-games terms again, the German government preferred an outcome that would correspond with the reason it had participated in the game to begin with: "love of gambling" and "pleasure of the game." The French government, like a typical gambler's wife, wished to prove to the "whole world" that, indeed, "we" were dealing with not just a player, but a chronic gambler, that the Germans were indeed "German"—in other words, breakers of agreements, violators of international law, threateners of peace and security. Like many an aging couple, their preferences just happened to coincide. The result: a highhanded unilateral denunciation of the treaty provisions, followed by immediate increase in armaments [30] and strong protests on behalf of France.

---

of all the participants that is to be greater than any individual member. Thus, equality of armaments of the major actors should be maintained not only in theory but also in practice. The British view was that an agreement revising part 5 of the Treaty of Versailles should be reached with Germany (Kennedy, supra note 28, at 67).

30. In his memoirs Churchill notes that the French were well informed of what was coming, and that they "had actually declared the consequential extension of their own military service to two years a few hours earlier, on the same momentous day" (W. Churchill, *The Gathering Storm* 117 [1961]). It was in the interest of the German government that the French government be informed in advance of its next move so that the possible French reaction could be learned. The French

For a while, it seemed as though the French government had managed to achieve its primary objective. Great Britain, Italy, and France, and later the Council of the League of Nations, it may be recalled, joined in strong formal declarations reaffirming the principle of unanimity in treaty termination, condemning Germany's denunciation of the treaty, and committing themselves to close collaboration in opposing future repudiation of treaties "in Europe." Thus, in this case again, supposedly in protest to unilateral treaty termination, and under the guise of sacred legal principles, Britain and France acquiesced in the "unilateral" repudiation of Italy's treaty obligations in regard to Africa.[31]

Such a dressing-up of a political skeleton to clothe it decently for ideological internment is by no means rare in protests against unilateral decisions. Thus, one is justified, if nothing else, in reaching a conclusion that some unilateral terminations, even when strongly protested against but not seriously objected to, can be regarded as mutually agreed outcomes. Indeed, the cases discussed above suggest that formal protests are the symptoms of such behavior, and not, as claimed, its very negation.

### On the Simplicity in Application of the Traditional Principle

The notion that all unilateral terminations are unlawful, forces the student to focus on only direct conflicts among parties and to ignore the often more salient common advantages not directly related to the immediate physical issues in dispute. This mode of convenient but rather unrealistic analysis is also found in strategic theories such as game theory. Thus far, the most developed model in game theory is the two-person zero-sum game. The zero-sum condition is the requirement that the gains of the winners exactly equal, in absolute amount, the losses of the losers.[32] Even with

government's decision to extend the period of conscription had been announced a day before the German decision was announced. It meant that the French government had decided to take only long-range measures against Germany. In announcing its decision to establish a national compulsory military service, the German government referred to the French decision as "the last straw that had broken Germany's camel-like patience" (Toynbee, supra note 23, at 142).

31. See also p. 42 supra.
32. Luce and Raiffa, supra note 3, at 64; Riker, supra note 24, at 15.

respect to games, this means that the players' individual and common pleasures of exercising skills—"suspense," "joy in gambling," the "atmosphere of the game," or "companionship"—are simply not considered as part of the game situation. Yet, as Riker observes, "these pleasures, perhaps even more than the desire to win, are what generate the game situation to begin with, are what reconcile losers to their losses, and are what induce winners to risk their gains and reputations in repeated engagements." [33]

The justification for overlooking various common advantages in certain strategic theories is that they do not seem capable of being defined in exact numbers, as required by the mathematical formulations of game theory. Similarly, this difficult and sometimes almost impossible task of measuring qualitative factors in the making of decisions seems to be a common reason that legal scholars overlook such a wide variety of factors in treaty termination. Traditionally, legal scholars in general, and those in international law in particular, have sought hard-and-fast rules for decision making. One solution frequently adopted is to enunciate rules of a flat "yes-no" nature. A rule of refusal (for example, all unilateral terminations are unauthorized) is definite in the sense that it renders a "no" decision and has the impact that it can be precisely carried out without further delegation of discretion.[34] The simplicity in application stems from viewing "termination of agreement" as a unitary concept, referring to the reallocation of the physical values disputed, as determined by the treaty provisions, and excluding the elements of and the conditions surrounding the decision process itself. Thus viewed, "termination" becomes a quantitative concept: what the claimant state gains by the decision, the objecting side presumably loses. Unilateral termination is arbitrarily regarded as the winning of a conflict, where the notion of "winning" itself is subjected to definite certainty. Possible gains for the objecting side are totally ignored.

Not all decisions, however, are susceptible to statement in such terms. Some observers who have been aware of the complexity of the decision-making process pertaining to termination, have tried

---

33. Riker, id. at 29.
34. See generally Friedman, "Legal Rules and the Process of Social Change," 19 *Stan L. Rev.* 786, 824 (1967).

to escape the problems by ignoring them altogether. The approach is slightly different but the result is quite the same. The "political-question" doctrine, according to which treaty termination is an extralegal decision, has been a rule of legal refusal, capable of statement as a simple "no."[35] Once the principle banning all unilateral termination is abandoned, of course, no simple "yes" decision is possible. The answer as to whether termination is or is not authorized will depend on a host of qualitative factors. But can one justifiably apply rules to direct political and economic conflict alone, without considering the context of cooperation in which conflict usually occurs?

## Advantages of Losing a Conflict

Following the interdependence of the participants' decisions implied in the concept of strategy, it is possible to distinguish between two main categories of benefits accruing to a party through participation in a conflict. The first category includes the immediate values at stake, as well as other direct advantages that the parties seek to maximize by initiating a conflict and/or by winning it. These benefits are termed "primary gains." Once an undesirable event has occurred, however, such as when the material conflict is deemed lost, a party may realize that there are certain advantages the event still brings with it. The participant, therefore, may accept the opponent's decison, which in any case he may be unable or unwilling to prevent, and thus obtain some gains from it. Such indirect advantages, as we have seen in the case of the rearmament of Germany, result from the parties' efforts during the development of the conflict to make the best of a bad bargain. They can be conveniently termed "secondary gains."

This phenomenon of secondary gain is rather common in everyday life. It is also a fruitful source of private litigation. Being incapacitated by illness or accident, for instance, has certain advantages, among the most obvious being financial compensation for accidents and the plea of insanity as a legitimate excuse for killing people.[36] Illness and other kinds of misfortune may also

35. For additional discussion of the "political question" approach to treaty termination, see p. 36 supra.

36. E. Berne, *Games People Play* 159ff. (1967). " 'What do you expect of someone

provide a legitimate excuse to avoid unpleasant duties and to disregard pressing responsibilities. They provoke sympathy and attention and assure the sufferer a privileged position.[37] Some of the pleas people use to excuse symptomatic behavior are colds, alcoholism, "broken home," "situational stress," "society," "modern living," and the economic or political "system." Parallel justifying symbols in international activities are "underdevelopment," "have-nots," and the "innocent victim of aggression."

Similarly, a participant may try to obtain from the opponent's unilateral decision a bonus, by way of additional benefits that could not be obtained without it. Particularly among traditional opponents, as in the case of Arabs and Israelis and, perhaps, in relations between the Eastern and Western blocs, perceptions of conflict are usually exaggerated. Each side tries to get the best it can from every incident by portraying its opponent as the unscrupulous breaker of agreements and violator of international law—in short, as having aggressive intentions. The tactic is to incorporate the immediate issue into the general conflict of ideologies. The point was made earlier that the incentive to act politically is greatly enhanced by crisis. Citizens, allies, and friends can be more easily rallied against an opponent for a general, clear-cut principle than for a particular cause. This it not to say that parties to disputes can be said to prefer illusory ideological advantages to material gains. But in the context of traditionally hostile parties, winning a conflict materially usually requires some sort of highly coercive act, one that is often dangerous, sometimes disastrous. The example given above of the rearmament of Germany is particularly instructive, since, because of the overwhelming military power of France, the outcome was clearly preferred by the French government more for its ideological value than because of military factors.

The German rearmament case also illustrates another point. Secondary gains are influenced by the extent to which every one

---

as emotionally disturbed as I am—that I would refrain from killing people?' To which the jury is asked to reply: 'Certainly not, we would hardly impose that restriction on you!' " (id. at 159).

37. For a detailed discussion of the psychoanalytical concept of "secondary gain" upon which the present discussion is drawn, see Katz, "On Primary and Secondary Gain," 18 *Psychoanalytic Study of the Child* 9 (1963).

else is willing to tolerate the parties' conflict. In the case of the individual, the reality of society provides compensation for injuries and illnesses; psychiatric therapists, relatives, and friends are still "only trying to help" when he shows signs of definite progress on his own. Thus, for some people, the exploitation of misfortune may represent a better adaptation to reality than they had previously been able to make.[38]

International interaction abounds in similar cases. During the interwar period, for example, it was universally believed that colonies and other conquered territories were necessary to enable a country to achieve sufficient land and raw materials for its existing and prospective populations. German and Italian claims that they were "have-nots" therefore drew much sympathy.[39] It was also believed that for true collective security to be established, the major powers of Europe should be somewhat equal in resources. At the same time, the collective security system promised universal sympathy to any state that might be a victim of aggression, although before the occurrence of a specific act of aggression the members were expected to be neutral. The French in 1935 tried to cling to their favored position by projecting an image as a victim of unilateral termination of international obligation, thus creating an advance identification of friend and foe for future interaction.

The secondary gain is merely part of the parties' efforts to exploit the possibilities for the maximization of preferred values. The participants' maximizing efforts are essentially a never-ending process. They start with the formation of a conflict situation and continue with its development. The terms "primary" and "secondary" gains, therefore, should be used without any implication as to their relative importance or motivating strength. To be sure, the initiation of a conflict itself may be influenced by the knowledge that it will lead to secondary advantages. However, there are cases in which the conflict comes to have certain value to a party only after its development.[40] Thus the analysis of particular con-

38. To answer such questions, criteria for adaptation and maladaptation are needed (id. at 37).

39. Cf. F. Dunn, *Peaceful Change* 4–6 (1937).

40. If secondary gains moves are seen as a further elaboration of primary gains (and vice versa), and thus as an expression of the parties' total maximization

flicts in terms of their dynamic antecedents usually shows that gains from being a victim are merely a defensive and adoptive elaboration of the gains from conflict formation, and vice versa.

Many of our established legal notions and so-called precedents against the unilateral termination of international agreements have been arrived at by disregarding this self-perpetuating process and by focusing too exclusively on the obvious advantages a participant derives from a particular conflict. A systematic treatment of the concept of "unilateral termination" should start with an elucidated contextual model of all the relevant decision sequences. With the aid of these devices, we can proceed to describe why in past situations of particular conflict a specific solution was adopted, why secondary gains were retained and primary ones dropped, and what causal relationships existed between them.[41] Such an analysis

---

efforts, then the problem of when and how to interpret them becomes more complex. In the search for factors that influence secondary gains objections to the explicit resolution of conflicts about termination, the impact of the initial defensive efforts of the objecting side (ch. 4 infra) should be explored. In the Berlin crisis of 1961 the French government objected to direct negotiations on the Soviet demand. The West, therefore, defined in broad ideological terms the pragmatic issues involved in the crisis. The tactic of issue escalation was deliberately adopted as a commitment not to yield to the Soviet central demand and to the proposal to enter into direct talks. The Berlin Wall fulfilled the ideological image which the West had sought to impute to the East. The Western powers, of course, made the best out of this "unilateral" act. The question, however, may be raised whether the Wall did not represent some primary gains at least to France, since French high officials may themselves have a strong preference for a permanent division of Germany.

41. For one thing, the secondary advantage may have to be bought at a considerable price. In the case of Germany's rearmament, the immediate price paid for rallying Italy's support was Ethiopia. Furthermore, the Germans had built the foundation for rearmament long before they officially terminated part 5 of the Treaty of Versailles. This was done by getting everything set for a large-scale production of arms rather than by actual armament. France could therefore maintain its military superiority over Germany in the future only with the combined military power of Britain. But the rearmament of Germany in defiance of treaty obligations was, in itself, not sufficient to induce the British government to plan for the production of armaments on a large scale. This was done only in 1936 after the so-called unilateral remilitarization of the Rhineland by Germany.

The Rhineland conflict was in many aspects a repetition of the rearmament conflict. Germany won the material gains and France the secondary ones. There was, however, one important difference between the two disputes. While in 1935 France could apply its overwhelming power to Germany with a relatively low cost, in 1936 it required general mobilization to stop the German army from occupying

may refute some common beliefs. It may become clear, for example, that the objecting side often does not lose because it can gain on the secondary scoreboard. On the other hand, some conflicts are so badly conducted that, despite appearances of their successful resolution by means of secondary gains, they actually result in a net loss to the objecting side, and, in the longer term, to everyone concerned.

### Original Purpose of the Rules: To Minimize Secondary Gains

Once the totality of the conflict situation is considered, the "gains" may turn out to be one-sided, or mutually disadvantageous. Secondary gains cases constitute the most serious world crises: those which are made up of recurrent conflicts and do not vanish with a single resolution. Such are the effects of "solutions" to conflicts that, although they settle particular immediate issues, they result in a regrouping of the participants in sharper confrontation in future conflicts.[42]

---

the Rhineland. The French position in 1939 was even worse than in 1936. Because of a delay of two years in British plans for mass productions of arms, the German government was able to continue tearing up the treaties of Versailles and Locarno (Kennedy, supra note 28, at 95–96).

42. The magnitude of the parties' involvement with major goals is generally one of the key factors in conflicts about termination. In evaluating possible solutions for these conflicts one should consider the level of the achievement goals for which a government or a country strives. Experiences of success in previous conflicts usually lead to rising aspirations (Siegel and Fouraker, *Bargaining and Group Decision Making* 61–62 [1960]). The combined effect of psychological and material gains in 1935 was to transform the German aspirations from the level of an empty dream to that of a promising enterprise and a project emanating from established expectations. This interrelationship between psychological advantages and material gains became rather evident in later disputes. In 1938, when the balance of power in Europe became rather tenuous, France and Britain abandoned secondary advantages and focused on the primary gains. At Munich the German central demand was satisfied by way of an explicit agreement. But at this late stage of the overall conflict the explicit appeasement of Germany could only be interpreted as a further sign of weakness. Furthermore, the fact that the Allies at long last abandoned their secondary gain strategy added to the primary gains of Germany. The Allies appeared to desert an ally and to engage once again in unprincipled negotiations. They ended up being accused anyway of arming themselves in anticipation of war, despite Munich's seemingly amicable agreement and "peaceful change." France and Britain might have been better off reaching an explicit agreement on rearmament with Germany, deferring the exploitation of

Ironically, the very principle that agreements should be terminated only by the expressed consent of all parties originated from a desire to minimize such harmful effects of secondary gains. In the nineteenth century, it may be recalled, the participants cherished the ideological value of stability. When important unilateral terminations nevertheless occurred, the parties tried at least to clothe them with the legal appearance of mutual consent.

The Russian remilitarization of the Black Sea in 1870, for instance, was not only made unilaterally but was also presented as a fait accompli. Nevertheless, such a bold act could not just be ignored, for it involved a vital issue that concerned the very existence of the European system of balance of power. Thus, a seven-power conference, held at London three months after the Russian decision had been made and carried out, was engaged to find an acceptable face-saving formula for the great powers concerned. The outcome was the famous Declaration of London, which states that it is an essential principle of the Law of Nations that treaties can be terminated or modified only by a new and amicable agreement between the parties. Accordingly, the dead letters of the denounced treaty were also abrogated in the conference by amicable agreement.[43]

For cases in which an agreed face-saving formula was not forthcoming, the fiction of the implied clausula was convenient, a fiction according to which every agreement contains a tacit assumption that the commitment will automatically cease to be binding when circumstances change.[44] Thus, often in practice and always in theory, unilateral termination was concealed beneath the formal consent of all parties. This was another expression of the recurring

secondary advantages to later conflicts. The latter could cultivate the atmosphere of crisis necessary for effective preparations for the coming war.

43. H. Briggs, *The Law of Nations* 913 (1952). For additional discussion see ch. 1 supra; Tseng Yu-Hao, *The Termination of Unequal Treaties in International Law* 75 (1931); Corbett, "Social Basis of a Law of Nations," 85 *Recueil des Cours*, vol. I, 471, 504 (1954). Since then, the Declaration of London has commonly been considered as the authority against unilateral denunciation or termination. Cf. E. Hoyt, *The Unanimity Rule in the Revision of Treaties* 7 (1959). It should be emphasized that the desire to paper over a unilateral breach of a treaty with a seal of mutual consent was less an act of hypocrisy and concern with the past than a concern to communicate a shared intention to police treaties in the future.

44. Ch. 1 supra.

theories of social contract. Such fictions purport to describe the unique feature of social living: that people must "consent" to continue participating even though they are on the losing side in particular decisions. When governments are aware of the possibility that fundamental relationships may break down, and at the same time share the desire to avoid such an occurrence, decisions are generally not portrayed in a winner-take-all manner.

Such seems often to be the case in the contemporary loose bipolar or tripolar international system as well. In many instances of political shift of a state in a bloc alignment, there may be a common incentive to discontinue some treaties, but both sides may be reluctant to concede the preference openly. In some instances, such treaties simply pass tacitly into disuse, while in others they are terminated unilaterally without serious objection.[45] Even among bloc members, it is often politically unwise to vindicate treaty rights on grounds of law enforcement. Protests against unilateral denunciation among members of Western coalitions, as in the 1966 Franco-American dispute discussed below, are therefore often couched in conciliatory terms which are intended to influence sympathetic audiences within the other state to bring pressures on the terminating government to revise its position.

## ALTERNATIVES TO THE PRINCIPLE OF UNANIMITY

What alternatives can be found to the discarded principle of unanimity in the bargaining on termination of international agreements? Many people tend to confuse so-called unilateral decision with coercion. We have seen, however, that although there may be

45. Kaplan and Katzenbach, supra note 9, at 245. This tendency may be reinforced by the recent attempts of Secretary of State Kissinger to reconstruct a global balance of power system.

A great number of international agreements fall into desuetude: they are tacitly terminated because the parties lose interest and decline to invoke them, or they simply drift into oblivion without a formal act of termination. What has been regarded by the U.N. Secretariat as the "lapse" of obligations concerning minorities through the operation of the principle of rebus sic stantibus, seems actually to be the cause of these treaties and declarations falling into desuetude. Compare U.N. Sec. Gen., *Study of the Legal Validity of the Undertakings Concerning Minorities*, U.N. E/CN 4/367 (April 7, 1950) with Feinberg, "The Legal Validity of the Undertakings Concerning Minorities and the *Clausula Rebus Sic Stantibus*," 5 *Scripta Hierosolymitana* 95, 116 (1958).

substantial differences in degree of the parties' consent to termination in particular conflicts, the supposed distinction between unilateral and formally unanimous termination often does not correspond to any real difference in the shared character of the outcome or the strategies and tactics employed. On the other hand, the concept of strategy or bargaining, when used in a broad contextual frame, allows us to concentrate on the sequences of reciprocal choices rather than, narrowly, on the demonstrative form of the outcomes and the self-characterization of acts by the parties.

These insights have immediate application to the making and appraising of termination sequences. A coercive strategy, as generally defined for criteria of unlawfulness by McDougal and Lasswell, is one that offers its target few alternatives at high costs, with a low probability of gains. Conversely, persuasive strategies are those that offer their targets many alternatives at low costs with high probability of gains.[46] We should exercise a high preference for persuasion as opposed to coercion in assessing lawfulness. Specific principles of authority—to be further advanced in later chapters—should focus, among other things, on the extent to which the particular strategies employed in a conflict narrow or broaden the range of the parties' choices.

Any decision, whether it results from coercive threats or persuasive promises, requires some idea about the alternative courses of action. The foregone alternatives represent the costs (or gains) of the chosen activity. The evaluation of such costs is crucially affected by the parties' previous experiences with each other. Both in threats and promises, the question is usually whether a party's past history justifies belief in its word. The very fact that a unilateral demand for termination is made by the promisor often suggests that a party's additional promises on the same matter, and with regard to the future, are equally unreliable. This may partly explain why a great many conflicts about termination, as we shall see, are settled mainly by tacit bargaining rather than by direct talks.[47] While offers, promises, and collaborative acts play a central role in direct negotiations, in tacit bargaining the parties, mainly through threats and unilateral moves, seek solutions that may leave each side with the immediate possession of its gains.

46. McDougal, Lasswell, and Miller, supra note 3, at 13.
47. Additional reasons are discussed in ch. 5 infra.

Since threats and promises, conflicting and collaborative acts, are all simultaneously or alternatively present in many conflicts about termination, it is hard to draw a clear-cut line between coercion and persuasion in the handling of these disputes. Further, a certain degree of coercion is present in any decision to terminate, since it must always result in some deprivation.[48] Thus, any proposed criterion for lawful decision-making that is based on the degree of coerciveness of decisions is not amenable to direct and easy application. It depends on a wide variety of factors and on an ability to discern cooperation in a conflict, to which the sloganized thinking of the average citizen is blind.

Parties to conflict, on the other hand, are usually in quest of hard-and-fast so-called authoritative principles that can serve them in their ideological struggles. The enforcement of such principles only by propaganda strategies, however, is primarily negative in character, since it merely intends to deprive parties of approval after a decision has already been made. Too often, deprivations involving denials of formal legal recognition are selected as sanctions because they are the simplest—and sometimes the only— ones available under the circumstances. Their very application in termination conflicts implies the inability or unwillingness of the objecting side to apply other measures. The fact that the target of a respect sanction in international affairs generally resists such an application might suggest that it perceives itself as threatened.[49] However, against the legal principles that justify the application of the nonrecognition sanctions, the targets usually find some other principles to justify their acts. Fundamental policies of authority appear to be formulated in complementary pairs—rebus sic stantibus v. pacta sunt servanda—so that justifications are easily found. When authoritative principles are invoked too often for the sole purpose of formal nonrecognition against what are obviously uncontested outcomes of conflicts, authority itself, we have seen, is disrespected, and law ceases to play a constructive role in the conduct of disputes.

Law operates at many different levels and can perform innumerable functions in decision. In the most subtle sense, authoritative principles are operative when they formulate issues and pro-

48. For additional discussion of this point see ch. 3 infra.
49. McDougal, Lasswell, and Reisman, supra note 2, at 297.

vide the symbols for claims. A critical function of rules in termination disputes is to temper the severity of the strategies employed. In this specific respect, one may say that principles and rules are effective in proportion to the degree they influence the strategies employed; they are ineffective when they provide the parties with no more than self-fulfilling negative ideological images of their opponents, or with convenient face-saving formulas after a conflict has been lost. Their impact should be to increase the interdependence of the parties' choices in the handling of conflicts, to stabilize the patterns of reciprocal choices, to strengthen the bargaining position of one side or another, to supply provisional guidelines for the content of choices involved, and thus to influence the parties' choices, the outcome of the dispute, and the long-range effects the dispute has on the general advancement of international law. International rules may have differing degrees of such influences, depending, in part, upon their strength in activating expectations of authority during conflicts. The purpose of part 2 is an increased understanding of the mechanics of the conflict situation of termination, and the identification and manipulation of those events that can activate expectations about authority most effectively and economically.

# PART 2

# The Decision-Making Dilemma

# 3 Defining the Conflict

The major aspects of a bargaining situation may be summarized in the simplest form as follows: A party is in a situation from which one of several possible outcomes will result with respect to which he has certain personal, varying, and sometimes inconsistent, preferences. He does not have full control over the variables that determine the outcome. Another party or other participants who also have personal preferences among the possible outcomes, have some control over these variables.[1]

## COLLABORATIVE CONFLICT

One way to measure conflict and collaboration in decision-making situations is by reference to the parties' preferences. Where all parties have the same preference pattern over outcomes, and one of them cannot achieve it singly, they will cooperate in order to do so. This is a case of pure common interest, which results in *complete collaboration*. The opposite extreme is a situation, for instance, in which if a party prefers outcome A to outcome B, the other prefers B to A, and if one party is indifferent between A and B, then so is the other party. In such a situation we may regard the parties as sworn adversaries of each other who are engaging in *strict competition*. In game theory such pure conflicts are known as two-person zero-sum games. Since the parties have strictly opposing preferences for the outcome, the expected utility of one of them is in effect the negative of the expected utility of the other; that is to say, the interests of the parties are in direct and absolute conflict, so that one's gains exactly equal the losses of the other.

Situations that involve pure conflict or pure common interest are not common in human reality. It was noted in the previous chapter that, as applied to any social interaction (parlor games included), the category of pure conflict seems to be too gross a

1. See J. von Neumann and O. Morgenstern, *Theory of Games and Economic Behavior* 11 (1953).

miscarriage of the mathematicians' and analytic jurists' privilege of abstraction. The only kind of international situation that may meet the conditions of strict competition is total war. Perhaps it is not pure conflict even when each side demands unconditional surrender from the other; it becomes one only when each side aims at the total annihilation of the other, and also prefers mutual annihilation to a stalemate.[2]

The other extreme situation of complete common interest is also rare in social interaction. Love is perhaps such an example, if the lover regards his beloved's gains as his own—a purely collaborative situation which lends credence to the colloquial expression that love is the only game two can play and both win. However, another phrase from a popular song, Boulding points out, gives succinct expression to a mathematical model which suggests a close resemblance between the phenomenon of falling in love and the phenomenon of an arms race: "Lay down your arms and surrender to mine."[3] In situations in which the outcome preferences of the parties were perfectly matched for all time to come, there would be, of course, no need for binding agreements. At the global level, the first approximation of strict collaboration is a state of extreme emergency, a last stand against an encircling enemy. In such a situation, perhaps, there should be no thought of measuring contributions. The appropriate organizing principle would be "one for all and all for one."[4] These situations are indeed rare. Furthermore, political or military collaboration in itself is a product of conflict with an external enemy. Demands for the termination of alignment agreements are usually put forward as soon as the external threat diminishes. In short, international affairs always involve mutual dependence as well as opposition, which renders even the fiercest conflict non-strictly-competitive.

Such mixed-motive conflicts are those in which at least some of the parties' choices during bargaining do not conflict with each

2. R. Luce and H. Raiffa, *Games and Decisions* 59–60 (1957).

3. K. Boulding, *Conflict and Defense* 30 (1962), and see his discussion of Richardson's mathematical model.

4. Cf. L. Fuller, *The Morality of Law* 21–22 (1964). Upon this situation the theory of collective security is based. The balance of power theory, on the other hand, stresses conflict.

other, so that if one party prefers A to B, the other does not prefer B to A. Winning such conflicts, when realistically viewed, should not mean gaining relative to one's competitor but relative to one's own value system. Even in the conduct of war there still may be much for all the parties to gain by setting geographical and other limitations upon it, or, more narrowly, by observing the Geneva Convention regarding the treatment of civilians and prisoners. For wherever one party has some effective measure of control, the range of alternatives is not totally foreclosed, and there exists the possibility of some bargaining, tacit or express. At the minimal level, bargaining consists of avoiding what is for a party an uneconomical infliction of damage on the other.

### The Bargaining Situation of Termination

Our first step toward formulating the problems involved in treaty termination is to limit, according to the degree of competition and collaboration involved, the class of bargaining to which they apply. Some conflicting and common interests may be traced to the original agreement. Cases of treaties concluded by extreme coercion must be excluded, for by virtue of their incorporating no interests common to both parties, there could have been at the time of their conclusion not much to negotiate for. Similarly, cases in which there was no conflict to begin with must also be excluded, because there could have been nothing to negotiate about.[5] It may even be that, at the time of the original agreement, the common preferences for collaboration in the production or allocation of the particular valuables were stronger than the conflicting ones. However, a conflict about termination may later arise when one party, or both, comes to regard the burdens and benefits from the treaty as being unbalanced. Such a disequilibrium in gains and losses may result from subsequent changes in objective circumstances or from a rise in subjective expectations of a party who is no longer willing to accept an original inequality. Be that as it may, because of this inequality at the time of the termination dispute, the party contemplating default would still profit even if the other side did the same in retaliation.[6] In other words,

5. F. Iklé, *How Nations Negotiate* 2 (1964).
6. This in itself does not necessarily mean that the agreement is not enforce-

termination of the treaty, either by a new agreement or through unilateral acts, will operate to the clear advantage of the claimant party. Hence the essential characteristic of this type of termination controversy is that the parties exhibit opposing preference patterns in regard to the treaty's value allocation.

Following Schelling's distinction between the "efficiency," or mutually profitable, and the "distributional" aspects of bargaining,[7] *termination* conflicts belong in the latter category. They represent a situation in which the parties are interested in different things which they can only obtain from one another. Since a demand for termination is one for the redistribution of the particular valuables in favor of one side only, the guiding principle for the claimant party is usually to obtain from the objecting side as many of the disputed assets as it can. For the latter the motivation is to give as little value as possible. It should again be emphasized that it is the non-strictly-competitive conflicts that we are dealing with, since some sort of mutual gains outside of the immediate physical issues as represented by the treaty in dispute is always a possibility in their resolution. Nevertheless, in redistributional conflicts, the competitive interests are the principal objects of bargaining, whereas the common interests remain tacit or are related only to the details of the bargaining.

The opposite of bargaining on termination are negotiations whose objects are themselves subject to the common interests, and from which the parties can benefit only by joining together. The most notable examples of such arrangements, in which cooperation is a substantive aim in itself, are negotiations for the purpose of *innovation*. In the latter, the parties establish new

---

able. The parties' common interest in a treaty usually embraces more than their interest in the immediate arrangement it contains. Generally, within the international context, a breach may engender serious reprisals in other bargains, and thus not be worthwhile. A reprisal for a breach may in turn engender retaliation from the other side, and it often happens that the parties, through mutual actions and reactions, repudiate several prior agreements between them. Since unilateral acts pursuant to termination may initiate a chain reaction whose consequence might be undesirable to all parties, the parties usually have a strong common interest in setting limitations on the conduct of the dispute (chs. 8–9 infra). Our discussion of the parties' choices, therefore, must necessarily reflect their attempts to pursue simultaneously all their relevant interests, whether conflicting or common.

7. T. Schelling, *The Strategy of Conflict* 21 (1963). Iklé, supra note 5, at ch. 3.

institutions or economic arrangements through collaboration, and thus jointly increase production of values or restrict their dispersal in a mutually profitable fashion (for example, the Treaty of Rome setting up the Common Market and Euratom, and the Nuclear Test Ban Treaty, at least as between some of the parties).[8] There are, of course, many gradations between bargaining on pure termination, as defined here, and strict innovation—situations in which the change supposedly works to the immediate advantage of all parties concerned, but not to equal advantage.

## The Nile Water Dispute

A rather peculiar example, in which the parties seemed to oscillate between termination and innovation, is the case of the revision in 1959 of a former agreement between Egypt and the Sudan to allocate the water of the river Nile. In 1929 it had been agreed to distribute the water as follows: Egypt, 48 billion cubic meters; the Sudan, 4; the rest was considered to be lost. Since this unequal sharing was a reflection of foreign domination in the area, as soon as the Sudan gained its independence it put forward a claim for redistribution.[9]

The Egyptian government at that particular time was planning the construction of a new dam at Aswan, for which the Nile water dispute made it difficult to secure foreign financing. It was, therefore, pressing the Sudanese government for a negotiated settle-

8. Paradoxically, situations that are highly competitive do not necessarily pose legal problems of termination. Collaboration in limiting the harmful effects that result from high competition on an issue is made possible when the parties retain their freedom to repudiate the agreement whenever they lose by it more than they expect to benefit. See, e.g., Art. 25 of the Load Line Convention, July 5, 1930, 47 Stat. pt. 2, 2228, T.S. No. 858, at 32, and Art. 4 of the Nuclear Weapons Test Ban Treaty, Aug. 5, 1963 [1963] 14 *United States Treaties and Other International Agreements*, pt. 2, 1313, 1319. Theoretically, the terminable character of such treaties facilitates their revision despite the initial lack of unanimous consent. Parties supposedly may denounce or terminate the old treaty and then proceed to negotiate the conclusion of a new one. It is interesting to note, however, that in most of these cases parties regard denunciation or termination as too drastic a remedy, because they do not want to risk losing the degree of cooperation already achieved by the old treaty (E. Hoyt, *The Unanimity Rule in the Revision of Treaties* 49 [1959]).

9. L. Fabunmi, *The Sudan in Anglo-Egyptian Relations* 124 (1960). For the agreement see 93 L.N.T.S. No. 2103.

ment, and when the talks had reached a deadlock, it announced a
territorial claim concerning "all Sudanese territory north of the
twenty-second parallel." [10] In July 1958 the Sudan acted unilaterally by opening the Sennar Dam earlier than was annually
customary. Egyptian protests were met with the assertion that
the Sudan no longer recognized the old agreement.

In November 1958, after a coup d'état, a military government
seized power in the Sudan. It adopted a new foreign policy of
neutrality, which included acceptance of American aid, recognition of the Peking government, and strengthening of relations
with Africa south of the Sahara. These policy changes strengthened
the Sudanese bargaining position against Egypt: even the Soviet
Union pressed for an Egyptian-Sudanese settlement before committing itself to finance the construction of the Aswan Dam.

One might, therefore, have expected the Egyptian government
to resort to concessions in order to hasten the conclusion of an
agreement. Yet, because the Sudanese military regime needed
assistance from the Egyptian government to quell internal opposition, the conflict suddenly took an altogether different turn. Invoking "friendship," "cooperation," and "mutual benefit," the
parties entered new negotiations, of which the result was a sur-
prisingly rapid agreement.[11]

A Sudanese observer regards the dispute and the new agreement
as a modern application of the doctrine of rebus sic stantibus:

> In light of the above we may consider the 1929 agreement
> in the circumstances obtaining in Egypt and the Sudan in
> 1954. It is clear that the circumstances vitally changed and
> that a claim by *either* country based on *rebus sic stantibus*
> was reasonable. The population in *both* countries increased
> remarkably. The population in Egypt increased from 14
> million in 1929 to 19 million in 1954, while the population of

10. G. Barraclough, *Survey of International Affairs 1956–1958*, 367f. (1962). Egyptian threats of moves to occupy those territories were met by Sudanese counter-
threats of military resistance and a warning of an appeal to the United Nations—
the first time an inter-Arab question had been raised there.

11. Agreement Between the United Arab Republic and the Republic of the
Sudan for the Full Utilization of the Nile Waters, Nov. 8, 1959, in 15 *Revue
Egyptienne de Droit International* 321 (1959). See also Gamal Moursi Badr, "The
Nile Waters Question," id. at 94, 109.

the Sudan, which was 5½ millions in 1929, about doubled itself. Besides the increase of population, the modern technical and engineering techniques made it possible to harness the Nile on a larger scale than the conditions in 1929 could allow. The general world conditions are also important and should be taken into consideration due to their impact on the technical and financial ability of the nation-states in the Nile Basin to embark on large-scale agricultural production. All the above mentioned factors could have been advocated to justify a claim based on the doctrine of *rebus sic stantibus* in trying to terminate the 1929 agreement between Egypt and the Sudan.[12]

In this analysis much is again made of the mutual interest of both parties in modifying the old agreement. The conflicting interests are almost lost amid the various alleged changes in circumstances, which are portrayed as having symmetrical impacts on the economies of both parties, and which are said to have authorized a claim to termination by "either country." Certainly, the changes invoked in this passage could at most support claims for cooperation between the two countries in an innovative and more efficient use of the water. If the dispute was indeed one of innovation rather than of redistribution, it is hard to see why the negotiations had dragged on for so many years with recurring violent threats from both sides.

Such a presentation of the problem is indeed a faithful account of the official positions held by the parties in the final phase of the negotiations. For the new agreement itself, which reflected momentary political needs and not the specific issue at conflict, far from decreasing the Egyptian share in the water, provided both parties with additional water. Since Egypt was granted 55 billion cubic meters and the Sudan 18 billion, the new agreement cannot be regarded as one of reallocation, but only as one that distributes those waters which had gone to waste because of past technical difficulties. Though this additional water is allotted slightly in favor of the Sudan, the inequality of the former agreement has

12. Dafalla El Radi Siddig, "The River Nile," 1964 *Sudan L. J. and Rep.* at 171, 214–15 (emphasis added).

been preserved. Thus the Egyptian-Sudanese agreement of 1958 was not one of treaty termination or revision in any real sense, and it would be safe to predict that further changes in political conditions will start the controversy all over again.

### EXAGGERATED PERCEPTIONS OF CONFLICT OR COOPERATION

To say that for treaty termination to become a real conflict there must be a potential loss to the objecting party in the possible outcomes, is to imply that the given treaty is actually an asset to it. It should be emphasized here that the concept of value in bargaining is a matter of subjective, not objective appreciation. A desired event may be valueless from the perspective of an observer, yet for various unrelated reasons be given high value priority by one or all parties.

Furthermore, in the dynamics of interaction, events intensely valued by one party may acquire a value, or at least a relevance, for other negotiating parties simply because a counterpart pursues it. Especially in traditionally hostile contexts, the parties are sometimes more concerned with their relative value advantage than with the benefits they actually obtain. They may even prefer to avoid a beneficial change rather than appear to comply with an adversary's wish. "Opponents of a test ban agreement," Lieberman notes, "pointed worriedly at Khrushchev's kind words about Kennedy's proposal. 'If *they* think it's good, it must be bad for us.' " [13] In such cases, where the opponent's gains are seen as one's losses and vice versa, a party may hold onto an alleged treaty right solely because the other side loses by it, or simply because it "teases" the opponent.

The question, therefore, may often be raised whether a certain treaty in dispute really serves up-to-date interests of the objecting party, or whether termination is objected to merely from force of habit, and because traditional diplomacy requires one not to surrender "assets" unless their surrender brings compensating advantages.

The most interesting examples in this respect are conflicts about the termination of foreign military bases. Overseas bases

13. Lieberman, "Threat and Assurance in the Conduct of Conflict," in *International Conflict and Behavioral Science* 110, 117 (R. Fisher ed. 1964).

have a variety of important military, political, and economic functions. The expenditures connected with their construction and operations, for instance, are a form of economic aid, a form that is rather palatable to the U.S. Congress. For the purpose of the current discussion, however, it is sufficient to focus more narrowly on one important factor, namely, the exploitation of potential force involved in establishing political spheres of influence. Generally speaking, a nation's military strength is at its maximum at home. The further from home a government has to operate, the longer are the lines of communication, and thus costs of transportation rise, efficiency diminishes, and the less strength it can put in the area. Through overseas bases a government can increase considerably its operational strength in areas between its home base and its foreign bases, and in areas adjoining the off-territory base.[14] Examples of such practices are the overseas naval bases of Britain, the air bases of the United States, or the Soviet submarine base in Algeria.

General changes in conditions may decrease the importance for a nation of certain off-territory bases. For one thing, when the home strength of a nation declines in comparison to other nations and its sphere of influence shrinks considerably, it may no longer be able to hold onto those bases that are too distant from its base center. Britain, for instance, was forced in 1954 to relinquish its bases in the Suez Canal Zone, although they were still needed in case Egypt were to attempt to nationalize the Canal. Since then the British have been deeply in debt, and they have cut their overseas defense expenditures by terminating many of their other bases throughout the world. Some of the bases that Britain continues to maintain, such as the one on Cyprus and to a lesser degree the one in Gibraltar, are an economic liability since they no longer seem to serve a real military need.

They are a political liability too. With the base on Cyprus, Britain has been involved in a violent local quarrel. In 1964 British forces got rid of the thankless task of maintaining the peace between the Greeks and the Turkish Cypriots by handing it over to a United Nations force. Even so, the presence of British forces on Cyprus has implicated Britain in the dispute "by mere

14. See Boulding's theory of viability, supra note 3, at 229ff.

failure to give Athens or Ankara the support that is lying idle, and that each ally reckons to be its due." [15] The base on Gibraltar involves Britain in a treaty termination dispute with Spain. The preference of the local population, as determined by a referendum conducted by Britain, seems to go against Spanish rule. This is advantageous to Britain as long as it desires to hold on to the base, but may become a liability, too, as international pressures mount and the conflict between the two countries is enlarged.

A relative rise in the home strength of a nation, on the other hand, may expand its area of influence beyond its off-territory bases, which thereby outlive their military purpose. Furthermore, the usefulness of many such bases diminishes with the general progress of military technology. The termination of United States short-range missile sites in Turkey, and perhaps to a much lesser degree the termination of United States military bases and installations in France, seem to fall under this category.[16] In addition, cheaper and faster transport of troops and military hardware may render unnecessary some military bases in what hitherto has been a distant territory. The withdrawal of the United States naval base at Guantanamo, for instance, should have fallen into this category.

## Within a Generally Competitive Context: The Guantanamo Base

The Guantanamo military base treaties served a real interest for many years. With these treaties, as originally signed in 1903, the United States reserved the right to intervene militarily in Cuba "for the preservation of Cuban independence." [17] In 1934, when an amendment had restricted the use of the base to defense against

15. Monroe, "British Bases in the Middle East—Assets or Liabilities," 42 *Int'l Affairs* 24, 31 (1966). Thus, during the 1974 crisis Britain sought to transfer command of its force to the United Nations. *New York Times,* Aug. 11, 1974, p. 3, col. 6 (late city ed.).

16. But a strategic missile base in Cuba was, in 1962, more valuable to the Soviet Union than a comparable base in Turkey was to the United States. Horelick, "The Cuban Missile Crisis: An Analysis of Soviet Calculations and Behavior," 16 *World Pol.* 363, 367 (1964). U.S. bases in France were in 1966 particularly useful for the defense of Germany. See the following discussion.

17. "Relations with Cuba," May 22, 1903, 1 *Treaties, Conventions, International Acts, Protocols and Agreements 1776–1909,* 362, Art. 3 (1910). Article 1 restricted Cuba's freedom to contract with foreign powers. See also, "Agreement for the

external enemies,[18] it was still useful for the United States as a naval post for safeguarding the routes to the Panama Canal. Under modern military transport and technology, the protection of the Panama Canal and even possible United States operations against Cuba can be successfully conducted from places other than Guantanamo (the base was not directly involved in the Bay of Pigs invasion).

In such situations, in which there may be mutual incentive to discontinue a treaty and in which the objecting party is reluctant to terminate it formally, the treaty usually passes tacitly into disuse, or is terminated unilaterally without serious objection.[19] The termination of military bases in foreign territory, however, let alone those located in an antagonistic country, cannot pass unobserved, since such bases usually acquire a symbolic value far beyond their actual military utility. Termination involves problems of loss of face and broader implications of the acceptance of new states of affairs. The presence of United States troops in Cuban territory, for example, demonstrates to many in Cuba and to others in exile the continued willingness of the United States to fight the Cuban regime. From the perspective of the Cuban government, on the other hand, the continued presence of United States troops on Cuban soil illustrates to its people the undiminishing character of the external threat. Thus, for a variety of such side

---

Lease to the United States of Lands in Cuba for Coaling and Naval Stations," Feb. 16, 1903, id. at 358–59. "Lease to the U.S. by Cuba of Land and Water for Naval or Coaling Stations in Guantanamo and Bahia Honda," July 2, 1903, id. at 360.

18. The stated objective was to "enable the United States to maintain the independence of Cuba, and to protect the people thereof, as well as for its own defense" (Relations with Cuba, supra note 17, at 363, Art. 7). In 1901, Secretary of War Root assured a committee of the Cuban Constitutional Convention that the naval bases would never be used as points of observation of the national government of Cuba (H. Guggenheim, *The United States and Cuba* 90 [1934]). A new agreement was concluded abolishing, among other things, the right of intervention ("Relations with Cuba," May 29, 1934, 4 *Treaties, Conventions, International Acts, Protocols and Agreements 1923–1937*, 4054 [1938]).

19. The minorities' treaties and declarations, for instance, have not been invoked since the outbreak of World War II, although the opportunities for such an invocative were many. See supra ch. 2, note 45. The United States, because of political considerations, has generally shown restraint in dealing with unilateral treaty terminations by Cuba. M. Kaplan and N. Katzenbach, *The Political Foundations of International Law* 246 (1961).

benefits and difficulties, both parties seem to have an incentive to continue the base.

If, on the other hand, one were to believe that the Guantanamo base poses a material threat to Cuba, then it might also be true that the Soviet government itself prefers its continuation. Because Cuba is situated far beyond the geographical sphere of influence of the Soviet Union, the latter cannot directly control it and may, therefore, have to rely on such external threats in order to assure Cuba's continued dependence. Indeed, in the Cuban missile crisis of 1962 the Soviet Union attempted, without real chances of success, to tie the withdrawal of its missiles from Cuba to a demand for the withdrawal of United States missiles from Turkey. And even though the Soviet government asked and received American guarantees against attacks on Cuba, it did not put forward similar demands for withdrawal of the Guantanamo base.[20]

Although the actual behavior of all governments concerned show nonconflicting preference patterns as to termination of the treaty, their official statements stress conflict. They all seem to be in agreement, or so they have stated publicly, that the base is of vital military importance.[21] In the relations of hostile parties some form of intergovernmental comparison of values always exists: each party's preferences are determined to a great extent by its knowledge of the other party's preferences. In most situations a party's preference patterns are only partially known to its adversary, and falsifications and exaggerations of its true feelings and objectives seem to be an inherent and important bargaining strategy. For reasons to be explained later, this strategy is particularly common in termination conflicts.

### Within a Generally Cooperative Context: The NATO Dispute

Within political coalitions, both sides to disputes are kept reasonably well informed about each other's preference pattern for the possible outcomes of disputes. Furthermore, allies expect

20. Ch. 5 infra.

21. See Montague, "A Brief Study of Some of the International Legal and Political Aspects of the Guantanamo Bay Problem," 50 *Ky.* J.J. 459 (1962). For the legal arguments involved, see also Maris, "International Law and Guantanamo," 29 *J. of Pol.* 261 (1967). The base will probably be withdrawn as soon as circumstances permit face-saving.

sympathetic consideration of their views and respect for their desires. Thus, within such contexts, settlements of disputes are expected to depend more on mutual adjustment of objectives and compromises of individual preferences than on coercive threats and unilateral acts. Yet falsification of the parties' preferences is an inherent bargaining strategy even in such disputes. Precisely because allies are compelled to seek fair negotiative solutions that take into account all individual preferences, there may be an incentive for a party to disclose only that preference pattern which brings with it a more advantageous outcome.

Consider the 1966 Franco-American dispute regarding the French withdrawal from NATO's military organization and the corresponding demand for the removal of American military bases and installations from France. The bases in dispute had been established in the late fifties as part of the principal deterrent force upon which NATO's strategy of instant and all-out nuclear retaliation relied. Since then, however, the capability of inter-mediate-range missiles in Western Europe to survive a surprise nuclear attack, and hence their usefulness for effective deterrence, had diminished.[22] Even if they could be fully protected, by putting them on coastal steamers or on moving trains for instance, still, intercontinental missiles stationed outside of Europe could provide for the deterrence of massive retaliation at least as well.

Underlying this military policy of massive retaliation during the fifties had been the capacity of the United States, through bases in Western Europe, to inflict widespread devastation on the territory of the Soviet Union, which had been at that time in the inferior position of being unable to retaliate effectively upon United States territory. In 1962, however, after the introduction by both adversaries of nuclear intercontinental missiles, the United States, despite French protests, officially replaced it with a new policy of flexible, proportionate, and localized military response.[23] For the implementation of such a policy, the continued stationing of American forces in France was of prime utility, since it could place effective geographical and other possible limitations on American involvement in European armed conflicts.

The primary purpose for maintaining separate American bases

22. Cf. H. Kissinger, *The Necessity for Choice* 110ff. (1961).
23. H. Kissinger, *The Troubled Partnership* 117ff. (1965).

in France, then, was for the pursuit of a policy to which France objected.[24] Furthermore, one of the French arguments was that these nuclear bases, being an integral part of the United States Strategic Air Command, could involve France in armed conflicts that would not directly concern Europe and to which France was not a party.[25] To minimize these risks, it was argued, the United States nuclear forces in Europe should be put, if not directly under local national commands, under NATO's integrated command. Integrated command arrangements could have drawn a clearer distinction between United States strategic forces in general and those assigned to Europe. Such a distinction, no matter how formal and practically insignificant, would have served as a useful symbol of a geographically limited intention in the event of an armed conflict outside of Europe. However, complete integration of all forces, tactical as well as strategic nuclear, would have enhanced the decision-making power of Western European governments in regard to retaliatory policies. Because of its own desire to avoid involuntary military commitments, the United

24. The possibility of a conventional war in Europe does not appeal to many Europeans. The NATO nations cannot be expected to match the conventional forces of Eastern Europe. Once tactical nuclears were employed, it would be difficult to draw a clear line for limitations except for the geographical restriction. A nuclear war limited to Europe would have to exclude the territory of the Soviet Union from retaliation since the Soviet government will not accept American nuclear operations against its territory without striking back at American territory. For Western Europe, therefore, geographically limited nuclear war might mean a one-way nuclear war. Following the French demands, Rumania put forward similar claims to the Soviet Union. *New York Times,* May 18, 1966, p. 2, col. 4 (late city ed.).

25. "[B]efore we made our position known [France approved of the American measures during the Cuban missile crisis], and even though the NATO forces were supposed to be kept out of the conflict, American forces in Europe, including those in France, were put on alert—the highest degree of alert.

"Does that make you think? If one day there was conflict between the United States and Russia over issues that have nothing to do with France and her obligations under the alliance, who can maintain that the presence of American headquarters, communications, air bases and depots would not constitute an obvious and serious risk for us?

"We could not be forced to declare war I admit. But all this would turn us into a target for atomic bombs. Is this not what is really at stake?" Statement of Premier Pompidou before the French National Assembly on Apr. 20, 1966, as quoted in the *New York Times,* Apr. 21, 1966, p. 16, cols. 4, 5 (city ed.).

States refused to integrate its nuclear forces within NATO's command.

Such a contradictory preference pattern as to immediate physical issues in itself is not conclusive in disputes about termination, for much, we have seen, is also dependent upon the parties' ordering of preferences in regard to the broader context of collaboration between them. The North Atlantic relationship itself embraces a complexity of issues which do not deal simply with military matters, and on which there were mutual incentives to continue collaboration. Indeed, in claiming termination, the French government emphasized an intention to dissociate itself only from NATO's military arrangements, and to continue participation in the alliance's political organization.

The United States, however, rejected the distinction between political and military collaboration. It denied the validity of the claim to termination on the ground that the treaties governing the bases, although they had been separately concluded during the fifties, were integral to the Atlantic alliance and were legally binding for the duration of the North Atlantic Treaty of 1949.[26] Underlying this either-or argument was the assumption that the French government would regard an all-embracing termination of political relations as too drastic a remedy to the impasse of the particular dispute.

The French government's reaction was to demonstrate that if it had to choose between the status quo and no agreement at all, it would choose the latter. French arguments, accompanied by several unilateral acts, emphasized a high degree of conflict and indifference toward general political collaboration between the parties. Before the beginning of any talks on the issues, the French government removed some of its forces from Germany, implying that the rest would soon also be removed. And an official visit to

26. For a discussion and reference to the relevant provisions in the agreements, see Stein and Carreau, "Law and Peaceful Change in a Subsystem: 'Withdrawal' of France from the North Atlantic Treaty Organization," 62 *Am. J. Int'l L.* 577, 622–25 (1968). For a discussion of the arguments concerning the distinction between NATO's political and military organizations, see id. at 605. For additional discussion of the evolution of the alliance from loose political arrangements to centralized command, see M. Ball, *NATO and the European Union Movement* 31 (1959).

the Soviet Union by President de Gaulle during the dispute, in addition to other unilateral acts,[27] increased fears in the West that the next French move would be a withdrawal into neutrality. Consequently, the United States hastened to remove its forces from France before the prescribed French deadline expired.

France's advantage during bargaining partly arose from the fact that it had convincingly demonstrated, by deeds rather than words, that it would prefer removal of the bases and withdrawal from NATO's military organization above all other possible outcomes, while the United States, despite talks to the contrary, apparently preferred above all other possibilities, the preservation of at least the loose political arrangements of the North Atlantic Treaty of 1949.

## Conclusions

One reason why parties to disputes may not reach an optimum settlement, even if they reach agreement and do not resort to implementing threat strategies, is that they hide their true preferences (assuming that they even clearly know them). Outcomes that result from each side falsifying its true preference pattern and exaggerating the degree of common interests (for example, the Sudanese-Egyptian dispute) and conflicting interests (for example, the Guantanamo and NATO disputes) are frequently not what either side wants. Note that in the Franco-American dispute the alternate outcomes were presented by both parties in the form of "either-or." The issues of the bases and of participation in NATO's military organization were of course divisible. Within the polar alternatives, as presented by the parties, there were many other possible outcomes to the dispute, with differing degrees of military cooperation and nuclear vulnerability for both of them. For tactical reasons, however, both parties in different stages of the conflict chose to hold on firmly to a rigid position, refusing to enter into direct talks on the issues. The reasons for such a practice often seem to be structured into the mechanics of the termination conflict.

27. For these and other acts, see chs. 7 and 8 infra.

# 4   The Mechanism of Bargaining

Generally speaking, parties in bargaining continuously face the choice between three sets of alternatives: express or tacit agreement, further bargaining, or no-bargaining which, of course, in international relations is in many contexts a fiction. This three-fold choice requires many diverse estimates, which are stockpiled into three overall values: negotiators must continually compare all the available terms of a proposed agreement with all the likely consequences of no-agreement. At the same time, they have to evaluate continuously the uncertain prospects and risks of further bargaining. The objects of this evaluation (the content of the three general options) usually concern future events, and the decision maker's knowledge of them is therefore limited. They include proposed terms, threats, inducements, commitments, faits accomplis, reprisals, and so on. These are made, added, improved, withdrawn, strengthened, or weakened during the course of bargaining. Hence, even the parties' limited knowledge about their object of evaluation keeps changing during bargaining. This explains why during the course of bargaining they cannot hold to firm opinions in evaluating their choices.

## EVALUATING GAINS AND LOSSES

How do the parties evaluate whether their side would be better or worse off by accepting certain terms in an agreement, or by continuing to press for some other alternatives? In other words, what constitutes advantageous or disadvantageous outcomes? Obviously, to determine that each side needs to have some notion of what kind of outcome would mean to it neither a gain nor a loss —namely, what Iklé describes as a break-even point, dividing for a party the plus side from the minus side. As he points out, criteria of evaluation are as unstable as their objects:

> It is a common and cardinal fallacy to assume that these criteria exist independently of the negotiating process. Far from it, they are nothing but beliefs held by diplomats, their

government colleagues, and various bystanders, and they are continually modified by the bargaining process. Hence these criteria cannot form a firm basis for evaluating negotiations. Quite to the contrary, it is negotiation that develops and changes them. Diplomats not only fight about terms that they evaluate in a given way; they also fight about the way of evaluation in order to fit it to their preferred terms. Even evaluations of mediators and outsiders are affected by the negotiation process. International diplomacy, in contrast to parlor games, has no score sheets or poker chips that record the gains and losses for each side. This is one of the most essential facts in understanding how nations negotiate.[1]

The problem in bargaining, then, is not so much how to find a clear point of evaluation but, once it is adopted, how to hold to it firmly as negotiations develop. Interestingly enough, such points do not necessarily have to exist physically. Indeed, most of the time they are points of imagined equality whose strength consists in being focal points on which expectations can converge. In negotiations on termination, for instance, it is not uncommon for objecting parties to adhere firmly to the literal form of the old treaty, despite the fact that this, through the course of subsequent conduct and changing circumstances, has ceased to register the real distribution of values. Another frequently used evaluation point is the status quo. But again, "to the extent that a negotiator counts on things as they are at the moment, the ground is constantly shifting beneath him."[2] Faits accomplis during bargaining are usually aimed at the creation of new points of evaluation.

It is important in bargaining to adhere to relatively stable criteria of evaluation, imaginary or not. Like all symbolic elements, it is the degree to which it continues to attract expectations that is, perhaps, the best single measure of the strength of an evaluation point. Indeed, insofar as bargaining power depends much on one's ability to limit one's range of choice and to make one's opponent perceive that his range of choice is so limited, a strong bargaining power may be achieved by choosing a point of

1. F. Iklé, *How Nations Negotiate* 167 (1964).
2. Id. at 168.

high symbolic value from which a negotiator does not seem able to depart, as the yardstick for accepting certain outcomes.

At present we are not directly concerned with symbols as a source of conflicts, but rather with the question of how symbols influence strategic and tactical choices during conflicts—that is, with their conscious use in the context of reactions to treaties, alliances, threats, promises, bluffs, statements, and so on. Most of these represent not general data or phenomena of impersonal relations, such as the mechanics of a competitive market or arena,[3] but conscious attempts to change expectations regarding particular relationships. Strategies are employed in order to create subjectivities in particular targets. They communicate an image of how a party intends to act, and how his opponent should react if he wishes to maximize his gains or minimize his losses. The significance of symbols to this process is obvious. Because of their evocative power,[4] symbolic elements may have a strong impact on the basic attitudes of the negotiators concerned and the general public. And since the parties' strategic and tactical choices during conflicts are interdependent, commonly shared symbolic elements such as elements of authority may, in particular, have a strong influence on shaping the strategy sets of many conflict situations. At the moment authority is being described in a passive sense. It is clear that an appreciation of the mechanics of symbols can lead to their effective manipulation as an element of political control.[5]

3. The term "balance of power" itself is widely used by writers, not as a definable concept but as a *symbol* of realism, intellectual virility, and concern with the problem of power in international relations. See I. Claude, *Power and International Relations* 37 (1962).

4. The power of symbols over the behavior of people is partly related to the degree of the concentration of events the symbol represents and the sentiment—the attitude permeated by feeling—that it arouses. See H. Lasswell and A. Kaplan, *Power and Society* 103 (1965); K. Boulding, *Conflict and Defense* 96 (1963). See also C. Merriam, *Political Power* 104 (1934), in *Study of Political Power* (1956).

5. To play an influential role in conflict resolutions, signs of authority should provide parties with firm criteria of evaluation. However, since in the international arena the parties can usually contract out of normative directives, their utility for a committal strategy is somewhat restricted. Various works on treaty termination seem to have been influenced by this difficulty. Thus, it has sometimes been proposed that the principle that treaties should be terminated following material changes in circumstances, should be considered *jus cogens* ([1963] *Y.B. Int'l L. Comm'n* 142, 148, U.N. Doc.A/CN.4/SER..A/1963). Peremptory norms are directives from which individual states are not competent to derogate even by agree-

## Manipulations of Authority Symbols

The point of origin in the familiar type of the termination conflict is usually the disputed treaty—its culminating text or its
actual performance at a given moment—from which redistribution
is measured. Since, as was noted,[6] the objecting side stands to lose
those physical issues that the claimant party may win, the treaty
provides an initially convenient shared criterion of evaluation:
outcomes ranging from total termination to any sort of revision
are commonly considered immediate gains to the claimant and
losses to the objecting side, assuming for the moment no broadening of the context or change in circumstances. If the objecting side
wins the dispute and the treaty's value allocation is upheld, it is
neither a gain nor a loss to any side.

ment. (Articles 53 and 64 of the Vienna Convention on the Law of Treaties.
Schwelb, "Some Aspects of International *Jus Cogens* as Formulated by the International Law Commission," 61 *Am. J. Int'l L.* 946 [1967]). Normative directives,
out of which the parties cannot contract, narrow the parties' range of choice and
thus operate to strengthen the bargaining position of the party in whose benefit
the principle is applied. Such proposals seek in effect to prevent the parties at
the time of the agreement from expressly or tacitly excluding the future application of the general principle of rebus sic stantibus. It may be suspected that
similar considerations, but with regard to the time of termination, underlie the
fictitious definition of the doctrine in terms of a tacit clausula. The theory of the
implied term involves an automatic termination of the treaty ipso facto, as soon
as the circumstances that call the clauses into play arise (ch. 1 supra). Supposedly,
when the clause becomes operative the parties have no other option than to
accept the fact of termination. Similarly, doctrines of rebus sic stantibus, which
are defined in terms of changing circumstances that are injurious to the vital interest, the very existence, or the self-preservation of a state party to the agreement, reflect tactical consideration. When an issue is considered by a government
to be "vital," and is so perceived by the opponent, it narrows the range of choice
of the claimant party and thus enhances the credibility of threats and promises
(see ch. 1, text at note 35 supra).

These theories are based on a perception of critical problems and are in great
measure an endeavor to organize and clarify them. They are, however, too general to serve this need adequately. The mere labeling of a policy of termination
as *jus cogens*, or the make-believe that this policy is applied "automatically," does
not suffice to strengthen a party's bargaining power. For in most disputes disagreement may still exist as to whether the alleged changes in conditions justify
the application of the peremptory norm, or cause the treaty to be terminated.
Conflicts that involve vital interests are generally more intense, and hence more
difficult to resolve by authoritative means. The "political question" theory has
traditionally excluded most important disputes of termination from the realm of
authority, precisely because they involve conflicting vital interests.

6. Ch. 3 supra.

Thus, the initial bargaining situation clearly favors the objecting side, whose best strategy under these circumstances is to invoke the fact that "there is a treaty"—that is, that its possession or demands to exact performance are by clear legal right—while keeping out of any bargaining. The claimant, on the other hand, usually tries to undermine the validity of the treaty and to replace it through assorted bargaining tactics with another, more favorable criterion of evaluation. Occasionally, it may be possible for the objecting side to respond to the claim to termination by a counter-offensive, threatening to reinterpret the treaty provisions or to alter subsequent and established conduct relating to it. In such cases, even when the possible outcomes still focus on the treaty itself, they may represent gains and losses for both sides. However, the danger for the objecting side in such a strategy is that it may further obliterate existing arrangements and thus diminish their usefulness as criteria of evaluation. At the initial stage of the dispute—when relative strength and determination, as well as further developments, cannot be safely predicted—much of the bargaining consists of maneuvers to determine this initial point of firm evaluation.

Consider the Anglo-Spanish dispute over Gibraltar. For many years Britain has firmly rejected all Spanish demands to negotiate the termination of the Treaty of Utrecht of 1714 on the ground that the *treaty* had conferred upon it permanent sovereignty over Gibraltar. When the negotiations finally did start, the parties reached an impasse. In 1966 Spain obtained from the United Nations General Assembly a resolution directing the parties to enter into direct negotiations with the aim of *decolonizing* the territory.[7] Decolonization of areas held by Western powers is generally considered a fundamental development conforming with an established historical trend. Thus an outcome of negotiations on decolonization that simply continues the status quo is usually evaluated by the claimant as a loss and by the objecting Western government as a gain. To result in neither a gain nor a loss for either side, it should usually provide for at least some decolonization.[8]

Since the General Assembly's resolution had shifted the parties'

7. G.A. Res. 2231, 21 U.N. GAOR Supp. 16, at 74, U.N. Doc. A/6316 (1966).
8. Iklé, *supra* note 1, at 168–69.

criterion of evaluation from the treaty in question to the kind and extent of the desired change, Britain seized upon it to abandon its own treaty obligations. The treaty itself provided that, if Britain ever gave up the territory, it must return to Spain. However, on the assumption that colonized peoples are entitled to self-determination, Britain conducted a referendum in Gibraltar. Nearly all the inhabitants of the tiny colony voted to remain British subjects.[9]

### The Berlin Crisis of 1961

Symbols acquire authority when the image about particular patterns of common behavior that they evoke is shared by the relevant members of the group.[10] However, even with authoritative signals, much depends on the experience a particular person has had with the occurrences they symbolize. The image that is evoked by the symbol of the existence of a formal treaty ("seals" and "paper"), for instance, depends very much on what experience the particular parties have had in regard to the performance of treaties with each other. This may vary greatly from one context to another.

Consider again the example of the Berlin crisis of 1961. On the grounds of changing conditions and the need for normalization of the aftermath of World War II, the Soviet Union, we have seen, in effect demanded material redistribution and formal revision of the status quo in East Germany, namely, the conclusion of a permanent peace settlement. Since a de facto peace settlement had long existed, the issue concerned the expediency of its proposed modifications only. However, the normalization sought was not a return to a unified Germany but the abrogation of Western rights in West Berlin. The Soviet claim was that the relevant agreements at the conclusion of the Second World War, as well as other postwar inter-Allied agreements, were "null and void" because of their continued nonobservance and because of change in circumstances, and that therefore unilateral changes in the status of Berlin were authorized. The Western position was that the agreements in question were still in force, and that any unilateral action contrary to

9. *New York Times*, Sept. 11, 1967, p. 1, col. 1 (late city ed.). In another resolution the General Assembly declared the referendum to be in violation of its previous resolution. G.A. Res. 2353, 22 U.N. GAOR Supp. 16, at 53, U.N. Doc. A/6716 (1967).

10. See W. Reisman, *Nullity and Revision* 5 (1971).

their provisions would constitute a clear violation of treaty obligations.[11] It was made clear that a formal abrogation of the agreements by the Soviet Union would not be regarded as a lawful termination of the rights in question, and that unilateral changes would forcibly be opposed.

However, the United States, in a note of July 17, 1961 to the Soviet Union, based its rights in West Berlin primarily on the "unconditional surrender of Nazi Germany." These rights, it was emphasized in the note, "were not granted by, or negotiated with, the Soviet Union."[12] Similarly, in a statement of July 19, 1961, President Kennedy said:

> [T]he continued presence in West Berlin of the United States, the United Kingdom, and France is by clear legal right, *arising from war, acknowledged* in many agreements signed by the Soviet Union, and strongly supported by the overwhelming majority of the people of that city.[13]

A right is a signal of authority symbolizing both the events that led to its creation (for example, "bargained for") and the appropriate shared course of behavior in interaction concerning its subject matter. The emphasis by the United States that the source of the rights concerned was not a treaty indicates that treaty rights

11. Department of State, Press Release on Legal Aspects of the Berlin Situation in *The Soviet Note on Berlin: An Analysis* 36 (Dep. State Publ. 6757, 1959); Wright, "Some Legal Aspects of the Berlin Crisis," 55 *Am. J. Int'l L.* 959 (1961).

12. 45 *Dep't State Bull.* 224, 227 (1961).

13. Id. at 223 (emphasis added). "Inasmuch as these rights, including the right of access to Berlin, are not held from the Soviet Government, they cannot be ended by any unilateral action of the Soviet Union" (id.). A similar argument is sometimes made in regard to the American military base at Guantanamo. See Lazar, "International Legal Status of Guantanamo Bay," 62 *Am. J. Int'l L.* 730, 739 (1968). He believes that the United States' rights to Guantanamo do not arise from the treaty, but from its occupancy in the war with Spain: "Any attempt by the Republic of Cuba unilaterally to abrogate the governing Agreements could only result in a reversion to the legal relations obtaining in the international legal system prior to the establishment of the Republic of Cuba" (Lazar, " 'Cession in Lease' of the Guantanamo Bay Naval Station and Cuba's 'Ultimate Sovereignty,' " 63 *Am. J. Int'l L.* 116, 117 [1969]). This "right of occupancy" has not been invoked by the United States government itself, perhaps because in the context of Latin America it will backfire. Lazar's article itself has prompted the following review: "The ghost of colonialism has poked its haunting head once again into the American doorway." (Maris, "Guantanamo: No Rights of Occupancy," 63 *Am. J. Int'l L.* 114 [1969]).

were considered by the parties to be weaker than some other legal rights. Since the Soviet legal arguments about the previous non-observance of treaty arrangements were somewhat valid, the "un-conditional surrender" of Nazi Germany was a more powerful symbol than the "sanctity of treaties." In that context the former represented more, and hence evoked more.

In the relations between the United States and the Soviet Union in regard to Germany and other similar matters, the "sanctity of treaties" evoked the list of treaty provisions that had been tacitly or officially repudiated by both sides since the end of the Second World War. The "unconditional surrender of Nazi Germany," on the other hand, evoked a colorful and highly emotional image— a war in defense of freedom against totalitarianism. In particular, an image of a holy or just war for a big principle suited a commit-tal strategy. It made the West in the Berlin crisis of 1961 less willing to yield to Soviet demands, even if that had meant war.[14]

Against the big principle of freedom, the Soviet Union rallied support behind the big principle of peace. Old demands were injected into the symbolic image of a "peace treaty." The new threat of signing a separate peace treaty with East Germany in-cluded, of course, the old claims to unilateral abrogation of Western occupation rights in Berlin. The threat of making peace did not carry quite so clearly the stigma that the Western powers had successfully attached to the unilateral repudiation of the four-power agreement on Berlin. Furthermore, it exploited the very symbolic image of the Western claimed rights to Berlin by pur-porting to put an end to the everlasting "surrender" of Germany. Last but not least, of all the noble objects of war, peace is perhaps considered to be the noblest of them all. Indeed, in postwar West-East relations Berlin had not been perceived as a unique issue, divisible into small questions, but had become a test case for grand emotional principles. The city during the course of bargaining had acquired symbolic values far beyond its value in the currency of rational behavior, however defined.

## Gradual Erosion of the Treaty

We have seen that the *initial* conflict situation of termination favors objecting sides. Their preferred strategy under these cir

14. Ch. 5 infra.

cumstances is usually to invoke the fact that they have a treaty, and to try to keep out of active bargaining as long as they can.[15] Since there is a clear status quo in the form of treaty arrangements, the unavailability of bargaining should win over the existing state of affairs to the side that prefers this result. And since, at this initial stage, what the objecting side can usually expect to gain is at best that the treaty remain in force, there is, in the ordinary course of events, no apparent reason why it should desire to negotiate the matter at all.

## Direct Talks

Negotiation on treaty termination is a subject on which much of what has been written seems self-evident until examined more closely. It is, of course, unreasonable to assume that either party would generally accept less in the relatively more cooperative context of direct talks than it could guarantee itself in tacit bargaining. Nevertheless, practically every author on the subject requires the parties to enter into direct negotiations upon the forwarding of a claim to termination. Differences of opinion exist only in respect to the choices that should be available to the parties after negotiations fail. Some, it may be recalled, authorize termination only by mutual consent, or through adjudication.[16] Since resort to adjudication in disputes about termination is generally not compulsory, this view places a high premium on direct negotiations as the main method for reaching a final lawful settlement. While some disputes of termination might fall under the compulsory jurisdiction of the International Court, the court itself held that before submitting a dispute to adjudication, the parties should seek a solution by direct negotiations.[17] Similarly, writers who

15. This in itself is, of course, already a form of bargaining. A strategy is termed ideological or propagandist when communications are addressed to large audiences. Diplomacy, on the other hand, refers to inter-elite communications. (McDougal, Lasswell, and Reisman, "The World Constitutive Process of Authoritative Decision," 19 *J. Legal Ed.* 403 [1967]). When parties resort to diplomatic communications such as indirect talks, instead of using military or economic resources, a bargain is termed "explicit."

16. See David, "Faits Accomplis in Treaty Controversies," 6 *Int'l Lawyer* 88 (1972). For a discussion of the obligation to submit the dispute to a conciliation commission, see ch. 6 infra.

17. See, e.g., *Mavrommatis Case*, [1924] P.C.I.J. Ser. A, No. 2, at 15; *South West Africa Case* [1962] I.C.J. 319, 346; *Asylum Case*, [1950] I.C.J. 266; *Request for*

allow for unilateral termination see in it a strategy of last resort, to be used only after the parties have reached a deadlock in negotiations.

Of the many pacific methods that are listed in Article 33 of the United Nations Charter for settling disputes,[18] negotiation is the most noncommittal. To require parties to enter into direct talks does not necessarily mean that they must reach an agreed settlement of the dispute. It is therefore commonly assumed that, since the possible outcomes of negotiations depend on mutual consent, governments would always be willing to resort to, if nothing else, at least this method of resolving conflict.[19]

Furthermore, direct negotiations may have beneficial effects besides those of reaching an agreement. The side effects of diplomatic talks assume great importance, particularly in a crisis. They include maintaining nonviolent contact between fierce adversaries, gathering intelligence about the opponent's will and capabilities, communicating accurate interpretations of the actions and utterances of each side during the conduct of conflict, and so on. Diplomatic talks in themselves may serve propaganda (e.g. focus public attention on or away from one's position), military (e.g. enhance or retract the threat power of the parties), or economic (e.g. promises of future benefits) purposes. Even when the parties are initially recalcitrant, cooperation may be enhanced a great

---

*Interpretation of the Judgment of November 20th, 1950 in the Asylum Case,* [1950] I.C.J. 395, 402; *Haya de la Torre Case,* [1951] I.C.J. 71. In the *Peace Treaties Case* the International Court stated: "The mere denial of the existence of a dispute does not prove its non-existence." [1950] I.C.J. 65, 74. *The Right of Passage Case,* [1957] I.C.J. 125. *The North Sea Continental Shelf Cases,* [1969] I.C.J. 3. For a discussion of these cases and the policies relating to the principle of the exhaustion of anterior processes, see Reisman, supra note 10, at 359ff.; Goldie, "The North Sea Continental Shelf Cases—A Ray of Hope for the International Court?" 26 *N.Y.L. Forum* 325 (1970); 1 Rosenne, *The Law and Practice of the International Court* 96ff. (1965); Schwebel and Wetter, "Arbitration and the Exhaustion of Local Remedies" 60 *Am. J. Int'l L.* 484 (1966); Bourquin, "Dans quelle mesure le recours a des Négociations diplomatiques est-il nécessaire avant qu'un différend puisse être soumis a la juridiction internationale?" in Basdevant, *Hommage d'une Géneration de Juristes* 43 (1960).

18. Article 65 of the Convention on the Law of Treaties directs the parties to settle disputes about treaty termination by the pacific means indicated in Article 33 of the Charter (ch. 6 infra).

19. Cf. Holsti, "Resolving International Conflicts: A Taxonomy of Behavior and Some Figures on Procedures," 10 *J. Conflict Resolution* 272, 277 (1966).

deal at the conference table, and many examples seem to indicate that—other things being equal—the availability of direct negotiations will usually elicit behavior of a lower degree of coercion.

However, the fact that in the long run explicit negotiations may be valuable to all concerned does not seem, standing alone, to induce parties to engage in them in particular disputes. Another condition should usually be satisfied before submission to talks, that is, the submission should not prejudice the party's bargaining position in regard to the central demand without at the same time benefitting it in some other concrete way. Put differently, any of the outcomes that may possibly be agreed upon at the talks should, at least, not be expected to yield less for a party than it could more-or-less obtain by refusing to enter into the talks to begin with. However, that in most disputes about treaty termination we encounter strong demands and refusals to negotiate, suggests that this is often not the case and that the question whether negotiation should or should not take place is considered by parties to be of highest strategic importance. Negotiations are usually unappealing to the objecting party because, by the very fact of their occurrence, the claimant can conveniently turn the outcome of the dispute to his own advantage.

### Disadvantages of Direct Negotiations

There are certain risks that the objecting side runs by consenting to negotiate on the claim to termination. It is the confrontation of explicit proposals that distinguishes direct negotiation from tacit bargaining and other types of conflict behavior. Thus, a consent to resort to explicit negotiation implies a consent to somehow change the status quo, and in cases of termination the change presumably operates to the advantage of the claimant state. But what is there to negotiate about when the defending side objects to the termination of the treaty and refuses to accept any change whatsoever? Furthermore, to consent to negotiation upon the argument that a treaty is terminable on some legal grounds, may from the outset of negotiations be taken as a tacit admission that there is some validity to the adversary's claim.

Even when such an admission is not the mutual understanding, the claimant may propagandize the fact of negotiation to his own advantage. An offensive government is often faced with the problem of how to change people's expectations. However dynamic a social process may be, momentum should be taken into account in every conflict of this sort. This is the element of habit, custom, and resistance to change. The old treaty, being a symbol of authority concerning particular arrangements, represents expectations of continuity which the conduct of negotiation on termination may gradually frustrate. Expecting changes in the former arrangement, third-party states, as well as many people in the bureaucracies and outside them, thereafter may consider the treaty less valid. This change in expectations may later enable the claimant government to rally the necessary support for effecting termination by unilateral acts and faits accomplis.

For similar reasons, objecting sides usually do not even try at this stage of the dispute to make the best of it by way of counter-offensive through reinterpretation of the treaty provisions to their own advantage.[20] By literally adhering to existing arrangements, the objecting government can adduce behind its position the power of inertia and what in legal circles is known as the "normative strength of the actual."

Furthermore, to demand changes in the existing state of affairs is an innovation that not only needs strong justification in order to be widely supported, but also requires an indication that it is not going to lead to violence or other forms of extreme mutual damage. Third-party governments and public opinion are generally hesitant to support claims that may disturb the peace. On the other hand, direct talks may appear to relieve tension and therefore to enhance support behind the claim for change. There seems to be a certain acquisitive instinct operating in termination controversies. A party at times almost instinctively seeks to retain what it has, though it may gain no benefits from doing so and may, in fact, by its intransigence seriously worsen its position.

At any event, a negotiated settlement will presumably be

---

20. E.g., the so-called roll back strategy during the fifties. Such a strategy is usually possible only in few conflicts about termination. It may, however, be particularly called for where the claimant attempts to separate some of the treaty provisions from others.

reached only if the objecting side will make what the claimant party regards as a final and sufficient concession. The objecting side may accept certain proposals only when it is convinced that, because of some threats, unilateral acts, or promises on the same or other issues, the outcome by agreement is more advantageous than no agreement at all. Of course, the usual idea that a treaty either will continue wholly in force or will be completely terminated, mistakenly views a complicated range of possible outcomes as two simple extremes. There is usually some range of alternatives within which any point is better for both sides than no agreement at all. This might be termed the "acceptable" set of the negotiations.

For which of these points should a party settle? Each party is guided to a surprising extent by its expectations of what the other side might accept, and expectations are constantly changing during negotiations. "There is nothing either a gain or a loss, but negotiating makes it so!" [21] The formal allocation of physical issues appearing in the treaty, or the flow of practice embroidering it, are the main criteria for measuring gains and losses in termination, and they add a heightened dimension of expectations. Furthermore, like all symbolic elements, it is the degree to which the treaty continues to sustain expectations that is the best single measure of its strength. Once a party is felt to have departed from this by submission to talks, there is no end to the concessions it may be asked to make during negotiations. Hence, when a party is in such an advantageous bargaining position that it can hold onto a clear point which possesses authoritative symbolic value, it does not pay for it to relinquish it before it has some notion about the aggregate outcome that will be acceptable to the opponent. This means that even when the objecting side is prepared to accept some change, it may not agree right away to negotiate on the claim to termination.

This very question of whether the objecting side should have entered into direct negotiation at all on the Soviet claims to Berlin was a source of disagreement between the United States and Britain on the one side, and France on the other. In a speech to

21. Iklé, supra note 1, at 190.

the French National Assembly in December 1961, Foreign Minister Couve de Murville explained some of France's objections to negotiation:

> This problem, paradoxically, is whether the French, the Americans, and the British should take the initiative to propose to the Russians the setting-up of a four power conference. I say "paradoxically" because, after all, it is the Russians who have raised the question of a change of the status quo. Looking at it differently, it would mean that we should ask them to discuss their conditions for our staying in Berlin; that is, to discuss the concessions we would have to make to them so that they agree, to a certain extent and perhaps for a certain time only, that our troops can stay and that the freedom of West Berlin thus will remain more or less guaranteed.[22]

The United States and Britain also opposed the making of any concession to Soviet demands, but American and British officials held the view that negotiation itself, apart from any agreement, was of value. As stated by Secretary of State Dean Rusk a few months later:

> I think both sides still believe, as they have for some time, that maintaining contact on these issues [Soviet demands] is itself important, even though there has been no clear view as to how they might lead to a satisfactory solution.[23]

The dispute over Berlin could not have been separated from the general East-West conflict, and precisely because there was no lasting settlement in sight it was important, according to this view, for the major powers to be in such close contact that they could not be dragged into a war by some local misunderstanding. Negotiations were said to be acceptable to the United States and Britain because of their desire to keep a potential channel open for communication in an emergency, for the Soviets had threatened to resort to unilateral actions if their demands were

22. Quoted in Iklé, supra note 1, 34–35.
23. *New York Times,* July 13, 1962, p. 2, col. 7 (late city ed.).

not met. However, because of the insistence of France, formal negotiation did not take place at that time.

### SPIN-OFF CONFLICT

Such are the mechanics of bargaining over termination that, in the usual course of events, the objecting side is expected to resist even ordinary talks on the claim. Since the most it can expect to gain from such a move is what it already has, and since it stands to lose a great deal by it, the objecting side may prefer to remain "immobile"—keeping out of any real bargaining. If changes are nevertheless mutually effected in such situations, whether by formal agreement or by a fait accompli tacitly acquiesced to, the reason is to be found in the relative power, strategies, and tactics involved. These tactics introduce new elements into the situation and thus operate to change the parties' criteria of evaluation. Promises and threats (explicit or implicit in the situation) introduce into the conflict the possibility of mutual gains and losses. Their immediate effect is usually to interject extraneous issues into the bargaining situation. Promises on behalf of the claimant party to compensate for the given treaty termination in another matter introduce for the first time the possibility of gains for the objecting side. Threats of causing "worse consequences" introduce into the possible outcomes of the dispute the element of risk for both sides. For the claimant party a threat opens the possibility not only of gains, but of losses. For the objecting side a threat means the possibility of greater losses than what is initially at stake. This possibility of extraneous bargaining is what the particular agreement, whether remaining in force or terminated, costs the parties; it represents the values obtainable through alternative activities foregone in pursuing the given one.

The outcome of the conflict will usually be determined by the varied resort to such threats and promises concerning the issues initially in dispute or other originally unrelated matters, as well as by their gradual implementation. Hence an ancillary dynamic: lateral expansion of dispute, or spin-off conflict. In the aforementioned dispute over Gibraltar, the United Nations General Assembly instructed the parties to settle by negotiation. In the negotiations that followed the resolution, Britain proposed to submit the question of the termination of the Treaty of Utrecht to the International Court of Justice. Spain refused to resort to adjudication, insisting on direct talks as prescribed by the resolution. To force Britain into negotiations, Spain implemented a threat to terminate British treaty flight rights over Spanish territory. However, following the Spanish move, Britain consented to enter into negotiations, not on the Spanish central claim as might have been expected, but only on the question of the flight restrictions.[24]

Treaty termination becomes a dynamic conflict when threats are issued or faits accomplis are made. While such threats and unilateral acts are not necessarily aimed at fulfillment of the central demand but only at forcing the adversary to negotiate about the demand, they may still shift the parties' evaluation criteria from the given treaty to some other matters, and thus may crucially determine the outcome of the dispute. The dilemma of whether to launch a counteroffensive instead of remaining passive usually arises for the objecting side when the adversary has already managed somehow to undermine the validity of the treaty. At this point, however, the conflict, as will be further explained, is usually laterally expanded and includes promises, threats, or unilateral acts in other issues. Attempts to apply sanctions within the treaty where possible cannot be successful at this stage of the conflict escalation, and the counteroffensive, if at all, has to be made outside the treaty. The objecting side can expect to make some limited gains within the treaty only after the claimant has failed in pressing its central demand. But even then, such an exploitation of victory by further undermining the authority of the original agreement may lead to a revival of the claim and enhance its future success.

There is a danger here that the primary motivation for maximizing one's demands and shunting all possibilities for a negotiated settlement will result not from a realistic assessment of

24. However, the negotiations on the flight restrictions broke down, since Britain refused to accept Spanish demands regarding Gibraltar. *New York Times*, June 10, 1967, p. 2, col. 3 (late city ed.). But in the Berlin crisis of 1958, the United States proposed in the negotiations specific concessions on the central issue, see p. 140 infra.

the conflict situation but rather from thinking about dynamic relationships in terms of static facts. Indeed, all facets of bargaining process are in a state of flux; the facts of this moment are not the facts of the next. The claimant state, when confronted with strong adherence to the status quo in the form of a refusal to enter into direct negotiations, may, if it is unable to satisfy its claim unilaterally, still be able to erode the other side's expectations by its unilateral actions. While it is true that many disputes over termination cannot be resolved by unilateral acts, a fait accompli may create a new focal point for expectations to converge on, and may thus make further value redistribution more attractive to the objecting side.

In the Berlin crisis of 1961, we have seen, the central Soviet demand concerned more the free access of the Western powers to West Berlin than the right to free movement within all of Berlin. Since negotiations on Berlin had been taking place for quite some time before the emergence of acute crisis, and since it was clear from the United States' position that they might be resumed sometime in the future, the Soviet chose to make a fait accompli that, among others, could be used as a device for extracting new concessions on the central demand. The erection of the wall was probably intended, in part, to reiterate and provide a symbol for the idea that the division of the city, indeed of the whole country, was final and permanent. Since then, Western governments and the public have no longer tended to view the new situation as a departure from earlier agreements, but as a new status quo from which improvements are evaluated.[25] Negotiations on Soviet demands are now acceptable to many more people in the West, since the removal of the Wall is regarded by them as a proper, bargained-for consideration. In other words, the spin-off conflict has become part of the major complex of contention.

25. Iklé, supra note 1, at 168.

# 5 Negotiating a Settlement

No matter how thin you slice it, it's still baloney.

Alfred E. Smith

During the discussion in the previous chapter a certain characteristic of negotiations on termination was noted: they frequently
take the form of negotiations about what the parties should negotiate about. A major problem in termination is the spread of
benefits or the division of costs which are inherent in this type of
decision. If the issue of termination or modification is kept separate, it remains, no matter how divisible the object of negotiations
is, a gain for the claimant state and a loss for the objecting party.
But if two simultaneous negotiations can be brought into a contingent relationship with each other, a means of compensation is
available. And since the principal means of compensation are concessions on some other subject, the agenda assumes a particular
importance in negotiations on termination. Agreeing on what the
issues for talks are, therefore, may alone require more time and
effort than settling them.

## Termination as a Topic

It was demonstrated in the previous chapter that for termination
to be a topic for negotiation, both parties must first agree on the
question of whether the agreement should be terminated. But this
is precisely the point on which the parties may be divided. Moreover, even if the defensive party is willing to settle for the termination of the agreement, there is no reason why it should relinquish
its advantageous position by implying its consent to termination
before at least knowing the kind of settlement that will be reached.
This is particularly true when the objecting side demands, in return for termination, concessions on some other issues that are
extraneous to the original agreement. For the objecting side to

agree to negotiate only on the claim to termination is, then, usually to make an important concession from the outset.[1]

In most cases negotiations, in which the termination of the treaty is the *only* issue for decision, are already the outcome of a basic agreement (tacit or expressed) between the parties concerning the validity of the claim, and the desirability and extent of the change (the accuracy of this observation will be tested throughout the discussion). For this reason, parties who object to the claim to termination, if powerful enough, usually object to entering into explicit negotiation on the subject. They may agree, at best, to participate in "discussions" concerning the validity of the claim, provided these are clearly distinguished from actual bargaining on the central demand.

Consider, for example, the following report concerning the Franco-American dispute about the removal of American military bases from France:

> The United States has decided to end the exchange of diplomatic notes with President de Gaulle and turn to oral discussions. . . .
>
> As one official put it today "We don't advance anything by making debating points in diplomatic notes."
>
> The administration now intends to pursue the matter in quiet discussions. But officials made clear that the administration had no intention of acceding to the French demands for immediate discussions or withdrawal of American bases from France.[2]

The United States asked to discuss "questions of legality" first, and not the "practical arrangements" for withdrawal of the bases as suggested by France. To discuss the legal validity of the treaty and the opponent's claim instead of negotiating on the claimant's demand is, of course, not to concede the central point from the outset. There is no reason, however, to prefer oral discussions to the exchange of notes for the purpose of making "debating points" on questions of legality, except that in "quiet talks" officials can

1. This is so partly because governments traditionally see the matter in this way. Changes in perspectives may enable parties to be more flexible.

2. *New York Times*, Apr. 26, 1966, p. 17, col. 1 (late city ed.).

freely negotiate on any issue without committing themselves in advance to a specific settlement. In such talks the parties may make demands, propose concessions, and occasionally even threaten and warn each other more freely. And particularly in bilateral meetings not of the pageant type,[3] the parties may not feel constrained to observe strictly the agenda agreed on.

This does not imply that questions of legality are relevant only as an instrument to ideologize one's position in public discussions. But precisely because of the importance of their ideological impact on the bargaining positions of the parties in the instant dispute (and on similar disputes in the future), the party that objects to the termination may try to avoid an open submission to negotiation on the central demand, and hence avoid the implication that it affirms the claimant's contention that the treaty should be terminated. For, if the parties were to reach a deadlock during negotiation, the party objecting to the termination might be accused of breaking its promise to terminate or modify the treaty, of negotiating in bad faith, and of attempting to preserve intact a treaty that it had already implied was obsolete. Third-party governments, as well as many people, would thereafter consider the treaty less valid, and the claimant state might make use of the argument in order to justify a unilateral termination of the agreement. Moreover, the possibility always exists that the claimant state is not interested in a compromise solution to the dispute but rather in the side effects of the negotiations—namely, in compelling the other side to admit that its position regarding the central demand is not firm, and in finding out its possible reaction to unilateral termination. In addition, the claimant state is always in a stronger legal position [4] and usually also in a stronger bargaining position regarding unilateral termination after a deadlock is reached than before the start of negotiations.

The aforementioned reasons for the objecting side's refusal to negotiate on termination are generally valid for many situations. They are, however, more compelling in a context of traditionally

3. In pageant-type oral negotiations—such as the Paris talks on Vietnam and the similar previous talks during the Korean War—the content and style consist in great part of exchanges of oral hostilities.

4. Partly because unilateral termination is presumably authorized—if at all—only if and after the parties reached a stalemate during the negotiation (ch. 6 infra).

hostile parties. Hostile participants more often make physical moves while talks are being conducted. That is to say, submission to negotiation cannot guarantee the objecting side the absence of unilateral acts and faits accomplis by the opponent. Allied governments, on the other hand, since they are required to respect one another's preferences, are far more restrained in their negotiations, and it is also much harder for them to refuse to talk about an ally's claim. Furthermore, difficulties in formulating the topic for negotiations can more easily be avoided, since between allies ongoing discussions are usually taking place.

But there is another side to the coin. Since allied governments cannot overtly coerce but have to demonstrate respect for one another's wishes, it may be advantageous in conflicts within a political coalition for a party to disclose a desired preference pattern and to have a prior reputation for inflexibility. If a friendly government claims termination and demonstrates its commitment (for example, a cabinet's disclosed decision "to terminate"), then the objecting side is forced to yield to the demand unless it can persuade the claimant government in "quiet discussions" to change its position. Paradoxically, in such a situation it is the claimant and not the objecting party who may try to avoid direct talks on the claim. In the dispute over the American bases in France, the French claim was presented in the form of a final decision. As it turned out, the French government itself objected to negotiations on terminations, for such would only have detracted from the appearance of finality that the claim assumed.[5] It is obvious that the word *final* has different meanings in different contexts.

Something more than the appearances of a commitment may perhaps be involved in refusal to negotiate in such a situation. In a context of traditional enmities it is usually advantageous to threaten an adversary in public. This adds commitment to the threat, enhances its credibility, and may rally both allies and citizens as a result of the atmosphere of crisis that it creates. In a generally cooperative context, on the other hand, to threaten an adversary in the open is self-defeating. If a party wishes an ally to continue with political or military collaboration and yet publicly

5. See also ch. 7 infra. For a game theoretical analysis of a similar bargaining situation, see Luce and Raiffa, *Games and Decisions* 91 (1966).

threatens to hurt him badly if he does not cooperate on certain issues, the party may trigger a process of commensurate response. A public challenge may, in certain contexts, require your counterpart to bring into question the fundamental basis of prior collaboration. It is therefore possible that a party might prefer not to have the privilege of quiet discussions on a particular subject matter, for with them would come the possibility of threats from its opponent. One should, of course, be careful not to exaggerate this argument. In a period of elaborate communication systems between governments, it is almost impossible to cut out communications on an issue merely by refusing to discuss it.[6] Particularly between allied governments, there are usually diplomatic contacts and ongoing discussions on many issues, which may provide a convenient means for communicating demands and threats on any issue. Still, being a radical departure from the status quo, termination is usually regarded as an important matter, which should, naturally, be negotiated only by the highest officials. There are only few forums that can provide both the secrecy and the authority needed for bargaining on such an issue.[7]

Furthermore, warnings and threats are moves made by a party for the purpose of changing the opponent's expectations and consequently influencing his choices. In redistributional conflicts between traditional opponents, threat strategies are relatively inflexible. Central demands are presented in the form of an ultimatum, threats are specific, and a definite date is often set for

6. But see *New York Times,* Aug. 31, 1967, at 5, col. 1 (late city ed.) regarding a dispute between Britain and China on Hong Kong. The British foreign minister addressed a "personal message" to the Chinese foreign minister. Communications between the two governments, however, were "disrupted," and the message "was sent to Peking by commercial cable and an attempt was made to give a copy to Shen Ping, the Chinese chargé here, at the Foreign Office. He refused to accept responsibility for transmitting the message and would not take the copy.

"Britain's diplomatic radio facilities were destroyed in the burning of the Peking mission. In return the Chinese diplomats here have been barred from using their diplomatic radio transmitters" (id.).

7. Paradoxically, between traditional adversaries quiet discussions may be needed in order to communicate genuine promises. Such promises, when communicated in the open, may run risks both that they will be perceived by the opponent as a mere propaganda maneuver, and that they will be resisted by the promisor's internal pressure groups as well as external allies.

their implementation unless the central demand is satisfied before then. For the purpose of such threats it makes little difference whether they are communicated during and as part of direct negotiation on the issue, or are "just communicated" to the other side. In a generally friendly context, on the other hand, the parties cannot threaten highhandedly. Because they try not to jeopardize the cooperation they already have, serious threats, if any, should always be relatively flexible. In these situations threats are often disguised as objective warnings about the "natural" consequences that may result from each side pursuing its exclusive interests. This is not to say that everyone really believes that it is never the warner's actions that cause or contribute to the adversary's loss, and that therefore the threatened party may comply with the threat and still save face. The point is that the parties try to show that in case of disagreement these actions will have to be taken for reasons other than causing loss to the other party. In other words, such threats or warnings should not only be flexible but should preferably be connected to the details of the issue at hand.

It is, thus, during the exchange of arguments ("The natural consequences of your demand will be . . . , which will cause both of us damage but which will probably hurt you more") and proposals (". . . but to prevent these losses . . .") in the generally cooperative context that occasions arise for successful threats and warnings. Since such threats should preferably be transformed into arguments and proposals, the capacity of parties to threaten one another is enhanced by the participation in direct negotiations of officials who are competent to make decisions on the issues involved. In the Franco-American dispute, the French finally agreed to multilateral discussions on the matter within NATO. For that purpose, the foreign ministers of the alliance met at Brussels for a special conference. There the French foreign minister insisted on an agenda that would include only "future cooperation" between the participants, not "former arrangements." When pressed by the United States to enter into bilateral talks on the claim to termination, the French government insisted that the matter should be discussed on a low governmental level, for instance between military officers of the two countries. These officials, it was argued, could best resolve the "practical problems" (like transpor-

tation of withdrawing troops and storage of equipment that would
be left behind) involved in the French "final decision."

This case is perhaps not typical of disputes between political
allies. For one thing, such parties expect sympathetic response to
their views, an opportunity to present these views if they are not
understood or readily agreed with, and an assurance that efforts
will be made to avoid or at least mitigate the adverse impact of
national decisions upon their economies. To present a claim in the
form of "this is what I'm going to do; make up your mind and do
what you want" may bring short-term advantages in an isolated
case, but when repeated may adversely affect the future of the
alliance. Negotiations within coalitions are generally more readily
available, and agenda difficulties can easily be avoided. Indeed, the
French attitude was allegedly a reaction to similar practices by the
United States.[8]

Second, certain important features of the Franco-American
conflict seem to have made the success of the French decision
possible. France, a relatively powerful state, is, of course, a Western
European country with which genuine future cooperation was
highly preferred by the United States. Such a demand for termination of military bases might, in a different case, have been treated
by the objecting party as a defection to the rival coalition, in
which case there would neither be incentive to submit to the
claim nor to negotiate on the demand.

To the extent that a refusal to negotiate is influenced by the
somewhat remote possibility of exposing oneself to more serious
threats, a solution to the problem cannot be found wholly in the
formulation of an acceptable agenda for talks. The fear of threats,
however, does not seem to be a decisive motive for refusal to
negotiate, and cases in which such a reason may be suspected are
usually accompanied by other reasons. Furthermore, these cases
do not call for international regulation. Such refusals to negotiate
are symptoms of the collaboration and common interests inherent
in a situation. And if by resisting negotiations threats and coercive
acts could be averted, then we might as well dispense with the
negotiations.

8. Ch. 8 infra.

## NEGOTIATING ON REVISION

Termination as a claim implies an all-or-nothing outcome. It is therefore an unacceptable topic for negotiations. By agreeing to negotiate on revision instead of on termination, both parties presumably abandon their maximum strategy (both as to claims and related unilateral acts) without at the same time prejudicing their bargaining positions in regard to totally unacceptable outcomes. Revision (or modification) is a more acceptable topic because it assumes that the parties will replace their former arrangement by a new one through negotiation. A further advantage of this formulation of the issue is that it suggests an outcome not of either-or, but of more-or-less, and commits neither party in advance to the kind and extent of the concessions that will presumably be "mutually" made. The outcome of negotiations on revision—unless extraneous issues are introduced or claims by the objecting side for an innovative interpretation of the treaty provisions are discussed—may vary from a complete termination of former arrangements to a continuation of the former agreement in a new form (a face-saving formula).[9] But here again, submission to negotiation presupposes agreement that the former arrangement is obsolete, and focuses the negotiation on the question of the extent of the desired change. Once the validity of the treaty as an evaluation point is departed from, and unless another such point upon which the expectations of the parties can converge during the negotiations is clearly established, there is no end to the concessions that a party may be asked to make. And, since any change arrived at by revision would also presumably benefit only the claimant state, many of the difficulties encountered in bringing the parties into the conference room for negotiations on termination also arise in negotiations on revision.

To the extent that officials of the objecting side feel that they "must" enter into negotiations or else suffer losses, revision is definitely a more advantageous topic. The fact that the parties have settled on revision after prolonged bargaining on the question of negotiation indicates that the claimant party intends to negotiate conservatively—to guarantee itself a certain security

9. See, for example, the Egyptian-Sudanese dispute, ch. 3 supra.

level concerning the possible outcomes rather than to maximize its demand. This is sometimes made explicit by the parties before they enter into talks. Hence the following problem arises: at the end of the first phase of bargaining (about whether to enter into direct talks or not), the claimant government usually realizes that its opponent has made serious "mistakes," thereby allowing the claimant to increase its minimum level concerning the outcome. The most obvious and familiar such example is the case in which the objecting side is forced into direct talks by a threat of some worse consequences if it does not submit to the talks. Thus, the claimant now faces the dilemma of whether he should really negotiate conservatively, thereby guaranteeing himself his latest security level, or should anticipate the objecting side's future mistakes and capitalize on them by negotiating less conservatively. It would be very tempting for the claimant to demand his maximum in the negotiations even if this might lead to a deadlock. After all, by agreeing to negotiate, the objecting side has manifested a susceptibility to threats: since it yielded to a threat at the outset of negotiations, why should it not yield to future threats in connection with the central demand? At any rate, the claimant state, it may be recalled, will usually strengthen its bargaining position and will always improve its legal case regarding nonconsensual termination after a deadlock is reached in negotiations rather than before the start of negotiations.

The difficulty here is that the tactical choices made at an early stage in the bargaining influence those of later stages. In deciding whether to enter into direct negotiations, the objecting party—indeed both parties—have to make simultaneous choices which not only concern gains and losses at that particular stage, but also concern the parties' bargaining positions in the negotiations themselves. A certain circularity resulting from the mutual mistrust between the parties is involved in making choices in these situations. Each party's choices depend on his opponent's choices, and these are not necessarily known to him.

The answer "we do not, as a matter of principle, agree to negotiate under threats or pressure" is thus quite familiar in conflicts about termination. In the dispute over Gibraltar, for instance, Britain consented to talk only about the Spanish threat to terminate British flight rights over certain parts of Spain, but not about the Spanish central demand.[10] Similarly, in the dispute between the United States and Panama concerning the Canal, the United States refused for a long time to enter into direct negotiations on the revision of the treaty. It continued to reject such negotiations even after an outbreak of violence in and around the Canal Zone and Panama's severance of diplomatic relations between the two countries. Less than a year later, and only after relations between the two countries seemed to have returned to normal, did the United States announce its willingness to enter into negotiations on revision. In announcing the decision President Johnson added:

> Last January there was violence in Panama. As I said then, "violence is never justified and is never a basis for talks."
>
> But while the people of the United States have never made concessions to force, they have always supported fair play and full respect for the rights of others. So from the first day I made it clear that we were ready to sit down and seek answers that would be just and fair and right—without precondition or precommitment on either side.[11]

Some months earlier, when the parties had convened to discuss the resumption of diplomatic relations, the United States had rejected a formula designed by a team of mediators from the Organization of American States, which provided for discussions or negotiations on the treaty. Consequently, the parties had agreed at the time on a formula for talks that would not mention the disputed treaty but would broadly "seek the prompt elimination of the causes of conflict between the two countries without limitations or preconditions of any kind." [12] Although the agenda specifically excluded any limitation or precondition, so as to refute any implication that it concerned the renegotiation of the Canal Treaty, the resulting eight-month talks were nothing but

---

10. *New York Times*, May 18, 1967, p. 15, col. 1 (late city ed.); June 6, 1967, p. 4, col. 3 (late city ed.). See also ch. 4 supra.

11. Statement of President Johnson, *New York Times*, Dec. 19, 1964, p. 10, col. 6 (city ed.).

12. Id. at col. 2.

negotiations on the preconditions that would accompany a consent by the United States to renegotiate the treaty.

### PRECONDITIONS TO TALKS

Parties which oppose claims to termination are, then, inclined to reject proposals to enter explicit negotiations on termination, or even negotiations on the revision of a treaty. Even if in principle they are willing to agree to the central demand in return for some other concessions, they may insist on knowing beforehand what the quid pro quo, compensation, or amelioration for the deprivational effects of the decision will be. It goes without saying that before negotiating with the other side they cannot possibly know the details of these concessions. In this situation it may be advantageous for the objecting side to disclose its strategy at the outset of negotiations and to commit both itself and its adversary to it. One such way of being assured of a minimum level of an outcome, or of a suitable side compensation, is for the objecting party to insist on subjecting the negotiations to certain substantive preconditions. For example, when the United States finally agreed to negotiate (not only to "discuss" and "debate") the revision of the 1903 Panama Canal Treaty in December 1964, the consent was coupled with the precondition that any settlement arrived at would enter into force only if an agreement was first reached (whether with Panama or with another country) on the reconstruction and maintenance of a new canal. Obviously, there were material and tactical advantages for the United States even in this formulation.

Accompanying consent to enter negotiations with preconditions cannot always be a good solution. For one thing, preconditions, if they are to be effective, must be relatively clear and specific. Conditions that are ambiguously phrased—for example, "proportionate contributions," "sharing of costs," or "just and adequate compensations"—cannot be of much value for the purpose of a committal strategy. In addition, reaching an agreement on a concrete formulation of preconditions may in itself require a long process of negotiations, to a point where the term "preconditions" will no longer fit. Indeed, President Johnson's statement on the Panama Canal appeared to be more of a mutual agreement on

what the new treaty should include in principle than a proposal
to negotiate accompanied by unilateral preconditions:

> Such a treaty would replace the treaty of 1903 and its amend-
> ments. It should recognize the sovereignty of Panama. It
> should provide for its own termination when a sea-level canal
> comes into operation. It should provide for effective discharge
> of our common responsibilities for hemispheric defense. Until
> a new agreement is reached, of course, the present treaties will
> remain in effect.[13]

Note that the consent is not merely to negotiate, or to negotiate
on revision, but to recognize the sovereignty of Panama over the
Canal and to conclude a new treaty that would provide for its
own termination. The old treaty, on the other hand, granted to
the United States the perpetual and total administration of the
Canal Zone.

Preconditions, then, may in themselves require lengthy negotiations, and hence they cannot always provide for a solution to the
dilemma described above. It is not surprising, therefore, to find
preconditions accepted from the outset of real negotiations in
situations where the objecting side is relatively much more powerful, for it can better endure the losses from a continued stalemate
than its adversary who, in any way, by accepting the conditions
stands to improve its initial position considerably. There may
nevertheless be serious disadvantages to insistence on preconditions. When the concessions sought concern matters that are foreign to the treaty in question, as may often be the case, the

13. Id. at col. 4. For these and other developments, see 2 A. Chayes, T. Erlich, and
A. Lowenfeld, *International Legal Process* 879ff. (1969); Hoyt, "Law and Politics
in the Revision of Treaties Affecting the Panama Canal," 6 *Va. J. Int'l L.* 289
(1966). However, the new talks were broken off in 1967. In 1973 the conflict erupted
again. The United States vetoed a proposed U.N. Security Council resolution directing the parties to enter into direct negotiation on treaty termination or revision.
Nevertheless, the parties entered into so-called important conversations and
reached a new agreement on "a set of fundamental principles which will serve
to guide the negotiator in the effort to conclude a just and equitable treaty
eliminating, once and for all, the causes of conflict between the two countries"
("Statement by U.S. and Panama on New Canal Treaty," *New York Times*, Feb. 8,
1974, p. 2, cols. 5, 6 [city ed.]). Though it is more detailed than President Johnson's
1964 statement, the 1974 joint statement reiterated a similar set of interrelated
principles.

objecting party will be accused from the outset of negotiating in "bad faith," of trying to "dictate" a settlement, and of "imposing" a treaty in whose application it has no further immediate interest.

## COUPLING DISPUTES

It is possible to attribute to any particular conflict a certain minimum size in factual or in physical terms. Conflict, as we have previously noted, is generally defined and measured by the inconsistency between the events desired by the parties. A conflict between two or more participants who simultaneously want the same object, can, of course, be reduced if division of the object is possible. If, on the other hand, the objectives of the parties are so narrowly defined that further division of the issues is not possible, the outcome will have to accommodate one party only, and there may therefore be less likelihood of negotiation and agreement. Furthermore, when a government is already committed to the narrow object in dispute (for example, "termination" or "revision"), any division of the immediate issue that aims at redistribution must be at its expense. There are, of course, numerous other dynamic factors that may widen the gap between the parties' positions, and they will be considered at the appropriate time.

Paradoxically, some gaps may be narrowed by widening the frame. The chances of settling an issue when one party's gains mean another party's losses are increased, either by lateral expansion of the immediate subject matter in dispute until it includes enough ground to enable the settlement to benefit both parties, or by the introduction of issues materially unrelated, for which, however, there is an identity of parties.[14] The latter technique is known as a "tie-in" or "package deal." [15] The issue of the termination or revision of the treaty in question is specifically linked with other issues which are pending negotiations between the same

14. Roger Fisher discusses mainly five dimensions that measure the size of an issue: "(1) the parties on each side of the issue; (2) the immediate physical issue involved; (3) the immediate issue of principle; (4) the substantive precedent which settlement will establish; (5) the procedural precedent which settlement will establish." Fisher, "Fractionating Conflict," in *International Conflict and Behavioral Science* 91, 94 (R. Fisher ed. 1964).

15. See generally F. Iklé, *How Nations Negotiate* 233–34, 244–45 (1964). For the relation between tie-ins and compensation, see T. Schelling, *The Strategy of Conflict* 32 (1963).

parties and in which the positions of the parties are reversed. In other words, a concession on behalf of the objecting party need not only mean an acceptance of the opponent's position with regard to the disputed treaty. Rather, the conceding party may suggest alternative outcomes that will not require him to make further concessions in other rounds of negotiations on different issues with the same parties.

## The Theory of Exchange

The interjection of extraneous issues into the negotiation may, therefore, make the resolution of the claim possible by compensating from "outside" the treaty in dispute for the deprivation attendant upon its termination. This creates a new and different kind of bargaining situation, in which the relation between the claimant and the objecting side is analogous to that between two parties who have commodities to trade. In the new bargaining situation of exchange some values will presumably be traded for others. It is therefore possible for both parties to gain.

The theory of exchange is relevant wherever something is given up for something else, and no matter whether the exchangeables are physical commodities or, for instance, clauses in labor contracts, treaty provisions, or even quiet understandings and tacit agreements. Its point of origin is usually the status quo, or no-exchange, which is, of course, often a fiction, since the availability of such a point must in practice already assume a predetermination of the immediate values that may or may not be exchanged. By an "exchange" is usually meant the actual reapportionment of this joint bundle of commodities, either by conflicting or trading moves. The former is any exchange that is expected to make at least one party worse off. The latter, on the other hand, means mutual benefits, but not necessarily equal advantages to both parties.[16]

In any such bargaining there may, of course, be a great many possible alternative trades. These are mainly determined by the various possibilities of first determining and then dividing the commodities involved. But while in the initial situation of ter-

16. K. Boulding, *Conflict and Defense* 15 (1963). For a discussion of tacit connection of disputes, see chs. 8 and 9 infra.

mination (before the coupling of issues), a threat of no-agreement operates only to the advantage of the objecting party, in the new exchange situation either party can threaten to force the outcome of the dispute to be less favorable for both sides by refusing to agree. The likelihood that the parties will reach an optimal agreement—a trade that is better for each party than the status quo, and that is not inferior to any other feasible trade—is therefore substantially increased.

### Packaging and Untying

In contrast to the austere purity of theory, practical difficulties do arise. By interjecting extraneous issues into a termination conflict, the parties in effect abandon the treaty as the main criterion of evaluation. Realizing that the expansion of the size of the dispute is a promising solution to the bargaining problem in termination, the parties usually engage in a lengthy bargaining to determine a new such point (described in the theory of exchange as the status quo), which should consist of all the component values that will presumably be tied together.

This may often prove to be a difficult task.[17] As Roger Fisher observes, "[i]ssues between people and between governments do not have objective edges established by external events. These problems of life lie in a seamless web of interrelated facts and circumstances."[18] Almost anything in the world can be related to anything else, and it is up to the parties themselves to choose which congeries of events and objects should be considered as a unit for the purpose of working particular relations with each other. Events and objects may be treated jointly for some purposes and separately for others, the choice being primarily tactical, depending, as we shall further see, on similar reactive tactics of the opponent and a variety of other contextual factors.[19]

17. Parties not only bargain on terms that they evaluate in a given way, but also bargain on the criteria of evaluation in order to fit it to their preferred terms, (ch. 4 supra).

18. Fisher, supra note 14, at 92–93.

19. Hence, the initial step of coupling disputes may in itself require a lengthy process of hard bargaining. Ideally, each party should concede points in issues about which the adversary has a stronger preference. However, both in the generally cooperative and adversarial contexts each party's preferences are influenced

It is clear, however, that in conflicts about termination in which both sides do seek a negotiated settlement, the technique of "tie-ins" may prove useful for reaching an agreement. On April 28, 1967, for instance, an agreement between the United States, Britain, and West Germany was reached on the level of American and British troops in West Germany, and on their support costs. The main points of this agreement, which ended a long period of unseemly public bickering and private threatening, represented a patchwork of both connection and division of issues. Being essentially quantitative, the issues of monetary expenditures and the level of troops were inherently divisible. It could therefore be agreed that 30,000 of the 225,000 American troops and between 5,000 and 6,000 of the 59,000 British troops in West Germay would be withdrawn. As to the foreign exchange costs for maintaining the troops, the West German government undertook to purchase military equipment in the United States ($300 million). In addition, the German Bundesbank was supposed to invest in American securities ($500 million). Furthermore, West Germany promised to buy British goods ($125 million). The United States increased its previous commitments to purchase in Britain, and undertook to station in Britain some American troops that had been withdrawn from France.[20]

Between allied governments there is usually a tendency not to press for immediate radical changes. Instead, big issues are divided so that they can more easily be settled by a process of on-

---

by the adversary's. In negotiations between allied governments, the parties are presumably favorably influenced in the direction of attaching some weight in their own preference-map to the fact that their ally prefers a certain outcome. This facilitates the reaching of an agreement on what issues to connect. Difficulties may arise, however, in negotiations between traditional opponents, where the connection of issues often involves problems of relative advantage and intergovernmental comparison of values. It should, of course, be emphasized that the terms "generally collaborative" or "adversarial" contexts, though useful in indicating the general tendency of particular relationships, tend to reduce the variety of interaction into two categories and may, in many contexts, be too broad to be useful. Collaborative or competitive governments are seldom friendly or hostile all across the board. It is useful for the purpose of dynamic coupling of disputes to make further distinctions according to a variety of additional contextual factors, such as the relative importance of particular issues and the relative power of the parties.

20. *New York Times,* Apr. 29, 1967, p. 3, col. 1 (late city ed.).

going discussions. It was also agreed, therefore, that these complicated arrangements would run for a period of one year only. Demands for more drastic cuts in troop levels and for a wider sharing of expenses were thus left for further rounds of negotiations. The significance of the 1967 agreement lay, then, not so much in the immediate settlement it contained as in the strong bearing it may have had with regard to further negotiations between the parties.

The British and American demands for troop withdrawal and support costs represented an important departure from the arrangements that had been in effect for almost twenty years. In such a situation any change, however slight it may be in material terms, operates to create expectations that additional changes in the same direction will be effected in the future. In agreeing to meet some of the foreign exchange costs of the troops, the German government may have been concerned, not only with how much it would lose immediately by yielding on that point, but with how much it would lose by way of precedent. Thus, by tying the question of sharing in military costs to other financial and commercial transactions between the parties, the German government maintained a clear and firm position against direct financing of the foreign troops on its behalf.[21]

In sum, it may be advantageous for all parties to broaden the issue or couple different disputes and then subject them to a piecemeal settlement. The ability to define the issues in the "prenegotiation" phase, and to size them so as to put the dispute in the intermediate range that is optimal for negotiability, enhances the willingness of the parties to negotiate. Fractionating a conflict at the negotiation phase while at the same time coupling the narrower and separate issues with *other* divisible issues between the parties, may eventually facilitate an agreement on the larger issues. A piecemeal settlement may bring moderate changes in the status quo, in the mutual hope of winning a series of small gains over a protracted time. It may reduce the tension that usually follows

21. Similarly, in pressing for the temporary agreement, the American and British governments were interested not only in the immediate settlement it contained but also in its effects on future negotiations. As the first significant withdrawal of troops from Germany since troops had been committed there, the agreement established a valuable precedent.

the sudden abrogation of a demanded and expected order, and thus may gradually decrease opposition by the public and third-party governments. In addition, such a solution may enable the parties to overcome feelings of mutual mistrust (for example, reluctance to accept long-range promises of great benefits), to experiment with new ideas and to learn from the experience (for example, testing the reaction of the Soviet Union to Western troop withdrawal from Germany). This can be done by stretching out the negotiations (broadening issues and expanding benefits) and solution phases (small gains over protracted time), while shortening the time of the implementation phase.[22] And the resulting agreements on the narrower coupled subjects may provide the parties with common and stable criteria for evaluating future settlements.

## LATERAL EXPANSION OF ISSUES

Since formulating a topic for direct negotiation on joint issues may usually require difficult and prolonged bargaining, it might be highly impractical for the parties to insist on reaching a formal agreement on the subject for talks before they enter the conference room. For this reason, parties that are eager to settle a dispute by talks may wish to defer the explicit connection of particular issues until a later stage of the negotiations. Instead, they may agree before entering the conference room merely on a broad and vague definition of the subject matter of the dispute. The broadly defined agenda should cover enough ground so that both parties may benefit from possible exchanges of issues. How broadly the agenda ought to be defined depends on the subject matter of the treaty in question and on its relative importance.[23]

If a treaty is important enough, the topic for negotiation may be formed in a most general way to include the "betterment of

22. See generally L. Randolph, "A Suggested Model of International Negotiation," 10 *J. Conflict Resolution* 344, 350 (1966).

23. When the issues are too broadly defined, an agreement may be more difficult to reach since it involves greater changes in the status quo and may, therefore, be objected to by third-party governments, the public, and other pressure groups. Indeed, the overexpansion of issues, as will be further explained, is often used by parties as a way of committing themselves to evade negotiation on an unappealing demand.

relations" between the parties without explicitly mentioning the termination or revision of the disputed treaty.[24] The advantage of such a general formulation is that it avoids the difficulties that stem from the desire of the objecting side, sometimes of both sides, not to commit themselves to a specific outcome in advance. Another benefit from forming the subject for talks as normalization of general relations between the parties instead of treaty termination, is that it may thus avoid the psychic dysphoria which usually follows claims for the abrogation of an expected and demanded order. The parties presumably seek an integrated solution to the particular dispute rather than a mere compromise, if not a strict fulfillment of their mutual demands.[25] This, too, may be conducive to successful negotiations.

Between the too narrow formulation of an issue as termination or revision of a specific treaty provision, and a formulation that embraces all relationships between the parties, there are an infinite number of formulas, depending on the level of generality in which such an issue can practically be defined. Since the terms in which a dispute is described may have a strong impact on the outcomes, even when the conflict is eventually settled by tacit bargaining, each party usually defines the issues according to its political objectives and various other tactical considerations. Defining the issues is most difficult, however, when the parties both have to agree on an agenda that will provide a mutually accepted basis for direct negotiations.

Consider the following example. In diplomatic notes of November 27, 1958 to the Western powers, the Soviet Union declared that it regarded the international agreements of 1944 and 1945 concerning the zones of occupation in Germany and the administration of Greater Berlin as no longer valid. The Soviet government demanded the withdrawal of all military forces from West Berlin and instead proposed the establishment of a demilitarized "Free City." A period of six months was given in the note

24. See the agenda chosen in the above discussed Panama Canal conflict.

25. In integrative settlements the parties usually define the conflict situation symbolically, so that the result cannot be clearly perceived by the parties in terms of "wins" and "loses." Lasswell, "Conflict and Leadership: The Process of Decision and the Nature of Authority," in *Conflict in Society* 210, 214 (de Reuck and Knight ed. 1966).

for compliance with this demand. By the end of that period, it was stated, the Soviet government would conclude an agreement with the East German government granting it full sovereignty "on land, on water and in the air," which in effect meant on all approaches to Berlin.[26]

The Soviet notes also included a proposal for the conduct of negotiations with the West within the period of the ultimatum. Interestingly enough, while the maximum demand for the demilitarization of the city was exact and specific, the minimum demands for direct negotiation and for reaching an agreed solution were couched in ambiguous language. The period of six months was referred to in the notes as "fully sufficient to provide a sound basis for the solution of the questions connected with the change in Berlin's situation." This period, it was added, should be used for reaching an "adequate agreement." The central demands were probably included in a more exact form in order to make acceptance of the lesser demands for direct negotiation on the matter more likely. Such a deliberate tactic is typical for claimant parties in termination; for, as was noted earlier, the fact that negotiations on a claim to termination take place is by itself advantageous to the claimant side. The objecting side, because it refused to meet the central demand and because it is concerned about its threatening nature, may find direct talks on a more appealing topic more attractive.[27]

The Western powers, in joint official declarations, insisted that the presence of their forces in Berlin was based on agreements with the Soviet Union, and that the latter could not terminate those agreements unilaterally. It was further emphasized in separate diplomatic notes to the Soviet government that the West was unwilling to negotiate on this issue under menace or ultimatum. However, the Western governments also pointed out that the form of government in Berlin was "only one aspect and not the essential one" of the German problem, and that they were ready to discuss with the Soviet government such broader issues as re-

26. The Soviet note is reprinted and commented upon in J. Smith, *The Defense of Berlin* 166ff. (1963). For how the denounced agreements had been concluded, see P. Mosely, *The Kremlin and World Politics* 155 (1960).

27. See H. Speier, *Divided Berlin* 12 (1961).

unification and European security "as well as the peace treaty." [28] By enlarging the issues to include, among others, the Soviet central demand as well as the Soviet ultimatum, they hoped to keep the Berlin crisis within diplomatic bounds.

Though this question of the appropriate subject for talks was not officially resolved, a conference of foreign ministers was held in May at Geneva. In this conference the Western powers made some proposals that contained important concessions regarding the size of their troops in Berlin and East German control of the access routes to the city. But the Russians, whose confidence had considerably increased following their previous success in forcing the West into negotiations on changes in Berlin, rejected these proposals. Another explanation of why the Russians missed this opportunity for a new agreement favoring their demands, is that they did not really want a reduction in the size of Western forces in Berlin, but only to generate an atmosphere of crisis in order to justify, among other things, the continued presence of their forces in East Germany.

## AN AGENDA TOO BROAD

### In the Generally Competitive Context

The technique of formulating the topic for negotiation in terms of the overall relationship between the parties is used particularly in the termination or revision of treaties of power and security. It was employed in the aforementioned dispute between the Allies and Germany concerning the German claim in 1932 for the termination or revision of the Treaty of Versailles's disarmament provisions.

Negotiations on European disarmament had been taking place for some time without yielding any material results, and as a consequence Germany withdrew from the disarmament conference, pressing for the termination of its own unilateral obligations. Only after a five-power pact was signed on December 11, 1932, did

28. Four Power Communique on Berlin of Dec. 14, 1958, and NATO Declaration on Berlin of Dec. 16, 1958, U.S. Dep't of State, *The Soviet Note on Berlin: An Analysis,* Dep't of State Publ. 6757, at 50 (1959). See id. at 32 for the U.S. note of Dec. 31, 1958, replying to the Soviet note. For analysis, see Speier, supra note 27, at 16–17.

Germany agree to resume participation in the discussions. This was not an agreement on the substantive issues of the dispute but only on the agenda for talks. The pact consisted of a compromise formula, agreed upon after prolonged negotiation, in which the "equality of rights" of Germany was recognized in principle "in a system which would provide security for all nations."

The general idea of the equality of all states in a political system of collective security was, of course, as old as the obligations of the Treaty of Versailles, but in addition it was stated that:

> This declaration implies that the respective limitations of armaments of all states should be included in the proposed disarmament convention. It is clearly understood that the methods of application of such equality of rights will be discussed by the Conference.[29]

Since this formation of the questions for negotiation necessarily included the revision of the Treaty of Versailles, it was advantageous to Germany. The French, however, were determined at the time to resist, even by the use of force, any attempt to revise or terminate the treaty. Nevertheless, the declaration was acceptable to the French government because it was explicitly understood that the establishment of a satisfactory system of collective security would precede Germany's release from its treaty obligations. The prospects for reaching an agreement on general disarmament and collective security "for all nations" were nil, and the French saw no harm in recognizing Germany's equality of rights in principle, of which the practical application might be postponed indefinitely.[30]

In this case, however, the French tactic failed. As could have been expected, once the negotiations were resumed, their central

29. Reprinted in A. Toynbee, *Survey of International Affairs* 1932, 288 (Royal Inst. Int'l Affairs, 1933).

30. See also the Four-Power Pact of 1933 between Germany, France, Great Britain, and Italy, committing the signatories "to make every effort to pursue, within the framework of the League of Nations, a policy of effective cooperation . . . [and] to insure the success of the Disarmament Conference." For a comment on this "pseudo-agreement"—"An example, now almost forgotten because the treaty was so meaningless"—see Iklé, supra note 15, at 17. Some contemporary observers recognized the emptiness of this treaty but commended it "chiefly on the ground that it seems harmless" (id.).

topic became Germany's specific claim for release from the treaty obligations rather than the general and rather vague idea of a world-embracing collective security. Unsuccessful negotiations had lasted for more than two years, after which not much was left to be said against a unilateral termination by Germany of its obligations. Collective security, of course, had been postponed indefinitely.

Although it was clear from the beginning that the prospects for an agreed solution of the dispute were nil, both France and Germany were still interested in the negotiations for the sake of side effects. The French preferred that the issue be defined broadly as a deliberate defensive maneuver in the hope that the negotiations, if dragged out long enough, would postpone unilateral rearmament by Germany. Germany, being powerless at the time, was interested in entering into talks in order to establish a common recognition of the expediency of treaty revision. Besides, the Germans at the time were unofficially rearming in violation of the treaty.[31] Thus, France's defensive maneuver was accepted by Germany, since the negotiations on the agreed agenda provided both the means for it to cultivate expectations favoring unilateral termination, and the time necessary for it to acquire some effective power to implement such a decison.

Linking the grave conflict between France and Germany to the lost "issue" of universal disarmament, however, did not expand the immediate physical issues between the parties in any real sense. Rather, only the ideological terms in which the participants viewed the dispute were enlarged. Since the subject matter of the dispute concerned the total distribution of military power between the opponents, it transcended from the beginning most issues that could possibly be interjected into the negotiations. This case, however, clearly illustrates an important point: despite the seemingly aggressive posture implicit in a presentation of issues in

31. The so-called secret violation of the treaty by Germany was commonly known at the time, see W. Churchill, *The Gathering Storm* ch. 7 (1961). The British government, however, was not prepared to use force for the enforcement of the treaty, and the Germans themselves were very cooperative; they listed their military air activities under the head of "civil aviation." The British government preferred the secret violation of the treaty to formal termination, since it felt that the extent of the first would be smaller than the latter.

broadest terms, the technique may nevertheless be used as a deliberate defensive tactic. By connecting the material issue of Germany's rearmament to the illusive one of world disarmament, France scored an ideological gain: the dispute was not viewed simply as one about concrete issues between two rivals, but rather as involving the larger problem of the world's security. By means of the broad agenda for negotiation, then, Germany was once again politically isolated as the world's everlasting potential aggressor, on whose disarmament world peace supposedly depended.

A more explicit use of the same technique was employed by the United States in 1961 in the dispute with the Soviet Union over Berlin. One should note the different objectives in using the tactic in the two conflicts. While in the Franco-German dispute the immediate issue was enlarged in order to enable the parties to participate in talks, in the latter conflict the same technique was used for the opposite objective of resisting the resumption of direct negotiation. In both cases, however, the broadening of the ideological terms in which the disputes were viewed was aimed at resisting the opponent's demands.

In tacit bargaining the "agenda," though not formally defined, assumes equal importance and can be used for a variety of ideological purposes. The United States has defined the transit of forces from West Germany to West Berlin, not in terms of a group of narrow and pragmatic questions based on specific treaty provisions, but in terms of freedom versus communism. According to this view any interference with Western access to Berlin would be serious enough to justify a war, including, perhaps, a nuclear war. Thus, the small issues of the particular case were turned into a test case involving a major principle, making it more difficult for the United States to make concessions to Soviet claims.[32]

These two cases do not involve the lateral expansion or connection of different issues in the sense previously described, but rather a description of the issues in broad terms of the conflict of dogmas. The issues of German armaments and of the presence of allied forces in Berlin are explicit and precise. The "issues" of collective security, the triumph of democracy, or the victory of socialism, are vague and general. When major conflicts are ex-

32. Fisher, supra note 14, at 105. See also ch. 4 supra.

amined in restrospect it often becomes apparent that the alleged issues were not the underlying bases of the conflicts but only their symptoms.[33] However, unlike the case of the rearmament of Germany, which was from the beginning a big pragmatic issue, the escalation of the issue in the Berlin crisis from the pragmatic to the dogmatic has also meant a material escalation of the conflict between the parties.

### In the Generally Cooperative Context

Generally, within political coalitions the big principles that may be involved between the parties to a dispute are general friendship, cooperation, or collaboration rather than the victory of good over evil. It may therefore be advantageous in certain such disputes for *both* the claimant and the objecting sides to escalate the size of the conflict, even by describing it in broad ideological terms. Thus President de Gaulle, in a letter dated March 7, 1966 to President Johnson, tied the termination of the old treaties concerning American military bases in France together with a new agreement concerning the future relations between France and her Western allies:

> It goes without saying that for the application of these decisions [termination of old agreements] she [France] is ready to settle with the allied governments and, in particular, with that of the United States, the practical measures that concern them. Furthermore, she is disposed to reach an agreement with them regarding *the facilities to be mutually made available* in case of a conflict where she would be engaged at their sides, and regarding the *conditions of the cooperation* of her forces and theirs in the event of a common action, especially in Germany.[34]

Since, as fervently argued by the United States, the military bases in France were crucial for the defense of Germany,[35] and since

---

33. See generally Rapoport, "Perceiving the Cold War," in *International Conflict and Behavioral Science* 13 (R. Fisher ed. 1964).

34. Reprinted in *New York Times,* March 25, 1966, p. 7, col. 1 (city ed.; emphasis added).

35. Baldwin, "Outlook for NATO: Use of French Land Appears Vital to Any Defense of West Germany," *New York Times,* May 2, 1966, at 12, cols. 1–2 (late city ed.).

the French proposed some agreement in regard to the facilities to be made mutually available in case of a future war, the French could expect by enlarging the agenda not only to overcome some of the objections of the United States to treaty termination, but also to have some of the installations and equipment transferred to them, to say nothing of evading payment for the great expenses in property loss, shipment, and relocation of the bases.

Indeed, the United States government responded to the French initiative by asking to postpone negotiation on the removal of the bases from France until an agreement could be reached between France and Germany on the future stationing of French troops in German territory. However, by tying the question of the removal of the bases to the conditions for future military cooperation between the two countries, the French in effect also expanded the area in which inducements, pressures, and threats could be used. Before the beginning of such negotiation, the French removed some of their forces from Germany and unilaterally changed the previous routine of an annual grant to members of NATO to fly aircraft over French territory to a monthly permission subject to abrupt cancellation. Thus they implied that, if pressed during the negotiations, they might pull their forces out of Germany and terminate the overflight rights altogether.

The effect of these and other similar pressures and threats was to create the impression that the French, far from making concessions, might add new demands to their initial claim. Faced with the choice of continuing negotiations and catching up with France's rising demands, or yielding to the French claim for immediate removal of the bases, the United States elected to do the latter. Obviously, the enlargement of the issues for talks in the French note of termination was not really intended to propose the conclusion of specific and narrow commitments in regard to future cooperation, but only to serve as a reminder of the mutually harmful consequence of no-agreement in the instant dispute.

### Between Great Powers and Small States

In certain contexts the ordinary sanctions of reciprocities and retaliations cannot be relied upon to induce parties into a negotiated agreement. Some issues, we have seen, because they are inherently so vital that they overshadow all other issues between the parties, cannot be further expanded in any concrete term to include enough common ground for a negotiated settlement. Similarly, the range of issues upon which a negotiating party can freely draw for purposes of strategic expansion may simply not exist for a small country or a ministate. The asymmetry in the power of the parties usually works to the detriment of the smaller state, even when the great power does not employ physical resources to achieve its desired outcome. In such situations, if the issue is important enough (it may often be the main relationship between the parties), there may simply be no other issues that can be interjected into the negotiation by the smaller state. Thus termination or revision cannot be made more attractive to the objecting side. Since the small state in such cases cannot move the great power either by promises or by threats, the latter will simply refuse to negotiate or even to consider the claim to termination. Instead, expectations of coercion prevail, and this may lead to various minor acts of violence.

To compare the above-discussed case of the rearmament of Germany until 1935 (as distinguished from the remilitarization of the Rhineland in 1936) with the cases of the Panama and the Suez canals, is instructive. In all three cases there was the same overwhelming disparity of power between the objecting and the claimant parties, while at the same time the issues were important enough to disrupt the general relations between them. For many years the United States had refused to negotiate on Panama's claim for the revision of the Canal Treaty, even in the face of demonstrations, riots, and other disturbances in and around the Canal Zone. It was noted earlier that as a result of these incidents Panama broke diplomatic relations with the United States, unsuccessfully attempting to press the latter into accepting the revision of the 1903 treaty as an immediate subject for negotiation. Since the main issue in the interaction between the two countries was the canal, the reestablishment of diplomatic relations could not ordinarily be regarded as an adequate quid pro quo for a United States concession. The United States government accepted negotiations on revision of the previous treaty only when the canal became outmoded and interest arose in building a second canal, possibly in Panama. Indeed, both issues were eventually tied in the same negotiations.

Another example in which a tie-in was foregone is provided by British negotiations with Egypt in 1954 concerning the latter's claim for the withdrawal of British troops from the Suez Canal area before the time specified in the Anglo-Egyptian Treaty of Alliance of 1936.[36] The conflict had been taking place for quite some time, and in 1947, after failing in previous negotiations, Egypt even brought the matter before the Security Council. There Britain invoked pacta sunt servanda, "the most fundamental principle of international law and one on which, after all, the Charter itself depends." [37] The British government contended that the real issue (the validity of the 1936 treaty) was a "legal question," with which the Security Council was allegedly incompetent to deal. It thus managed to prevent even the adoption of a mild resolution recommending to the parties that they "resume direct negotiations, and should such negotiations fail, to seek a solution of the dispute by other peaceful means of their own choice." [38] The result was, indeed, a resort to violence in the Canal Zone in the form of guerrilla warfare and other disturbances. Following these incidents, which were increased in 1952 due to revolutionary changes in the Egyptian government, a new agreement on evacuation of British forces was reached in September 1954.

Once British troops were out of the Canal Zone, it could have been expected that the next Egyptian demand would be for the nationalization of the canal. Yet the British did not demand guarantees against nationalization in return for the withdrawal of their troops. Since nationalization of privately owned foreign property is authorized in international law (the disagreement concerns the existence and scope of a duty to compensate), an Egyptian promise not to nationalize could have reenforced British interests in the canal. Whatever the legal merits of a specific use of force to implement a treaty obligation, British military intervention against a breach of such an Egyptian promise not to nationalize might have been easier to justify at home and harder for the

36. Reprinted in 31 *Am. J. Int'l L.* 77 (1937 suppl.).

37. U.N. SCOR, 2d year, 176th meeting, at 1772 (1947). J. Halderman, *The United Nations and the Rule of Law* 6ff. (1966); Briggs, "Rebus Sic Stantibus Before the Security Council," 43 *Am. J. Int'l L.* 762, 764 (1949).

38. Supra note 37, 189th meeting, at 2109. Failing to reach an agreement on the resolution, the Security Council postponed further discussion of the matter while technically retaining it on the agenda. For additional discussion see ch. 7 infra.

United States to oppose. Moreover, as observed by Iklé, if "Egypt had refused to give such a promise, the British-Egyptian conflict would have come to a head at a time far more favorable to Britain: there would have been no need to attempt a landing of troops in the Suez Canal Zone, for the troops were still there." [39]

One reason why the British did not seek to tie a promise not to nationalize to the removal of their forces may have been that they were anxious to reach an agreement because of the guerrilla warfare conducted against their forces in the Canal Zone, in addition to the mounting pressure from the United States. Moreover, the validity of such a guarantee could have seriously been questioned. One of the claims for the termination of the 1936 treaty was that:

> Egypt was not a free party in concluding the Treaty of 1936. First of all, its territory was occupied at the time by United Kingdom troops. Secondly, the Government of the United Kingdom left no doubt in the minds of the Egyptian plenipotentiaries as to the consequences of their failure to agree to the United Kingdom demands.[40]

The same argument, of course, could have been applied to the guarantee against nationalization.

The effects of duress on treaty obligations were more controversial at that time than currently. But whatever the merits of legal arguments, with the process of decolonization reaching a culminating point and with the growing invocation of the doctrine of unequal treaties, there would have been no reason to believe that a promise imposed by the presence of British troops in Egypt amid violent uprising would not be broken as soon as those troops were gone. Indeed, the very fact that a guarantee was imposed on Egypt under such circumstances might have provoked an Egyptian decision to nationalize the canal. The British would probably have preferred not to bring the problem of ownership of the canal into the open, in order to make it easier for the Egyptian government to sign the agreement.[41] Furthermore, it could have been

39. Iklé, supra note 15, at 245.

40. U.N. SCOR, supra note 37, 175th meeting, at 1755.

41. The Anglo-Egyptian Evacuation Agreement of October 19, 1954, was a compromise that provided for the return of the English military, scheduled to leave in 1956, if any Arab country or Turkey was attacked (Article 4 of the agree-

expected that in return for a promise not to nationalize, the Egyptian government would ask for some concession regarding the ownership and administration of the canal. The British might have felt that by interjecting the issue of the ownership of the canal into the ongoing negotiations, they would not only open the door to Egyptian demands, but would also imply their lack of a firm position with regard to keeping the status of the canal unchanged. Generally speaking, the connection of disputes that divide the same parties along a common boundary does not increase the possibility of agreement, but instead sharpens the division between them.

### Redefining the Parties to a Dispute

In the relations between the United States and Cuba, for instance, the issue of the Guantanamo base is by no means central. However, since relations between the two governments have generally been disrupted, it has not been possible to tie the removal of the base to other issues between them. Indeed, the United States's economic and political pressures on Cuba during the sixties had not been applied with the objective of settling narrow and pragmatic issues, but rather with objectives so broad that they were impossible to attain by negotiations. The disparity in power between the parties is so great that a concession by the Cuban government short of an unconditional surrender, a radical change of "attitude," or a shift in bloc alignment, could not be acceptable to the United States government.

Broadly defining the subject matter of a dispute, or coupling a dispute with other issues, however, are not the only methods for extending the size of an international conflict. In addition, the size of issues can be broadened or narrowed by redefining the parties to a dispute. Since Cuba associates itself with the Eastern bloc, the Guantanamo issue can be settled along with other issues between the United States and the Soviet Union, an opportunity which

---

ment, in 10 *Revue Egyptienne de Droit International* 297, 298 [1954]). The agreement was denounced by radical Arab political movements as a betrayal, and their attempted coup was crushed by the Egyptian regime. For the negotiations of this agreement and the general reaction to it, see L. Fabunmi, *The Sudan in Anglo-Egyptian Relations* 306ff. (1960).

presented itself and was missed during the Cuban missile crisis of
1962. Instead, the Soviet government tried to connect the issue of
its missile bases in Cuba to that of United States missile bases in
Turkey.[42]

One reason why the attempt to connect these two issues (Cuba
and Turkey) failed, was that in both disputes the Soviet government was, in effect, the offensive side. By introducing nuclear
missiles into Cuba the Soviet government acted contrary to long-
established common expectations and mutual understanding with
regard to the geographical allocation of military strength. It
sought, in effect, to terminate a tacit agreement that had originated in a period of relative Soviet military weakness but that had
continued for many years. The secrecy with which the operation
was covered provides evidence that even the Soviets appreciated
the great significance of their move. They were caught, however,
before their new bases in Cuba were put in working condition.
The Soviet Union was, therefore, not in the position of a party
that had succeeded by a fait accompli in bringing about a new
situation, but rather in the more inferior position of a claimant
that had invoked—but did not yet fully exercise—its right to
effect termination. It thus seems clear why the proposal that Soviet
"concessions" in Cuba should have been reciprocated by "similar"
American concessions in Turkey could not be regarded as a proposal to couple issues in any true sense. In order to offer a common
ground for a negotiated settlement, a proposal to couple issues
should interject into a conflict, issues for which the positions of
the parties are reversed.

The interjection of the issue of termination of American nuclear
bases in Turkey into the Cuban missile crisis, however, sharpened
and aggravated a conflict that had been grave enough in its own
right. The stakes of each of the parties in the dispute were substantially increased. So also, the Turkish issue increased the number of participants that were directly involved in the Cuban conflict, since Western European members of NATO, while not

42. See generally E. Abel, *The Missile Crisis* 187ff. (1966); Lipson, "Castro on
the Chessboard of the Cold War," in *Cuba and the United States*, 178, 190ff.
(J. Plank ed. 1967); T. Schelling, *Arms and Influence* 8off. (1966); Horelick, "The
Cuban Missile Crisis: An Analysis of Soviet Calculations and Behavior," 16 *World
Pol.* 363, 366 (1964). See also ch. 3 supra.

directly involved in the Cuban missile crisis, had substantial interests in and direct commitments on the question of American military bases and installations in Turkey. Furthermore, defining an issue in broad terms is usually disadvantageous to an offensive adversary. Had the Soviet government backed its proposal for the alleged mutual withdrawal of military installations by a threat of using force, it would have cornered itself into the risky and far more inferior position of an offensive party that faced a decision whether or not to initiate hostilities on too broad a dispute. It would have been more difficult in such a situation to limit, geographically or otherwise, the armed collision that could have ensued.

The bringing in of the issue of United States bases in Turkey therefore did not offer any practicable terms for a negotiated settlement of the Cuban missile dispute. It would have been much more practicable for the Soviet government, if it so desired, to tie the question of Soviet bases in Cuba to the Guantanamo base dispute. The interjection of the Guantanamo issue into the negotiation would not have materially expanded the conflict between the parties, since no matter how narrowly the Cuban missile crisis could have been defined, it was naturally connected to the whole Cuban Problem.

### Risks in Conflict Expansion

The previous discussion demonstrates that the main problem in settling conflicts about termination is how to determine an initial position that will cover enough ground for mutually acceptable outcomes. Much of any direct negotiation on termination may thus concern this problem of defining the status quo that will be changed. Indeed, in most of the cases described above the parties sought to couple disputes or to expand them laterally by way of explicit proposals to the other side. The initial bargaining to determine the issues that will be joined together, however, may be conducted not only by an offer, promise, or threat, but also by physical moves and faits accomplis on issues that are not directly related to the treaty in question. Nevertheless, explicit proposals and demands for the connection of separate disputes play a key role in most such bargaining, even when the matter is eventually settled by various unilateral acts. They usually narrow and help define the areas in which pressures, threats, inducements, and faits accomplis can be employed and/or tolerated.

The outcome of this initial process of bargaining determines whether or not the parties will enter into direct talks on the central demand for termination of the given agreement. It has already been noted, however, that a great many conflicts about termination, perhaps the majority of them, are eventually not settled by direct talks but rather through tacit bargaining or a combination thereof.[43] Two more reasons for such a practice should be added in this context.

First, even when the coupling of disputes is initiated by an explicit proposal, it may easily be transformed into tacit bargaining by physical moves. To offer a settlement on some other "issue" is, of course, to imply that there exists a dispute regarding its subject matter, and that therefore it may involve some meaningful concessions on behalf of the offeror. Claimant parties, however, usually try to interject into the original conflict, issues in which they will be required to yield as little as possible (for example, the Berlin crisis of 1958). Sometimes they even try to join an issue from whose settlement they stand to gain rather than lose (for example, the Cuban missile crisis). And whether there exists a genuine dispute with regard to the subject matter that is sought to be connected to the conflict at hand may in itself be disputed by the parties.

The objecting side may therefore reject the particular proposal for connection of issues. It is tempting for the claimant side in such situations to resort to some unilateral acts, which changes the balance of burdens and benefits to its own advantage in the matter that is sought to be connected. By creating a dispute, the claimant party may render the proposed connection of issues more attractive to the objecting side (for example, the Berlin Wall and the termination of British flight rights over Spanish territory).[44] Although the purpose of such acts may be to make direct talks on the claim to termination possible, it is more likely that a process of bargaining which is initiated by unilateral acts will continue to be

43. Ch. 2 supra.
44. Ch. 4 supra.

settled by similar acts. Further, physical moves made during the bargaining and negotiating process increase the stakes, both with regard to the immediate physical issues and the principles involved. When such an issue becomes too big, especially when it involves some firm principles, it is less amenable to settlement by a negotiated agreement.

Second, while the coupling of seemingly unrelated issues (for example, Cuba with Berlin) might make it easier to draft an agreement between the parties, it is not always possible to connect such issues in the same negotiation. National positions must take account of ideological difficulties, and they are therefore increasingly expressed, not in pragmatic terms but in terms of principles. Since a great many international negotiations are conducted at least partly in the public view, governments find it exceedingly difficult to couple apparently unrelated issues in the same negotiation. It might appear as an unprincipled practice and might be objected to by both the public and third-party governments, particularly since the latter's own interests are usually involved. Connections of seemingly unrelated matters are therefore often made either by unilateral acts, supposedly in response to similar acts by the opponent, or in secret negotiations and subliminal tacit agreements. In these circumstances comparatively few limits on the components of packages exist.

If issues are joined by explicit offers, the process is constructive. Without such proposals, it may be difficult to conclude an agreement on either issue. If the issues are coupled with unilateral actions and threats on an otherwise unrelated matter, the process might be destructive. Coercive pressure produces counterpressures, and agreements may be terminated on either side. Sometimes the parties, through a process of tacit exchange—mutual breaches, reprisals, and retaliations—settle at an equilibrium point at which a given number of previous agreements have been repudiated by each side. Since this question of how termination of an agreement may be followed by other terminations is central to the subject of this book, it is discussed in more detail in chapters 8 and 9. It suffices here to note that the settlement of disputes about termination by tacit exchange usually aggravates the conflict between the parties. The more unrelated the response of one government is to the action taken by the other, the more difficult it is to limit the ensuing conflict escalation, and the parties may even approach the point of termination of "all" relations. In this respect, the expansion of termination conflicts resembles the process by which limited hostilities grow into all-out war.

Whether issues are coupled by way of explicit proposals or by unilateral acts is, of course, not the sole criterion for judging the usefulness of tie-ins in settling disputes of termination. It will subsequently be pointed out that some sort of unilateral action may occasionally be necessary even when the parties are constructively looking toward a negotiated settlement. This qualification is important but does not wholly detract from the usefulness of the distinction between tacit and explicit bargaining. The distinction serves to remind us that we are dealing with situations in which words are powerful. The action-reaction pattern that expands conflicts of termination is influenced by the way claims, offers, proposals, warnings, and threats are formulated.

There is a feedback between claims, proposals, and the conflicts they simultaneously reflect and influence. The preceding discussion demonstrates that the joining of issues, even when it is made by explicit proposals, tends to shift disputes from relatively narrow and pragmatic ones, to ones in which the only common denominator is the parties involved (like the Berlin crisis of 1958). The more issues a proposed solution covers, the weaker its focus becomes, and the less likely that the settlement will answer the problem which inspired the negotiation to begin with. Furthermore, the tendency of bringing in all possible issues between the parties shifts the focus from the specific issues to the parties themselves, their ideological images and relative power. The crude illustrations of the Berlin crises can hardly be regarded as good examples of a constructive attempt at settling a dispute about termination by an explicit agreement. Nevertheless, they illustrate a valid and important point. Both sides were aware of the necessity for broadening the initial, relatively narrow issue in order to keep the dispute within diplomatic bounds. They made proposals and threats regarding the extension of the issue by exchanging diplomatic notes. Yet the issue became so broad that only an acquiescently accepted unilateral act on a narrow and incidental matter could temporarily divert the conflict into an area where gains and losses did not involve what the parties themselves described as possible military confrontation. But the act of building the wall in Berlin did not settle any of the central issues in the Berlin crises. The conflict has merely been temporarily frozen.

At this point the reader should be reminded again of the relevance of the time dimension and intervening changes. The process of changing the scope of issues usually involves lengthy negotiations that must be leisurely stretched over a long period of time. Yet most conflicts about termination are crises situations during which the amount of time needed for such settlements is not available. Direct talks in a crisis may usually provide the parties with a cooling-off period; even so, events may move ahead of negotiation, if not because of the parties' unilateral acts and faits accomplis, then following changes in circumstances beyond the parties' control during the prolonged talks. Some of these intervening changes may move the negotiations ahead, while others may induce the parties to forego the attainment of their objectives by negotiation and, instead, to rely mainly on self-help measures.

The above points out the threat to peace and to general treaty arrangements between the parties which the tacit expansion of termination conflicts entails. In addition, settlements, no matter how peacefully achieved and even if they are not too destructive of other treaties, if arrived at by a process of unilateral actions, will usually fall short of an optimum solution. For a settlement to be an optimal one it has to provide for a detailed division of each of the combined issues, which may usually require a lengthy process of detailed negotiation. For tacit communications and implicit understandings to take place, on the other hand, the parties must hold onto clear-cut divisions and distinctions upon which expectations can easily converge. Also, parties to tacit bargaining have to rely more heavily on ideological tactics, which are intended to influence large audiences and to which it is much easier to present issues in a black-and-white form. For these and other reasons, outcomes that result from unilateral actions tend to be formed in an either-or rather than a more-or-less fashion, and thus may fully satisfy only one, or even neither, party.

Our analysis of *exchange* was motivated by the consideration that issues which are extraneous to the agreement in dispute should be interjected into the bargaining if a shared settlement is to be reached. The discussion reveals that a conflict about termination usually laterally expands and includes other terminations, and that the process often progresses more by way of tacit bargaining than by explicit negotiation and formal agreement.

If the side benefits are determined by explicit negotiation, they may usually involve promises about the future. Such settlements may satisfy all parties, and they necessarily involve some expectations of permanence and stability. In tacit bargaining on termination, however, the parties, through threats and unilateral acts, seek solutions that may leave each side with the immediate possession of its gains. When gains, however mutual, are related only to the decision at hand, they need not carry an implication of permanence. On the contrary, settlements that are arrived at by means of unilateral acts are often what neither side wants, and they produce tension and instability with regard to future interaction. The problem is that termination conflicts often overexpand and involve unilateral acts even when the parties initiate the process in a genuine attempt at a negotiative settlement. As Roger Fisher notes, "with international disputes, as with weapons, the bigger does not necessarily mean the better. . . . Arms are used only over issues. Perhaps more important than the field of arms control is the field of 'issue control.' " [45]

The task facing international regulation is, then, how to make the process of issue escalation more foreseeable and predictable. Some of these so-called abnormal situations consist of recurring crises (like Berlin and Panama). They have lasted long enough for their dynamics to have become patterned and reasonably understood.[46] For others, general rules have still to be constructed, made more explicit, or clarified.

45. Fisher, note 14 supra, at 93–94.
46. See Lipson, supra note 42, at 193. It should also be added that because agreements in heterogeneous communities are purchased by support for the enumerable preference of others, rule-making through multilateral treaty conferences may obscure common interests in ad hoc packages, tie-ins, and so on. Thus, customary international law may well prove in certain contexts to be a superior instrument for the clarification of community policy.

# PART 3

# Patterns in Formal Rule and Effective Decision

# 6  The Legal Procedures

Between two horses, which doth
bear him best;
Between two girls, which hath
the merriest eye;
I have perhaps some shallow
spirit of judgment;
But in these nice sharp quillets
of the law,
Good faith, I am no wiser than a
daw.

Shakespeare, *Henry VI*

The composition of the International Law Commission is traditional and legal. Thus it is no surprise that the ILC, in drafting
the Vienna Convention on the Law of Treaties, tried to judicialize
treaty termination. In this chapter a number of the institutional
efforts of the authors of the convention will be examined critically.
In the following chapter I shall resume investigation of the more
problematic dimension of termination by self-help.

## DUTY TO RESORT TO PACIFIC MEANS

The authors of the convention dealt with the strategies of
termination in their discussion of Article 65. A survey of the
various legal works on termination shows that Article 65 deviates
from the majority of these writings on only one point: it does not
specifically prohibit unilateral termination. A great difference indeed! But, then, the article does not refer to unilateral acts at all.
In using the canons of interpretation set forth in the convention
itself, one might arrive at several different feasible conclusions
in trying to construe the silence of the convention on this matter.
In regard to other problems concerning the settlement of conflicts
about termination, Article 65 is typical indeed. The ILC observed
with satisfaction that the current formulation of the controversial
article "represented the highest measure of common ground that

could be found among governments as well as in the commission on this question." [1] Article 65 in its final form appears to have been a compromise in which unresolved differences were neutralized in ambiguity.

The formulation of Article 65, therefore, is in itself symptomatic of many problems. Its first four subsections read as follows:

1. A party which, under the provisions of the present Convention, invokes either a defect in its consent to be bound by a treaty or a ground for impeaching the validity of a treaty, terminating it, withdrawing from it or suspending its operation, must notify the other parties of its claim. The notification shall indicate the measure proposed to be taken with respect to the treaty and the reasons therefor.

2. If, after the expiry of a period which, except in cases of special urgency, shall not be less than three months after the receipt of the notification, no party has raised any objection, the party making the notification may carry out in the manner provided in Article 67 the measure which it has proposed.

3. If, however, objection has been raised by any other party, the parties shall seek a solution through the means indicated in Article 33 of the Charter of the United Nations.

4. Nothing in the foregoing paragraphs shall affect the rights or obligations of the parties under any provisions in force binding the parties with regard to the settlement of disputes.[2]

The specific means of settling disputes indicated in Article 33 of the United Nations Charter, and through which the parties are bound to seek a solution, are: "negotiations, inquiry, mediation, conciliation, arbitration, judicial settlement, resort to regional agencies or arrangements, or other peaceful means of their own choice."

1. Int'l L. Comm'n., Draft Report, U.N. Doc. A/CN.4/L.116/Add. 6, at 4(4), (July 11, 1966).
2. Vienna Convention on the Law of Treaties, Art. 65, U.N. Doc. A/Conf. 18. 39/27 (1969), in 8 *Int'l Legal Mat.* 679, 703 (1969). Article 65(5) is discussed in ch. 7 infra.

This verbal commitment to peaceful resolution of disputes is not accompanied by analysis of specific policies that ought to guide or govern. Article 65 has sails but no anchor. Which of these methods should be given priority in the solution of conflicts about termination? [3] Suppose a party claims termination, giving proper notification. The other side objects. The claimant proposes negotiations. The objecting side, believing that adjudication is a more suitable method for preserving treaties, insists on adjudication. What then? To reach a deadlock a party has only to insist on a different method for settling the dispute.[4]

Any of the parties to the dispute may, in case of a deadlock after a period of twelve months following the date on which an objection to the claim was raised, set in motion the conciliation procedure provided for in Article 66 and the Annex to the Convention. This procedure, however, is a novelty in international affairs, and its future effectiveness in resolving conflicts cannot be taken for granted. The convention's annex provides for the establishment in particular disputes of an ad hoc conciliation commission within which the parties may argue and actually negotiate their differences. This commission seems to be a semiadjudicative-conciliatory organ. Its structure and functions have many advantages and thus may promote constructive settlements of particular disputes.

However, it will be pointed out later, the conciliation procedure also suffers from important shortcomings. The authority of the commission effectively to regulate the conduct of bargaining not only inside but outside the conference room is not clear. In addition, a period of approximately 21 months from the date of notification initiating the dispute may usually pass before the commission can even start deliberating. During this interim period tacit bargaining may develop and unilateral acts may be effected with the aim of influencing, or even effectively settling,

3. The ILC and the majority of writers seem to prefer adjudication. Indeed, the convention's orientation toward judicial settlement is expressed through its division into substantive and procedural articles. Article 65 is termed "procedural." The practical implications of this approach are discussed below. See also app. A infra.

4. Such cases, in which the parties reach a stalemate from the outset, are all too common in conflicts about termination (ch. 4 supra).

the matter from the outset of the commission's deliberations. Article 65(5), as will also be pointed out, seems to yield assent to such practice. Furthermore, the outcome of the commission's deliberations is not accorded the formal status of a binding decision but only that of so-called report and recommendation. This may raise additional problems of implementation. All these difficulties, of course, necessitate a more careful analysis of the convention's regulation of the bargaining process before coming to deal with the convention's conciliation procedure.

### Direct Negotiations

In light of the observations made in previous chapters, let us examine how Article 65 deals with the problem of bringing parties who hold extreme, and presumably irreconcilable positions into direct talks. A related question is whether we can attach to the article the implied condition that the parties are bound at least to seek a solution to the conflict through this least institutionalized technique.

In order for direct negotiation to begin, one of the parties, or a mediator, must take the initiative. There must be an explicit proposal to hold a conference or to begin diplomatic talks, or at least to have the new issue introduced into ongoing discussions. A party invoking a ground for terminating a treaty is, therefore, bound by the convention to notify the other party or parties of the bases upon which the claim is made, and the measures proposed to be taken with respect to the treaty. Since Article 65(3) also binds the parties to seek a solution by the means indicated in Article 33 of the Charter, such a notification of the claim can be regarded as a proposal to submit the question to one of these pacific means, of which negotiation may be said to represent to a party the lesser commitment.[5]

The three-month requirement for raising an objection to the

5. But see ch. 4 supra. The ICJ held that, before submitting a dispute to adjudication, the parties should seek a solution by direct negotiations (ch. 4, note 17 supra). Note also that Article 65 refers only to the pacific methods of conflict resolution provided for in Charter Article 33. The *renvoi* does not include the charter limitation about disputes that are likely to endanger the maintenance of international peace and security. For the procedures of forwarding a notification and the date on which it becomes effective, see Art. 78, supra note 2, at 709.

claim is important for the regulation of the dispute, since the stalling of a settlement by unexplained delays in answering correspondence indicates a desire not to resort to any of the methods indicated in Charter Article 33. Although Article 65 does not require the objecting party to submit a counterproposal, one wonders parenthetically why it does not require at least the giving of the specific grounds for any disagreement with the claim. It appears unlikely, however, that in the future governments will be permitted to dispose of a claim to termination merely by objecting to its legal validity, while at the same time refusing to resort to negotiation or any other pacific method of settling the dispute.

The objecting side is under an obligation to seek a solution to the question through the means indicated in Article 33 even when, and precisely because, it regards the claim as totally unfounded. The expression from Article 65, "a party which invokes a ground for terminating," is broader than "a claim based on." The latter may be interpreted as meaning that the object of such a complaint must be legally well founded. The International Court of Justice, even when confronted with the words "claims . . . based on the provisions" of a treaty, considered that these words "cannot be understood as meaning claims actually supportable under that Treaty." [6]

To some extent, then, this formulation may help to eliminate some of the obstacles of bringing parties into formal talks. Theoretically at least, since the parties will be required to do so merely because grounds for termination have been alleged, the fact of participation in talks, whether for the purpose of determining

6. But "[i]t is not enough for the claimant Government to establish a remote connection between the facts of the claim and the Treaty." However, "it is not necessary for that Government to show . . . that an alleged treaty violation has an unassailable legal basis" (*Ambatielos Case, Merits: Obligation to Arbitrate*, [1953] I.C.J. 10, 18). "These words ['Complaints alleging'] refer to what the complainant alleges—to that on which he relies for the purpose of supporting his complaint. . . . [I]t is necessary that the complaint should indicate some genuine relationship between the complaint and the provisions invoked, but that it is not required that the facts alleged should necessarily lead to the results alleged by the complainants. Any such requirement would confuse the question of jurisdiction with that of the substance" (*Judgments of the Administrative Tribunal of the ILO Upon Complaints Made Against UNESCO Case*, [1956] I.C.J. 77, 89).

which method will be resorted to for settling the dispute, for determining the issues at stake, or for reaching an agreement on the substantive issue, cannot be interpreted as a recognition of validity of the claim. Nor can direct talks be interpreted as implying a willingness to yield somewhat to the demand. The parties may issue a statement before entering into negotiations that in entering into talks, they seek only to comply with the "procedural" requirements of Article 65. Of course, one of the chief functions of traditional diplomacy—to persuade the other party of one's viewpoint—becomes extremely difficult when verbal declarations and publicized written notifications are discounted from the outset. But there can be no doubt that negotiation, however reluctantly assumed, is a useful process of persuasion, and that much is gained, even if only by giving each side a better picture of the strength of the other's convictions.

In general theory and broad outline, then, the convention's formula can be regarded as sufficient. However, its authors did not inquire into the difficulties inherent in this formula. The trickiest questions are raised by the use of evidence concerning the parties' tactical maneuvering during bargaining. In the first place, the question may again be asked whether, after failing to agree on the desired procedure for settling the dispute, the parties are bound to enter into negotiations on the substantive issue. The answer is not free from difficulties. Since at present almost every international dispute revolves somehow around a treaty provision, to require parties to enter into negotiations merely upon an invocation of grounds for nullity or termination is always to force defensive sides to submit to negotiation upon any demand for change, however offensive, aggressive, or arbitrary the demand may be. To suggest such an obligation is to attempt to bring about radical changes in international practice. This may not only be unfeasible for practical reasons but also undesirable on policy grounds.

This critical aspect of the problem of change is well illuminated by the Munich Agreement of 1938. It is now a matter of common observation that the efforts to resolve disputes during that period, supposedly intended to achieve peaceful change, were less the consequence of the equity of the claims than of the fear inspired by the claimants.[7] Thus, a decision maker should be able to distinguish between situations that justify an earnest attempt at change and those that call for the mobilization of forces to resist aggression. No doubt, a clear, strong demonstration that an arbitrary demand is not negotiable may help to deter aggression. One wonders in this respect, whether the convention's distinction between procedure and substance can really be maintained in such situations, and how helpful it can be in deciding whether to enter into negotiation on a demand for aggressive changes in the status quo. The answer to this may well be that if the objecting party enters negotiations because a multilateral procedural norm says so, perhaps his position is stronger—that is, he has conceded less at the outset—than if he had entered negotiations on the same subject without the guide of the norm.

Secondly, it seems doubtful whether, in its current formulation, so vague a duty to negotiate can be enforced. Suppose the objecting side does seek a solution through the means indicated in Article 33 of the Charter, and is formally willing to enter into direct talks with the claimant state. Since "negotiation" is not defined in Charter Article 33, it may still be asked whether the term should be interpreted literally as a process of bargaining. Can the objecting government send "negotiators" with authority to do no more than listen politely and object? In other words, is the insistence on "discussions" as distinguished from real bargaining to be considered a serious attempt at seeking a solution?[8] If such a practice would satisfy the requirements of Article 65, it is hard to see just what the new procedural safeguards that the convention supposedly contains are.

Finally, Article 65 was primarily intended to implement the basic policy that treaties, though terminable or invalid because of some specific grounds, should preferably be terminated by a new agreement between all parties concerned. Thus conceived, the duty to negotiate is directed primarily at the claimant state. Only when consent to enter negotiations or consent to the submission of the question to adjudication is not forthcoming, or after the

7. C. de Visscher, *Theory and Reality in Public International Law* 315 (P. Corbett trans. 1957).
8. For a similar practice see p. 121 supra.

impasse of negotiation, should the possibility of unilateral acts arise. However, the evasion of concreteness in the convention raises some difficulty even with respect to this fundamental policy. Suppose the objecting party does agree to enter into negotiations, or even insists on it. Whatever its meaning, the duty imposed by Article 65(3) is unqualified. Does the duty to negotiate extend to each and every topic the other side wishes to discuss? If not, what are the subjects that neither party may lawfully interject into the discussions over the objection of the other? Does the fact that the objecting side interjects extraneous issues into the negotiation— that is to say, insists on concessions which are unrelated to the treaty in question—permit the claimant state to refuse to negotiate? If not, is the claimant state allowed, in response to the other side's extraneous demands, to raise its demands beyond the restrictions and limitations of the substantive grounds for termination? [9]

## Unilateral Termination

Suppose the parties have complied with the procedural requirements, having lawfully stated their initial positions in formal notifications in due time, and having made impressive efforts to arrive at an agreed settlement of the dispute according to Article 33 of the Charter, but there are still no material results. The parties, either because they refuse to be moved from their initial positions, or because they cannot agree on the kind of compromise, reach a diplomatic stalemate. What then? May the claimant state nevertheless take the "measures proposed," and, if not, would the objecting party or parties be justified in enforcing the agreement against the will of the claimant state? In other words, is withdrawal from or termination of the treaty not authorized except by the mutually agreed act of all parties, or may they also be authoritatively made by a unilateral and noncollaborative act of the claimant state?

9. Neither in Article 65 nor in the *travaux préparatories* of the ILC and the Vienna Conference can one find answers to these questions, except for general statements such as that the authors of the convention sought not to be "involved in some measure and in one form or another in compulsory solution to the question at issue between the parties." [1966] 2 *Y.B. Int'l L. Comm'n* 263(5), U.N. Doc. A/CN.4/SER.A/1966/Add. 1.

Nowhere in the Convention on the Law of Treaties can an answer or a hint to the desired answer possibly be found. This question concerning unilateral action was, however, fervently argued by the authors of the convention. After prolonged consideration of the problem, the ILC, for example, concluded that the appropriate solution was to leave the matter intact. Thus, the most important and controversial issue in the law of treaties is ignored by the convention. The difficulties, as well as the "solution," are explained by Sir Humphrey Waldock in the commentary to draft Article 65, as follows:

> States in the course of disputes have not infrequently used language in which they appeared to maintain that the nullity or termination of a treaty could not be established except by consent of both parties. This presentation of the matter, however, subordinates the application of the principles governing the invalidity, termination and suspension of the operation of treaties to the will of the objecting State no less than the arbitrary assertion of the nullity, termination or suspension of a treaty subordinates their application to the will of the claimant State. The problem is the familiar one of the settlement of differences between states. In the case of treaties, however, there is the special consideration that the parties by negotiating and concluding the treaty have brought themselves into a relationship in which there are *particular obligations of good faith*. . . .
>
> The Commission did not find it possible to carry the procedural provisions beyond this point without becoming involved in some measure and in one form or another in compulsory solution to the question at issue between the parties. If after recourse to the means indicated in Article 33 the parties should reach a deadlock, *it would be for each Government to appreciate the situation and to act as good faith demands*.[10]

10. Id. at 262(2) and 263(5) (emphasis added). But see Briggs, "Unilateral Denunciation of Treaties, The Vienna Convention and the International Court of Justice," 68 *Am. J. Int'l L.* 51 (1974). He concludes that "with the exception of its *Namibia* aberration, the Court's consideration of the Vienna Convention on the Law of Treaties [*Jurisdiction of the ICAO Council* and *Iceland Fisheries Jurisdic-*

Thus, the procedural provision is drafted in as "objective," "impartial," and "neutral" a form as the substantive provision regarding changed circumstances. The convention's answer to the question whether, after negotiations have failed and before or after deliberations within a conciliation commission have taken place, termination by unilateral acts is authorized is, at best, a definite "maybe." [11] Since there is a danger of arbitrariness on the part of both sides, it was found impossible or undesirable either to authorize or to prohibit unilateral acts when the procedural requirements are met without yielding any result. Instead, a welter of safety-valve concepts and slogans fills the ILC commentary: "checks on arbitrary actions," "peaceful means in such a manner that international peace and security, and justice are not endangered," "particular obligations of good faith," and "to act as good faith demands," are variously put forth as remedies to the impasse of the dispute. However, the medium through which these phrases acquire meaning has proved much more difficult to identify. The impression is created that the missing ingredient is good will on behalf of nation-states and that, therefore, good faith is a "particular obligation."

This approach is, of course, not entirely new. Students of international affairs tend to identify peace, stability, and the quieting

---

*tion* cases] has been helpful in furthering the consolidation of the law against unilateral denunciation of international agreements without accountability therefor" (id. at 68).

11. See, for example, Article 4 of the Nuclear Weapons Test Ban Treaty, Aug. 5, 1963, [1963] 14 *United States Treaties and Other International Agreements* 1313, 1319 (which has become a model for similar provisions in other treaties): "Each party shall in exercising its national sovereignty have the right to withdraw from the Treaty if it decides that extraordinary events, related to the subject matter of this Treaty, have jeopardized the supreme interests of its country." The words "in exercising its national sovereignty" were inserted at the request of the Soviet Union. The Soviet government originally did not want a withdrawal clause on the ground that sovereignty permits the denunciation of a treaty in any event. See Schwelb, "The Nuclear Test Ban Treaty and International Law," 58 *Am. J. Int'l L.* 642, 661 (1964). At San Francisco, however, when the founders of the United Nations discussed the question of granting authority to the General Assembly to review and revise treaties, the Soviet government asserted that such a provision would contradict the principle of the sovereignty of states. National sovereignty, according to this view, prohibits the termination of treaties without the consent of the parties involved. L. Bloomfield, *Evolution or Revolution?* 100–01 (1957).

of conflict with notions of trust, good faith, mutual respect, and good will. But this view has certainly never before been put forward in so uncompromising a form. Not infrequently, writers impose this "obligation" on the party with whom they entrust the final decision of termination, as a safety valve and a last-minute reminder against arbitrariness. The convention, on the other hand, entrusts neither party (or either party) with the final decision; and yet it requires the making of the decision in good faith.

This point of view is valuable, however, at least to the extent that it encourages trust and good faith in the setting of ever-present possibilities of abuse. However, to be occupied with the problem of abuse is one thing; to be preoccupied with it is another. The problem of arbitrary action cannot be evaded by the pretext that no answer is possible until a better world is constructed and people start behaving differently. In order to provide effective answers, one would of course have to be more explicit both about the problems raised and about the desired solutions.

## THE OBLIGATION OF GOOD FAITH

Let us turn to a more specific examination of the meaning of the obligation of good faith in this context. Although the concept is widely used, it is susceptible to several conflicting interpretations. At least five different meanings might be given to the phrase from the ILC draft commentaries to Article 65 "to act as good faith demands," when it refers to the termination of an international agreement:

### Arbitrary Decision

The concept of "good faith" is often taken to mean the opposite of arbitrary assertion or action, and it is also used in this sense in the ILC commentary. Thus conceived, the argument of good faith in our context is nothing more than a rephrasing of the thought that governments should faithfully observe international law, treaties included. A comparison of Article 65 with Article 26 (pacta sunt servanda) will serve to clarify this point. The commentary to draft Article 26 states:

There is much authority in the jurisprudence of international tribunals for the proposition that in the present context the principle of good faith is a legal principle which forms an integral part of the rule *pacta sunt servanda*. . . . Accordingly, the article provides that "A treaty in force is binding upon the parties to it and must be performed by them in good faith." Some members hesitated to include the words "in force" as possibly lending themselves to interpretations which might weaken the clear statement of the rule. Other members, however, considered that the words give expression to an element which forms part of the rule and that, having regard to other provisions of the draft articles, it was necessary on logical grounds to include them. The Commission had adopted a number of articles which dealt with . . . the nullity of treaties and with their termination. Consequently, from a drafting point of view, it seemed necessary to specify that it is treaties in force in accordance with the provisions of the present articles to which the *pacta sunt servanda* rule applies.[12]

Thus the circularity of the official interpretation to Article 65 is evident: The meaning of pacta sunt servanda is that the parties are under an obligation to perform in good faith a treaty that is in force according to the provisions of Article 65, while according to Article 65 itself, whether the treaty is in force or not depends merely on the acting in good faith by the parties. To act in good faith in the context of treaties, then, is to act lawfully, but it is precisely the question of what constitutes a lawful termination that is at stake. This criticism is obviously based on the truism that to subject human conduct to the control of rules there must at least *be* some rules.

This is, of course, not to say that any reference to good faith should be avoided. The case of *Minority Schools in Albania*, which is referred to by the commentary to draft Article 65 as an authority for the obligation of good faith in the performance of treaties, may serve to illustrate the point. In a declaration made before the Council of the League of Nations on October 2, 1921,

12. Int'l L. Comm'n, supra note 9, at 211(2)(3).

Albania undertook to ensure that Albanian nationals belonging to minority groups would enjoy "the same treatment and security . . . as other Albanian nationals," and that in particular they would have "an equal right" to maintain private schools and other educational facilities. Albania contended that a new constitution (1933), which among other things had abolished private schools and offered instead free and compulsory elementary education in the state schools to all Albanian nationals, was not in violation of the equality of treatment clause, since it was of general application.

Though the new law purported to close all private schools in the country, it was clear that it had particularly detrimental effects on the capacity of minority groups to use their own languages in schools and to teach their religions freely. The Permanent Court, following its decision in the case of *Treatment of Polish Nationals in Danzig*,[13] had no difficulty in holding that the performance of the clause against discrimination must be performed in fact as well as in law, and that an act which is general in its application but is in fact directed against members of the minority constitutes a violation of the obligation.[14] Considering the circumstances of this decision, there can be no doubt that the inclusion of the concept of good faith in the performance of treaties serves a useful purpose, although the choice of words is perhaps inappropriate. It is clear from reading these two decisions that the difference between performance of a treaty "in law" and "in fact" is the difference between textual and contextual interpretations of the treaty and the parties' decisions following it in light of some common policies. In other words, a particular obligation must not be evaded by what amounts to a strictly literal application of the treaty provisions to the exclusion of all other legally relevant factors.[15]

13. *Case of the Treatment of Polish Nationals and Other Persons of Polish Origin or Speech in the Danzig Territory* [1932] P.C.I.J., ser. A/B, No. 44, at 28.

14. *Case of the Minority Schools in Albania*, [1935] P.C.I.J., ser. A/B, No. 64, at 1, 18–20.

15. However, the decision loses much of its force as a precedent since the phrase "in fact as well as in law" was embodied in the text of the original obligation itself (supra note 14, at 4). For an air transport dispute in which the Italian government, after losing in arbitration, terminated the agreement in accordance

If this was the ILC's point in the inclusion of the concept of good faith, it is certainly a valid one, though one wishes it had been made more explicitly, for it raises the most fundamental issues of treaty termination. It should, however, have been first stipulated that upon the fulfillment of the substantive grounds for termination and of the procedural requirements, and after a stalemate is reached, the claimant state is authorized to terminate the treaty. An arbitrary decision, that is to say, a decision contrary to the specific grounds which justify termination, would be regarded as a violation of the given agreement and the convention, and thus as unlawful.

Of course, the problem is much more complex, and it is doubtful whether all the difficulties can be evaded even with such a formulation. Many of the diplomatic stalemates have nothing to do with a lack of good will or ingenuity on the part of statesmen, and may arise from differing but genuine perspectives. The frustration of the "fundamental" purpose of a treaty, or the "material" violation of the other side, are usually not mutually satisfactory bases for termination, since their effect on the continual validity of the treaty may be easier for one party to perceive than the other. This is particularly true of the abstract formulation of

---

with its strict letters, see Bradley, "International Air Cargo Services: The Italy–U.S.A. Air Transport Agreement Arbitration," 12 *McGill L.J.* 312 (1966); Larsen, "The United States–Italy Air Transport Arbitration: Problems of Treaty Interpretation and Enforcement," 61 *Am. J. Int'l L.* 496 (1967).

Situations in which a government unilaterally, and contrary to the provisions of an air transport agreement, imposes restrictions on the operation of foreign airlines, raise typical problems of termination. The remedies that are available to the United States government in such disputes are limited. This is because foreign governments usually impose restrictions on American airlines whenever the latter benefit from the existing arrangements more than their own airlines do. United States airlines put pressures on their own government against negotiation and compromise, which in effect means surrendering part of the treaty already held, or granting additional privileges to the other airlines. Reprisals in kind cannot usually be effective against an airline that is already at a disadvantage. Consequently, denunciation of the agreement is more likely to harm American interests than others'. The only practical recourse left to the United States, short of enlarging the dispute by granting benefits or putting pressures on unrelated matters, is verbal persuasion and arbitration. The general policy of the United States government in air transport disputes of this type has been to reject explicit bargaining and renegotiation of existing arrangements, instead proposing arbitration or "consultation" within the framework of the agreement (Bradley, supra this note, at 313n.).

Article 62 of the convention (rebus sic stantibus), and perhaps of any possible doctrinal formulation of the grounds for termination based on fundamental change of circumstances. It is easy to sympathize, therefore, with the authors of the convention who shrank from explicitly authorizing nonconsensual termination on the pretext that the grounds for termination have been fulfilled. However, Article 65 is hardly a substitute for a clear principle of termination. For who is to judge good faith, and by what criteria, if not by the fulfillment of commonly agreed grounds for termination?

The academic question of whether a fundamental change of conditions has occurred is not the only or the most important one in conflicts about termination. What counts are many interrelated questions such as: (a) whether or not upon the occurrence of specific changes a decision to terminate a treaty is authorized; (b) whether the other side has the power and determination to terminate or to object to the termination of the treaty; and (c) whether the apparent gain deriving from a given, projected unilateral act will be more than offset by a comparable deterioration in the authority system within which it transpires—in other words, what the costs or penalties are for failing to reach a new agreement. And penalties, as those who are overconcerned with the possibility of abuse frequently ignore, go beyond a single win; they include losses to shared authority.

The relation between authority and control is complicated. The hypothesis is that the authorization or nonauthorization of nonconsensual decision making in case of a stalemate be an important reason why the parties reach a deadlock in settling a dispute. If powerful enough, the party that has authority on its side may have the incentive to resist an agreed solution of the dispute in the hope that its position may be strengthened after having failed to come to an explicit agreement. It cannot be assumed, following examples in national arenas where courts may eventually dispose of the case, that the parties may reach a compromise solution precisely because the legal situation is not clear,[16] for it is at least equally possible that one or both of the parties would prefer a deadlock for the very reason of the silence of authority. When

16. See R. Childers, *Equity, Restitution and Damages* xvii (1969).

there are no existing authoritative international standards in case of deadlock, the predominant criterion for evaluating the alternative outcomes of agreement or no agreement at all is necessarily the relative power of the parties alone. To give a solution of the problem that is neutral with regard to the question of whether specific unilateral acts may be authorized, while authorizing both sides to act in good faith, is in fact to place a premium on power. The relatively powerful party would then cause a deadlock to be reached and then, according to the ILC commentary, "it would be for each government to appreciate the situation." With the given hypothesis, it is not difficult to imagine the outcomes of such appreciation.

### Willingness to Compromise

Most writers, and the authors of the convention during the debate on Article 65, seem to imply that the parties should negotiate in such a manner that would make it highly probable that agreement would be reached. This essentially means that a party must lower its demands whenever the probabilities of reaching an agreement fall below its desired outcome. This view is in line with the frequently heard argument that, in order to demonstrate good will in international relations, the parties should observe certain rules of accommodation while negotiating, for example, the so-called rule that the parties ought to be flexible and that there should be a reciprocity of concessions to enable a compromise to be reached.[17] There is indeed considerable evidence that compromise, rather than the vindication of claims and counterclaims, was thought by the authors of the convention to be an essential part of the desired outcome.

Although willingness to compromise may prevent violence and other disruptions in specific situations, it is doubtful whether in negotiations on treaty termination or on invalidity in general it is really an essential ingredient of good faith. Viewing a demand as arbitrary or aggressive, a government may wish to object to any change whatsoever by putting basic principles and precedents in

17. For a discussion of this and other views concerning the concept of "negotiation in good faith," see F. Ilké, *How Nations Negotiate* 111ff. (1964); Cox, note 22 infra, at 1414ff.

jeopardy. If in the past a government successfully maintained the principle of the sanctity of treaties, or conversely, the rule regarding the invalidity of treaties imposed by force, it may adduce authority to its claim or counterclaim by continuing to adhere to that principle. By being willing, obliged, or forced to make concessions regardless of the substantive issues in the specific conflict, it risks the fundamental principle itself. Having pledged it, a government may persuade its adversary that it would accept a stalemate rather than capitulate the principle and invite similar demands in the future.

Moreover, since any change would presumably operate to the disadvantage of the defensive party, it may wish to negotiate an agreement on the revision or termination of the treaty provided its terms are met, but be quite unwilling to compromise on those terms. Another government may, for a variety of reasons, be so anxious to reach an agreement that it will be willing to compromise on whatever terms it may get. Which of these states of mind, or which of all the intermediate states of mind, is necessary to negotiate in "good faith"? With so many explanations for willingness or unwillingness to compromise, including the noble one of the sanctity of treaties, a finding on motivation that did not balance the claim and counterclaim, the proposals and counterproposals, in light of substantive international policies, would be sheer speculation.

If a compromise is indeed the desired outcome, some doubts arise as to the relevancy of the initial claims and positions of the parties. A party's claim to termination of a whole treaty, no matter how founded and justified, would result at best in some kind of a compromised modification,[18] unless demands in issues unrelated to the treaty in question were to be met. The logical criterion would be to scrutinize the reasonableness of the parties' proposals as a measure of their good faith. However, if an agreed solution is always to be found between the two starting points, it would be unwise for the parties to advance reasonable claims and moderate offers. The result of a rule of thumb such as this would likely be

18. "It is preferable to view the matter [rebus sic stantibus] as one of treaty revision rather than one of treaty termination, except in the most extreme instances of political significance," 1 D. O'Connell, *International Law* 297 (1965).

the opposite of what is intended. Governments would be expected to adhere strongly to obsolete agreements, even when they do not have an immediate interest in their further application. The more the hardship caused to the claimant state by continuing performance, the more profitable it would be to insist on strict performance. The gulf between substantive law and legal procedure would reduce the effectiveness of both.

### Concentration on Immediate Issues

It is sometimes argued that to negotiate in good faith on a claim to termination that is based on specific and defined grounds, is to consider only the issues directly involved without being motivated by or introducing demands for concessions in other issues extraneous to the treaty in question. This view may be criticized on the ground that it is both unrealistic and undesirable. For one thing, when the issue of termination is so narrowly defined, we have seen, every change must necessarily be perceived by the parties as a gain to the claimant and a loss to the objecting side. Without the introduction of issues from outside the treaty in dispute, there is usually no way in which the claimant may offer to make some meaningful concessions. Therefore, this view is contradictory to the view discussed above; that to negotiate in good faith means to make genuine efforts to find a mutually advantageous basis for agreement.

For another thing, governments are simply not accustomed to issuing declaratory recognitions of the legal validity of others' claims, doctrines to the contrary notwithstanding. It is instructive to note that there are virtually no cases in which the other party or parties to a treaty that one party claimed was terminated, were willing to admit that the doctrine of rebus sic stantibus, or other similar legal grounds as such, were applicable, though they were quite ready to agree in practice to revise the treaty in question or to accept its termination.[19] For the objecting side to admit before a solution is reached that the treaty is terminable on legal grounds is, in fact, to restrict its freedom to choose no-agreement in case its terms are not met, and to limit the areas in which inducements and pressures may be used.

19. Fitzmaurice, (Sec.) *Report on the Law of Treaties,* [1957] 2 Y.B. Int'l L. Comm'n 56, U.N. Doc. A/CN.4/SER.A/1957/Add.1.

On the other hand, once the parties reach an agreement, it makes little difference whether the treaty was revised or terminated on specific legal grounds, since parties to agreements may terminate or modify a treaty by a subsequent agreement for whatever reason they deem sufficient. Any agreed modification or termination of a treaty by definition implies a shared recognition that some changes in material conditions have occurred; otherwise, there would have been no need to revise or terminate the treaty. Any disagreement means the lack of shared recognition in the expediency of revision. The legal grounds for termination, then, are needed when the parties disagree, and they cannot arbitrarily be separated from the bargaining process by which this agreement is resolved.

### Commitment to Forego Self-Help Measures

Often the concept of good faith refers, not to the validity of the claim and counterclaim, but to the way the parties behave in the conflict with all its complexities, including their motivations, calculations, strategies, and tactics. Many arguments seem to be mainly concerned with the relative limitation on the coercive intensity of the four generic strategies used in conflicts: diplomatic, ideological, military, and economic. Though the parties may be relatively free, the argument goes, to manipulate whatever resources they command in the conclusion of treaties, by concluding the treaty they have brought themselves into a special persuasive relationship. The effects of this relationship should be to restrain their conduct in future conflicts relating to the treaty in question.[20] This distinction between the relationship and conduct of parties "within" an agreement and "outside" it, however, seems to be more imaginary than real. Since most modern international disputes revolve in one way or another around a treaty, it is often hard to draw a distinction between negotiations on the conclusion of a new agreement, and those on the revision or termination of an old one. Besides, these same parties often have other relations "outside" the treaty that are also being considered in the given case.

Furthermore, it is doubtful whether this view is correct even as a historical interpretation. Measures of self-help have always been

20. Int'l L. Comm'n, supra note 9, at 262.

a principal form of treaty enforcement, the sanction of threat of war included. The possibility of self-help measures cannot be excluded until some other forms of enforcement, institutionalized and less partial, are developed. The most immediate problem relating to sanctions is the need to appraise treaties to determine their projected validity and to evaluate the possible need for their revision. Sanctions should not be employed to enforce treaties that are judged deficient according to some common criteria.

International relations consist of a jumble of international agreements and understandings—some bipartite, others multipartite, some relating to trivial matters, others concerning issues of the highest importance. Some are the product of a mutual desire to further certain goals, while others are the result of coercion in various degrees. If treaties conflict with one another, or if there is doubt that a given treaty should be enforced, sanctions may operate at cross-purposes in effecting compliance with treaties pertaining to inconsistent matters, or for the preservation of a status quo that is regarded by one or more of the parties as inequitable.[21]

The growth in international organization in the last century, and the regarding of certain covenants as fundamental, work toward the systematization of the international treaty process. These organizations, however, do not yet provide an adequate mechanism for the enforcement of common policies and the common appraisal of treaties with the purpose of settling them into their relative order. The task of evaluation, enforcement, and revision is mainly left in the hands of the parties concerned. However, without common criteria of evaluation and first settling the question of the legal validity of certain treaties and the need for the revision of others, it is difficult to tell unfair practice from acting in good faith in negotiations on termination.

### ANALOGY TO COLLECTIVE BARGAINING

A comparison with United States legislative, judicial, and administrative decisions on labor-management negotiations may further illustrate the different viewpoints discussed above regarding the duty to negotiate in good faith, and hence provide hindsight for prospective international regulation. Indeed, treaty termina-

21. P. Wild, *Sanctions and Treaty Enforcement* 6 (1934).

tion and collective bargaining on renewal of labor contracts share many relevant characteristics.

First, both negotiations are usually conducted with the aim of redistribution. This has generally been true even though in labor negotiations, at least in the short run, both parties may sometimes win, since a raise in wages may be followed by a hike in prices. Second, in both situations the parties to negotiation are frequently organized entities, sometimes with overwhelming disparity in their power, which may effect both the willingness of the objecting party to enter into negotiations on the demand for a change, and the outcome of the dispute. The immense organization of trade unions in the last century also provides cases in which the unions actually have more power than the employer. Third, in both situations the objecting party may have similar reasons for resisting direct talks with the other side.[22] Fourth, unilateral acts during negotiations are analogous to both situations. When such actions are taken during negotiations or upon issues the other side wishes to negotiate, they interfere with the normal course of negotiations and may indicate that negotiation would be useless.[23]

Fifth, in both cases the basic policies in introducing legislation to regulate the dispute have been to encourage the parties to reach agreed solutions by free bargaining, and to check arbitrary and unfair procedures while not imposing involuntary substantive settlements on the parties, however just or desirable they may seem to be to the larger community. Sixth, despite the usual lack

22. Without statutory obligation employers refused to recognize unions as representatives of all the employees, even when a union represented the majority of workers. The denial of recognition and the refusal to enter into negotiations was particularly aimed at new unions that were too weak to effect a successful strike (Cox, "The Duty to Bargain in Good Faith," 71 *Harv. L. Rev.* 1401, 1408 [1958]). For a conception of international negotiation in good faith as drawn upon American collective bargaining, see Goldie, "The North Sea Continental Shelf Cases— A Ray of Hope for the International Court?" 16 *N.Y.L.F.* 327 (1970).

23. This is so whether the acts were intended to cause damage or to confer additional benefits. For example, by raising wages or making other concessions unilaterally, the employer shows the employees that they can secure advantages as great as, or possibly greater than, those the union can secure through collective bargaining. According to some decisions a unilateral action, unless taken after negotiations have reached an impasse, is an unfair labor practice." See Bowman, "An Employer's Unilateral Action—An Unfair Labor Practice?" 9 *Vand. L. Rev.* 487 (1956).

of compulsory adjudication on substantive issues in labor-management relations in the United States, there are nevertheless judicial or administrative permanent organs with compulsory jurisdiction specialized to decide what constitutes an unfair bargaining practice and to provide remedies for violations. In international relations no such permanent organ exists to which complaints of unfair practices in the termination of treaty obligations can be referred. This difference is important, since the National Labor Relations Board (NLRB) can order the parties to enter into negotiation, and if an unfair bargaining practice causes a strike to fail, the board can order the employer to reinstate the strikers in their former positions and to discharge replacements if necessary. However, the following passage by Cox points out that this difference is not really decisive:

> It is doubtful whether much is gained by retrospective review of the negotiations, however, when the parties have actually bargained together. Usually they will have signed some kind of an agreement. The union signs despite the employer's unfairness because almost any contract is preferable to a hiatus in which the union can offer its members nothing except the hope of winning an unfair-labor-practice case. The employer who is victimized by an unfair labor practice will ordinarily sign because he has no practicable alternative. If the contract is too one-sided, the loser may file unfair-labor-practice charges. A year or two later the NLRB may determine that section 8 (a) (5) or 8 (b) (3) was violated. After another twelve months more or less, the courts may enforce the NLRB decision. Will the decision accomplish anything at this late date? During the interval the parties will have had to go about their business. Conditions change. Relationships develop. I wonder whether the bargains struck despite "misconduct" in the course of negotiations are not likely to be more viable than any formal legal document addressed to a situation which is two or three years outdated.[24]

If it is still difficult to control the conduct of collective bargaining despite the availability of compulsory jurisdiction, it is cer-

24. Cox, supra note 22, at 1439–40.

tainly more difficult in international affairs, where agreements are generally considered valid despite the unfair practice (short of forceful coercion) that led to their conclusion.

It can be further argued that in labor-management relations the parties must always arrive at some sort of agreement because the dispute usually concerns the main, or the only, relation between the parties, and because almost any kind of agreement would be preferred by the parties to a breakdown of this relation by a continuous strike. On the other hand, interaction between states usually embraces hundreds and thousands of forms, patterns, and subjects, of which a particular treaty may constitute only a small, or sometimes an insignificant, part. Thus, states can better afford the failure to reach agreement on a particular point, since their intention may still be to influence bargaining on other issues. While this difference is certainly important, one should note that even in labor-management relations there are quite a number of separate issues that may form the subject matter of disputes. Wages, working hours, working conditions, social benefits, closed shop, union rights, personal relations, and so on are issues which embrace all categories of values and which invariably form the subject matter of disputes. Strikes also vary accordingly—from a walk-out or a sit-in, to a slow-down or a refusal to work extra hours.

On the other hand, there are treaties which, far from being a mere drop in the vast ocean of interaction between states, determine the major relationship between the parties and overshadow all other treaties between them. To this latter category usually belong treaties of power and security, such as peace treaties that impose unilateral disarmament on one side, allocate geographical areas, divide a country, or grant a specified territory of one state to the use of another. These treaties, when they cease to register the genuine shared expectations of the parties, can be terminated or enforced only by the threat or actual use of force. That is to say, disagreement on the question of termination or revision may result in war or in other more minor forms of violence.

One may wonder whether in such situations the parties really have much more of an alternative to accept or reject agreement than the employer and employees in labor negotiations. The common interest in both situations is similar. War is damaging to the defeated and the victor, as well as to states that do not actively participate in it. Likewise, from a strike, whether successful or not, not only the employer against whom it is directed suffers, but also the striking workers, and in many cases the overall community as well.

### The Duty to Bargain in Good Faith

The National Labor Relations Act provides that it shall be an unfair labor practice for an employer or a labor union to refuse to bargain collectively.[25] The act specifies that the representatives of the employer and the employee must "meet at reasonable times and confer in good faith with respect to wages, hours," etc., but "does not compel either party to agree to a proposal or require the making of a concession." [26] It was stated during the debates in Congress that all the bill proposed to do was to escort the union representatives to the door of the employer, that it does not seek to inquire into what happens behind that door. The duty to enter into collective bargaining was imposed on the assumption that even reluctant parties might exchange facts and arguments if forced to meet, and that such an exchange might increase mutual understanding and produce an agreement. However, in the early days of the act, a considerable number of employers politely met with the union representatives as required by the act, listened to their demands and the supporting arguments, and then rejected them. It was clear that the purpose of the act could be destroyed by going through the motions of negotiating almost as easily as by bluntly withholding any talks.

The concept of negotiation in "good faith" was incorporated into the law of collective bargaining as a solution to this problem. Since the phrase has no settled meaning, it was left to the NLRB and the courts to define it according to concrete situations. Thus, attaching conditions before entering into negotiations has been held to be an unfair practice even when the condition is that the

25. Labor Management Relations Act, 1947, 8(a)(5), 61 Stat. 141 (1947); 29 U.S.C. §158(a)(5). The duty to bargain collectively was originally directed only to the employers; National Labor Relations Act 8(5), 49 Stat. 453 (1935).

26. Labor Management Relations Act, 1947, 8(d), 61 Stat. 142 (1947); 29 U.S.C. §158(d) (1952).

union will abandon a strike.[27] The duty to bargain has been extended to each and every topic the union may wish to discuss, provided that it falls within the statutory phrase "rates of pay, wages, hours of employment or other terms and conditions of employment." The phrase "terms and conditions of employment" has been broadly construed.[28]

Furthermore, employers who merely went through the formal motions of negotiations knowing that they were a sham, were said to lack good faith and were held to be in violation of the act. "[T]here must be common willingness among the parties to discuss freely and fully their respective claims and demands and, when these are opposed, to justify them on reason." [29] To offer a union a contract saying "take it or leave it" has been held not to be a bargain in good faith within the meaning of the act.[30] Similar decisions have been rendered against withholding agreement upon trivial matters that are normally settled in a routine fashion.[31] Other decisions have even gone beyond merely requiring the parties to give the grounds for disagreement. In one case, for example, the company throughout the "negotiations" rejected all the union proposals but refused to offer counterproposals. It justified this approach on the grounds that, since it was not seeking anything from the union, it was up to the union to make the proposals. The court decreed a violation of the act, defining the relevant good faith provision as an "obligation . . . to participate actively in the deliberation so as to indicate a present intention to find a basis for agreement, and a sincere effort must be made to reach a common ground." [32] It was not sufficient to compel the parties to meet and discuss even the

27. See, e.g., American Laundry Mach. Co., 76 N.L.R.B. 981, 982–83 (1948), *enforced,* 174 F.2d 124 (6th Cir. 1949); cf. NLRB v. Hoppes Mfg. Co., 170 F.2d 962 (6th Cir. 1948). Cox, supra note 22, at 1410 n. 36. For similar practices in conflicts about treaty termination, see p. 130 supra.

28. See, e.g., The Andrew Jergens Co., 76 N.L.R.B. 363 (1948), *enforced,* 175 F.2d 130 (9th Cir. 1949), *cert. denied,* 338 U.S. 827 (1949).

29. NLRB v. George P. Pilling & Son Co., 119 F.2d 32, 37 (3d Cir., 1941).

30. NLRB v. General Electric Co., 418 F.2d 736 (2d Cir. 1969), *cert. denied,* 397 U.S. 965 (1970); Montgomery Ward & Co., 90 N.L.R.B. 1244 (1950).

31. Coronet Casuals Inc. et al., 5CCH Lab. L. Rep. §25, 921 (1973).

32. NLRB v. Montgomery Ward Co., 133 F.2d 676, 686 (9th Cir. 1943); see also NLRB v. Reed & Prince Mfg. Co., 118 F.2d 874, 885 (1st Cir. 1941), *cert. denied,*

broader issues without passing judgment upon the quality of the negotiations.

Thus, a meaningful test of what had originally been criticized as being an attempt to legislate a state of mind could not be subjective in any true sense. Theoretically, one first defines "good faith" and then proceeds to infer a lack of good faith, as so defined, from the activities that are claimed to interfere with the negotiations. In practice, however, attention has focused on particular items of conduct which have allegedly fallen short of accepted negotiating practices. Consequently, the parties have been asked actively to demonstrate their desire to reach a common ground. "[T]he employer is obliged to make *some* reasonable effort in *some* direction to compose his differences with the union, if § 8(a)(5) is to be read as imposing any substantial obligation at all." [33] However, many employers formally met this demand by proposing as the basis of an agreement "existing rates of pay, wages, and hours of employment," or even proposing an actual reduction in wages.

For the board and courts to regulate such conduct involved passing judgment upon the reasonableness of proposals and thus, inevitably, upon the application of pressure on the parties to make concessions. Though Congress added into the act the explicit reservation that the obligation "does not compel either party to agree to a proposal or require the making of concessions," subsequent decisions strongly implied that an employer bargains in good faith only when he is willing to make objectively reasonable concessions. Further, activities that were originally regarded as evidence of bad faith in a truly subjective sense, often have come to be sufficient for the board's intervention standing alone. The general direction of administrative and judicial interpretation and application of the act has been toward the formulation of particular required or prohibited acts, whose violation is now regarded as per se violation of the act. Such per se violations have

313 U.S. 595 (1941); Globe Cotton Mills v. NLRB, 103 F.2d 91, 94 (5th Cir. 1939). See also Cox, supra note 22, at 1412-14.

33. NLRB v. Reed & Prince Mfg. Co., 205 F.2d 131, 134–35 (1st Cir. 1953), *cert. denied,* 346 U.S. 887 (1953).

been: refusal to sign a written contract,[34] unilateral actions while discussions are taking place,[35] and withholding wage and financial data when the employer has argued that a demand is too expensive.[36]

These rulings have been arrived at through a purposive interpretation of the act. But while Congress clearly intended to influence negotiated solutions slyly and by indirection, in later decisions they have been sought and enforced openly and directly. Such an approach, when carried too far, may in effect come very close to a compulsory adjudication of the dispute.

## Conciliation and Adjudication

The general preference of international jurists for adjudication in solving disputes, and their uncritical tendency to judicialize all legal problems, may be suspected as two of the reasons for the inattention given in the convention to the problems arising in the course of bargaining on termination. Concluding that it is unrealistic to provide for compulsory adjudication of the dispute, and

34. See, e.g., H. J. Heinz Co. v. NLRB, 311 U.S. 514 (1941); NLRB v. Highland Park Mfg. Co., 110 F.2d 632, 637–38 (4th Cir. 1940). The latter decision suggests that if there had been good reasons for the practice it might not have been a violation. The refusal to reduce into writing any agreement that has been reached during the negotiations resembles the insistence to conduct "talks" and "discussions" officially distinguished from negotiation and bargaining on the termination of international agreements. The writing and joint execution in labor agreements are more important as a symbol than as a memorial of the bargain. They bear witness to the fact that the terms and conditions of employment are fixed not by the employer alone but *jointly* by the representatives of both the employer and the union. Similarly, in conflicts about treaty termination the objecting side, though willing or forced to accept a fait accompli, sometimes insists on signing a formal agreement terminating the old treaty. Compare the case of the rearmament of Germany with that of the Black Sea, ch. 2 supra.

35. Note 23 supra.

36. NLRB v. Truitt Mfg. Co., 351 U.S. 149 (1956), reversing 224 F.2d 869 (4th Cir. 1955), denying enforcement of the NLRB order: "Good faith bargaining necessarily requires that claims made by either bargainer should be honest claims" (351 U.S. 152). See also NLRB v. General Electric Co., supra note 30, at 752–53. The availability of financial data in international bargaining is of primary importance in negotiations on the revision of concession agreements. For these developments by which the NLRB has undertaken to regulate collective bargaining regardless of the parties' state of mind, see Cox, supra note 22, at 1430; Goldie, supra note 22, at 364.

that the problem is "the familiar one of the settlement of differences between states," [37] the ILC gave up further consideration of the question. This led to the unsatisfactory result that Article 65(3) has been drafted in a most general form, so that the obligation is to seek a solution through any and all of the available methods for settling disputes in international relations.

The association, in one short paragraph of such a wide range of alternative techniques for making the decision—institutionalized and organized, as well as informal—inevitably barred the way to further clarification of relevant policies.[38] It is clear that recommended policies for the regulation of the parties' conduct in relation to each of these different techniques should not only vary, but must necessarily contradict each other.[39] Thus, the convention's overwhelming reliance on all the pacific methods for conflict resolution must reduce the effectiveness of any such method.

### Why Not Adjudication?

Adjudication and arbitration (the terms being used here interchangeably), as *currently* employed in international relations, are not a suitable method for the resolution of most conflicts about

37. Int'l L. Comm'n, supra note 9, at 262.

38. The parties in negotiations are mainly engaged in setting terms for a new relationship. On the other hand, at least according to the prevailing myth, adjudicators should be mainly occupied with the terms of the old treaty. The procedures appropriate for adjudication and arbitration are those which can best assure each litigant a meaningful chance to present arguments and proofs for a decision in his favor. The procedures adequate for negotiation or mediation are those most likely to disclose that pattern of adjustment which will satisfy the interests of both parties. Fuller, infra note 43, at 24; Fuller, "Adjudication and the Rule of Law," 1960 *Proc. Am. Soc. Int'l L.* at 1.

39. Principles authorizing unilateral termination on grounds of changing conditions should perhaps be strictly defined. But there are no equal reasons to restrict the application of such grounds in disputes that are determined by adjudication. Articles 62(1)(b) and 70(1) of the Vienna Convention, for example, limit lawful termination to executory treaty provisions (ch. 1 supra). This limitation is called upon because of the relatively higher threat to peace that unilateral termination of executed treaties poses (ch. 7 infra). But the same policy consideration is not compelling when the dispute is settled by institutional decision making. Yet the convention and other works on the subject (ch. 1, note 22, supra) indiscriminately limit the application of the doctrine of rebus sic stantibus to obligatory treaties even by the International Court and arbitration tribunals.

termination. Many factors account for this, most of which have to do with the unique features of this type of dispute, discussed earlier. Most important, while the effective resolution of termination controversies usually requires a lateral expansion of issues,[40] the adjudicative process tends to limit and confine them. In traditional adjudication, much of the context surrounding the dispute is either held constant or taken for granted. This involves, among other things, a deliberate slicing and formal exclusion of relevant parts of the context while assuming the existence of others. These assumptions about the appropriateness of the contextual map are widely shared in domestic adjudication. Where these assumptions are untenable, adjudication breaks down (as in periods of labor unrest.) In international disputes about treaty termination, these suppositions are most relevant for an adjudicative decision, but they are at the same time most controversial. Thus the objecting side, we have seen, usually characterizes the dispute as a "juridical" (rebus sic stantibus) issue; that is, as raising a rigid and narrow question that excludes by definition a great many contextual factors which are, in turn, characterized as "political." The claimant, on the other hand, tries to widen the context of the decision by challenging the presuppositions upon which the adjudicative characterization of the problem is based.

Furthermore, the adjudicators are usually restricted to the record presented to them by the parties in the form of claims, evidence, and arguments at the adversary hearings. They are bound by formal rules of procedure and evidence.[41] These, too, usually

40. Chs. 4 and 5 supra. Gains from adjudication, of course, should be more broadly understood and may include gains to shared authority and comparable improvements in the authority system within which the decision transpires. But such motives in submission to adjudication are not common. Further, it is commonly assumed that since submission to adjudication and arbitration in international law is voluntary, a state will not submit a particular dispute to third-party settlement unless it has already reconciled itself to the possibility of losing the case, and thus will not resist enforcement. This assumption is unpalatable in many applications. Reisman, "The Role of the Economic Agencies in the Enforcement of International Judgments and Awards: A Functional Approach," 19 *Int'l Organization* 929 (1965).

41. It is commonly assumed that adjudication can function effectively only if the litigants have clarified and delimited by negotiation the disputed issue before

lead to a narrow focus of adjudication on the treaty in dispute, and to the exclusion of other supposedly extraneous factors, and make it difficult to resolve the controversy by allowing for some compensation for the deprivation attendant upon termination. (In traditional legal parlance this means that the court cannot replace the old treaty with a new one, a "legislative" function rather than a "judicial" one.) [42] Added to this is the fact that, in international disputes between states, monetary and similar equivalences are generally not accepted as compensation. Although particular issues may be equally justicable in national and international arenas, the international court and tribunals are thus far more limited in the range of alternative remedies at their disposal. This may partly account for the reference in Article 65 to such a great variety of decision-making techniques for settling termination disputes.

For these and other reasons, those who have been concerned with the failure of parties to resort to adjudication in conflict about termination may well have exaggerated the significance of the choice.[43] Some legal studies have even gone so far as attempting to make the lawful application of substantive rules of termina-

they enter the adjudication arena (supra ch. 4, note 17). This, however, is the most difficult task in disputes about treaty termination (supra ch. 5).

42. This is a telling point in favor of the bargaining process, but it too can be overstated. The distinction between the power to make and the power to interpret and apply law is one of degree. Courts often do exercise explicit prescriptive functions. "National courts have on occasion refused to decide on the ground that another decision process was more appropriate for the matter, or that information vital to rational decision was not available to the court but would be available to another process. This contingency is a rare luxury in the international arena. The capacity for formally 'binding' decisions is most often found in international tribunals. . . . The absurdity of an international tribunal speaking of a matter more appropriate for the international legislator requires no further illumination" (W. Reisman, *Nullity and Revision* 628 [1971]). The provisions of the Statute of the International Court are broadly formulated, and procedures of the court are governed by rules made by the court itself. This and other factors provide for potential flexibility (C. Jenks, *The Prospects for International Adjudication* 122 [1964]). The difficulties that confront courts in this respect are not only conceptual or technical but also political. For a court to promulgate innovative principles and new arrangements is to defy established expectations about the separation of power among the various departments of government. Its ability to make creative decisions that bear on broad matters of policy depends largely on its base of power in the community.

43. See, e.g., Larson, "Peace Through Law: The Rôle and Limits of Adjudication —Some Contemporary Applications," 1960 *Proc. Am. Soc. Int'l L.* at 8. Though he

tion contingent upon a decision of an international court or tribunal. Since the latter themselves are reluctant to assume responsibility, such a requirement must obviously be motivated by a strong bias in favor of traditionally objecting parties.[44] Indeed, there have been thus far only a few explicit judicial cases involving termination, and they have declined, on various procedural and other formalistic grounds, to pass judgment on the substance and merits of the dispute at hand (for example, *The Free Zones, Anglo-Iranian Oil Co., South West Africa* (second phase), and *Northern Cameroons* cases).[45] Such nondecisions—decisions refusing to decide—are real decisions despite judicial attempts to characterize them differently, and in this context of claims to termination they are in effect negative decisions—decisions that reject the claim. In all of these cases, the parties in actual possession of the disputed physical issues won the court-centered phase of the dispute by default of the court.[46]

mentions the Berlin and Suez conflicts as suitable for adjudication, the issues he formulates for such decisions are not really those of treaty termination.

Because of the connection and reapportionment of extraneous issues in termination conflicts, their settlement usually involves what Fuller describes as a "polycentric" task. (Fuller, "Collective Bargaining and the Arbitrator," 1963 *Wisc. L. Rev.* 3, 33). A polycentric ("many centered") problem is one to which there is no single issue or solution, or simple set of solutions, toward which the parties in court can direct their proofs and arguments. The difficulty lies in the fact that allocation of any single physical issue has implications for the proper allocation of every other issue, and the joining together of particular issues, when such a combination is called for, has implications for other issues and relations between the parties. If an optimum solution had to be reached through adjudicative procedures, the court would have to set forth an endless series of possible formulas for connection and division of issues and objects, and to direct the parties to deal with each other in turn. On the other hand, some legal questions concerning the invalidity of treaties—such as error, duress, and the effect of peremptory norms on a treaty—are particularly suitable for the adjudicative process. They essentially call for yes-or-no decisions. Some observers, however, see in compromise the dominant trait of arbitration (K. Carlston, *The Process of International Arbitration* 258 (1964); Dennis, "Compromise—The Great Defect of Arbitration," 11 *Colum. L. Rev.* 493 [1911]). Polycentric or integrative decisions contain, as has been pointed out, different elements than the regular compromise. In the *Free Zones* case, France and Switzerland, mutually dissatisfied with the judgement, empowered a joint commission to legislate in effect a new regime for the regime in question (L. Bloomfield, *Evolution or Revolution?* 80 [1957]).

44. See pp. 34–41 supra.

45. See supra ch. 1, note 68; Reisman, supra note 42, at 625ff.

46. Theoretically, a judicial decision not to decide a termination controversy does not change the status quo, and it therefore represents neither a gain nor a

## The Conciliation Commission

Following feverish last-minute negotiations at the Vienna Conference on the Law of Treaties, a complicated institutional procedure for the compulsory conciliation of most disputes about termination was interjected into the convention. Article 66 and the Annex to the Convention have not been given adequate attention by the ILC, along with other relevant provisions on termination, and they clearly do not form an integral part of the set of principles and procedures provided for by the authors of the convention. The substantive provisions, it has been noted, are narrowly formulated according to the explicit assumption that most termination disputes will not be settled within an institutionalized framework. The procedural provisions are too flexible pursuant, perhaps, to the same assumption. The added conciliatory provisions, on the other hand, assume broad contextual factors to be relevant for the decision, and in this regard they go far beyond what seems to be permitted by the substantive provisions. And they may even require passing judgment on practices that have been left unregulated by the procedural provisions.

The Annex to the Convention provides for the establishment in particular disputes of an ad hoc conciliation commission consisting of five members. Two of the members are appointed by each party to the dispute respectively, and may be of their own nationality. Two other members are also appointed by each party respectively, but from a predetermined list of qualified jurists drawn up and maintained by the secretary-general of the United Nations. Each member of the United Nations or a party to the

---

loss to any of the parties. In reality, however, such a decision is advantageous to the party in possession of the disputed physical values. A nondecision is in effect a decision that rejects demanded changes in the existing allocation of values. Once rendered and made public, it seems to acquire a kind of moral inertia that puts a heavier onus on the party demanding the reallocation (the rejected claimant in the judicial proceedings, which occasionally is the original objecting side, since a fait accompli in the interim may have changed this fundamental legal relationship [ch. 7 infra]). For a reaction along these lines in the aftermath of nondecision in the second phase of the *South West Africa* cases, see Reisman, supra note 42, 634.

convention can nominate two conciliators, and the names of those so nominated constitute the list. The chairman of an ad hoc commission is appointed from the same list by the four conciliators who have been chosen by the parties.

This procedure for the appointment of the commission is designed to achieve as far as possible both the impartiality and the flexibility necessary for rendering a mutually acceptable decision. To insure the smooth operation of this procedure, the secretary-general himself is required to make any appointment to a conciliation commission that the parties to the dispute or the four conciliators chosen by them fail to make. A commission should be fully constituted within a period of 180 days following the date on which the secretary-general receives the request for conciliation (at least 12 months from the date on which an objection was raised to the original notification of the claim), unless the parties to the dispute by agreement extend this period.

Note the marked differences in function and competence between this procedure of conciliation commission and the traditional adjudication or conciliation. The general principle dominating arbitral jurisdiction and procedures is one of defined powers limited by the parties' consent. The submitting states renounce no rights whatsoever except so far as may appear from the agreement to arbitrate (the *compromis*). But the jurisdiction of the conciliation commission is compulsory in the sense that it can be effectively invoked and initiated by any party to the dispute without any cooperation from the respondent in organizing the body of conciliators that is to pass upon the dispute, in setting the procedures, or in defining the questions at issue. The refusal of the respondent duly to designate members of the commission, or the latter's failure to appoint the chairman, do not bar further proceedings.

Furthermore, in examining the claims and objections, the commission is not bound by any formal rules of pleading or evidence but decides its own procedures: "The Commission may draw the attention of the parties to the dispute to any measures which might facilitate an amicable settlement." It "shall hear the parties, examine the claims and objections, and make proposals to the parties," again, "with a view to reaching an amicable settlement of the dispute." [47] These provisions, together with the particular way in which the commission is constituted, are obviously intended to encourage the parties to *negotiate* their differences within the institutionalized framework and under the auspices of a well-qualified board of conciliators.

In light of the above observations, one may characterize the machinery provided for in the Annex to the Convention as a type of compulsory mediation. The commission's functions, however, are not wholly conciliatory but also semiadjudicative. Its members are "qualified jurists." Its initial jurisdiction is limited by Article 66(b) to disputes concerning the "application or interpretation" of any of the articles of part 5 of the convention, which deals with invalidity and termination.[48] Furthermore, the commission is required to issue a report within twelve months of its constitution. It is said about this report that it may include conclusions regarding "the facts and questions of law," and in this sense the report resembles a judicial or arbitral award. However, it is stated in Annex (6) that the report or any of its conclusions "shall not be binding upon the parties and it shall have no other character than that of recommendations" to the parties.

### Advantages of Adjudicative Conciliation

The conciliation commissions and the decision functions accorded to them represent a more genuine step toward the constructive resolution of termination controversies than the traditional focus only on adjudication. While they put a premium on institutional mediation and negotiation, they do not rule out the possibility of an impartial decision by the semiadjudicative agency itself. However, because of the novelty of this procedure, it cannot yet be empirically evaluated. Future performance may fall short of the convention's envisaged scheme, or it may be that the decision dynamics of the ad hoc commissions will eventually develop an even more comprehensive decision-making organ and procedures than have originally been conceived. The potential advantages of such a mixed conciliation-arbitration procedure are many, some of which are summarized here.

47. Vienna Convention, supra note 2, at Annex, (4) and (5).
48. The exceptions are Articles 53 and 64, whose application and interpretation are subjected to the compulsory jurisdiction of the International Court.

First, it allows for the negotiative expansion of the dispute so as to cover enough ground for mutually acceptable outcomes. Recommendations of measures, and the making of proposals "with a view to reaching an amicable settlement of the dispute" include, of course, proposals for the negotiative connection of seemingly separate and extraneous issues.

Second, we have seen that currently a great many conflicts about termination are settled by tacit bargaining (unilateral acts) rather than by direct talks. The outcome of such practices is usually the tacit expansion of conflict and the termination of many agreements on both sides, which frequently is not what either party would ordinarily want. Furthermore, bringing up all possible issues between the parties, even when done by explicit proposals, tends, it may be recalled, to shift the focus away from the specific issues to the ideological images of parties. Under such circumstances formal agreements are difficult to reach. Within the new framework of conciliation procedure, these risks of mutually undesired unilateral acts and of the lateral overexpansion of conflicts could be substantially reduced. In addition, inherent problems in termination controversies of submission to negotiations and agenda formation could be eliminated.[49]

Third, termination is the kind of decision that usually brings about radical and innovative changes in the existing state of affairs, and as such it must always defeat at least some expectations and vested interests. Therefore, conflicts about termination are often crisis situations. A judicial crisis in this respect is a sudden demand upon a court or tribunal, different from past expectations; it puts the smooth and normal functioning of the court in jeopardy. In such cases, no matter how these demands are met or rejected, they will so alienate or disappoint an important segment of the relevant community that popular support for the court might be endangered. Courts must continuously weigh the authority and control factors in matters of jurisdiction so as to protect themselves, which partly explains the reluctance of the ICJ to decide termination controversies. Since in the newly created institutional procedure the immediate parties to the dispute will themselves actively participate in the decision-making

49. For all these practices see chs. 4 and 5 supra. For the tacit expansion of conflicts, see ch. 8 infra.

process (including the selection of the conciliators) and will actively share in the negotiated outcome, such crisis-producing cases will be less threatening to the decision-making institution. This, in turn, may enable the adjudicative agency to increase its role in the determination of particular disputes.

Fourth, the potential of a final decision by an external authority may impress on reluctant parties the wisdom of reaching an agreement, or the expediency of voluntarily accepting the proposals of the conciliatory panel. The shortcoming of the convention's conciliation procedure in this regard is that the commission's final report is not accorded the formal status of a binding decision but only that of a so-called recommendation. This may, of course, turn to advantage.

## A Proposal for Modifications

Having the above-mentioned advantages in mind, the conciliation commission's decision process may be further strengthened by the following modifications in its functions and procedures. Some of these modifications require the granting of explicit authority by an amendment to the convention, or else they may be adopted by special agreements between parties to particular disputes. Others can be dynamically developed as the commissions proceed in the future to settle particular conflicts, case by case:

First, the conciliatory commission should be explicitly granted, or assume itself, the authority to regulate the conduct of bargaining outside as well as inside the conference room; a function analogous to that of the National Labor Relations Board in the United States. The provision in convention's Annex (4) lends itself to such an assumption of authority. But according to Articles 65 and 66, fifteen months should usually elapse from the time a claim to termination is put forward until a request for setting the conciliation procedure in motion can be made. In addition, the Annex to the Convention allows a period of four to six months to pass before the commission is duly constituted in each particular case.

The two-year interim period, during which tacit bargaining is usually expected to develop, unilateral acts may be effected, and the conflict may be already laterally expanded, is too long to be left unregulated. Faits accomplis may be sought before the constitution of the commission with the aim of affecting, or even effectively settling, the matter from the outset of its deliberations. Article 65(5) of the convention, as will be explained in the following chapter, seems to yield assent to such practice. Reprisals may be taken against such practices, and retaliations are expected to follow. It is probable, therefore, that it will not be the initial, single termination conflict that will reach the commission, if any, but the host of agreements that will already be connected to each other by these unilateral acts. In order to prevent such developments, the interim period should be considerably shortened, or a permanent board should be created with the authority to supervise at least the bargaining moves of the parties before negotiations are institutionalized in the ad hoc commission.

Second, the partisan members of each commission (the ad hoc conciliators, two of whom may be nationals of the parties to the dispute) should be encouraged not only to advocate or uphold the point of view of the party which appointed them, as they will probably do, but perhaps also to engage in actual negotiations during the commission's attempts to arrive at a mutually agreed settlement.

Third, the conciliation commission should preferably be given the authority to make a final decision of a formally binding character in the form of a judgment or arbitration award, after attempts at conciliation fail. Annex (3) of the convention specifies that decisions and recommendations of the commission shall be made by a majority vote of the five members. Experience in tripartite arbitration in labor relations in the United States demonstrates that the partisan arbitrators, who are appointed by the parties to the dispute, cannot be wholly judges, for their function is to represent a viewpoint, a posture of interests. "If a majority decision is required, a proceeding that has the facade of arbitration is converted into a continuation of negotiation in an inept and distorted form, as the impartial umpire turns from side to side in an effort to induce one of the flanking arbitrators to join with him." [50] Because an adjudicative decision on termination is

50. Fuller, supra note 43, at 36. The procedure is not essentially changed if there is a five-man panel, with a neutral arbitrator, two appointed by the claimant

essentially a yes-or-no decision (this has to do with the special characteristics of the termination conflict mentioned above), the neutral umpire, if a decision in the form of a judgment or award is required, will eventually have either to join one side or the other of the partisan members, or work out some formal compromise in the form of nondecision.

Since, as has been noted earlier, the substantive outcome of adjudication on termination is currently fairly predictable, the party in possession of the disputed values may stall negotiations and refuse conciliation, expecting to win the dispute in the subsequent adjudicative decision. Similar tactics may also be profitable under the present formal recommendatory character of the commission's report. By empowering the conciliation panel, or preferably the neutral conciliator, to render a final and binding decision, the threat of an either-or decision may be felt more during the negotiative proceedings. The parties to the dispute may in this way be more inclined to accept a compromise, or any other proposal for an optimum settlement. To enhance unpredictability regarding the final adjudicative outcome, and in order to increase the possibility of a settlement by the parties' new agreement, the decision maker should be guided not only by the convention's rather narrow substantive principles of termination, but also by a variety of contextual and procedural factors, including such considerations as which party has the unreasonable attitude, unconciliatory mood, strictly legalistic approach, or is otherwise blocking agreement. There should be some penalty for refusal to cooperate in the conciliation proceedings.

Finally, it does not seem that further clarification of the convention's substantive provisions of termination (for example, Article 62 on changing conditions) is indispensable for the success of such a scheme. For one thing, it is doubtful whether substantive policies of termination are really susceptible to clear and precise definitional formulation. Nor can governments be realistically expected to agree on any such general definition unless it contains some element of ambiguity. For another thing, ambig-

---

and two by the objecting side. See also the discussion on United Nations' mixed armistice commissions in ch. 9 infra.

uity is indeed somewhat desirable for working out the proposed scheme; it makes the outcome of the dispute somehow less predictable and, therefore, the mixed mediation and arbitration proceeding more meaningful. Moreover, a pure conciliation board and a strict arbitration tribunal may have in practice to apply different and sometimes inconsistent standards of decision to conform to their peculiar purposes and procedures, none of which, in turn, may be suitable for a decision in a mixed arbitration-mediation organ. Insight may be gained and general standards of decision may gradually be developed by the new agencies as they proceed to settle disputes pragmatically, case by case. However, to enable the commissions to function successfully, Article 62 of the convention (and other similar substantive provisions) should be liberalized. In its current formulation the article rejects almost all claims to termination based on changing conditions.[51] This, of course, makes adjudication and mediation that are supposed to take the norms into account meaningless.

## Future Developments

The most profound difference between the regulation of the settlement of labor disputes in the United States and the regulation of disputes about nullity and termination of treaties in the world arena, is the availability of compulsory jurisdiction of a specialized and permanent administrative organ and the regular courts to supervise bargaining practices (as distinguished from decisions on the substance of disputes). These decision makers, while called upon to pronounce judgments upon violations of the relevant provisions of the National Labor Act, have been engaged in the further clarification, development, and creation of the law. Yet, despite this decisive difference, the relevant provision in the Convention on the Law of Treaties is less clear than the parallel labor provision. The obligation to enter into negotiations in the National Labor Relations Act is unequivocally stated, the topics for negotiation are defined, while at the same time the parties' freedom to elect no-agreement is expressly preserved.

Even so, the act could not provide answers to problems that arose in concrete situations. The NLRB and courts, refusing to

51. Ch. 1 supra.

be halted by the ambiguity of the act, found in the provision an intention to create a genuine obligation of collective bargaining. "Good faith" was interpreted as the duty to desire agreement. But the test in the course of application has become objective rather than subjective, per se violations instead of an inquiry into into the state of mind. The board has not been satisfied with the duty to refrain from abuse but has proceeded to require the doing of specific acts. While Congress might have intended to regulate only the mechanics of negotiation, later decisions, without openly admitting it, had actual influence on the substance of the disputes.

Some commentators believe that this development has gone beyond original congressional intent. Others argue that there has been no departure from congressional intent for the very reason that such intent cannot be clearly inferred from the legislative records. Both in Congress and in the ILC and the Vienna Conference, the specific problems were obviously not thought of while the provisions were adopted. One thing seems to be clear from the foregoing comparison: if the congressional act in itself, despite its relative specificity, could not be of much help in specific conflict situations, the formulation of the Convention on the Law of Treaties will certainly not suffice.

The ILC's and the Vienna Conference's records on the subject are disappointing. Not only was the attention devoted to the specific problems scant, but the considerations they did receive were themselves symptomatic of the problems rather than an earnest effort to answer them. The reference to the duty to negotiate was much too casual to indicate that subsection 3 of Article 65 was intended to embody such a duty. The obligation is to "seek a solution through the means indicated in Article 33 of the Charter"—nothing more. It makes little difference whether or not the framers of the article were intent upon requiring negotiation procedure, for they failed altogether to provide any means for settling the empirical questions on the basis of policies involved.

Article 26 and the Commentary to draft Article 65 are clearly authorities for the contention that the parties' good faith is required, but there is a total failure to indicate the content of such a standard. In fact, the paragraph quoted earlier,[52] in stressing the complete freedom of the parties, might well be taken to negate any intention that the criterion of good faith should be used as an indirect means of coercing acceptance of the claimant's proposals, no matter how unreasonable the objecting side's position may be. In short, the authors of the convention, which prescribed the duty to submit the matter to one of the pacific means indicated in Article 33 of the Charter, did not make a substantial contribution to its meaning.

Both the problem and its ultimate solution seem to be virtually inevitable. Like all bargainings, "negotiations on termination" is a variable concept. It assumes recognition of a need for a change in a given value allocation, or at least a willingness to accept "some" change and bargaining without compelling a particular outcome or, in fact, any agreement at all. The outcome of particular cases depends on the particular preferences, artifice, resources, strategy, skill, etc., of the parties in formulating their demands and proposals; on the factors governing the reshaping of threats and promises during negotiations; and on the combination of these and other factors (public opinion and other pressures from the world community) entering into a decision. The duty to engage in such a process can hardly be susceptible to legal enforcement unless it is given a more pragmatic meaning. Three possible meanings are: (a) that it simply requires formal motions of negotiations; (b) that it requires that, plus the making of objectively reasonable proposals; and (c) that, in addition, it would be required of the parties to perform other specific acts which are conducive to reaching some kind of desirable agreement.

These are all theoretically workable, though the second notion (b) is fraught with problems not present in the first. It also presupposes that objective international standards of reasonableness can be found, an assumption which many governments still deny even in regard to third-party adjudication. Inherent in the third possibility is the difficulty that, because it is independent of the actual state of mind, it requires the performing of acts that have meaning when done voluntarily but that, when coerced, deviate

52. Supra p. 167.

from past voluntary expression.[53] None of these courses is entirely satisfactory, and perhaps there is no practical course that could be wholly so. The NLRB and courts in the United States have ultimately proceeded in the direction of the second and third possibilities. They have at least achieved the "result of taking provisions barren on their face and clothing them with life and meaning." [54] Unfortunately, the international community has no such organs to which this task can be delegated.

It is unlikely that the regulation of the conduct of negotiations on treaty termination will be subsequently developed in the way it has been developing in the United States. There are several reasons for this. First, in the world arena there are no permanent organs specialized to supervise at least the negotiation procedure (a truism that would hardly need to be mentioned if it were not for the ILC and writers who prescribe rules as if institutional decision makers would dispose of the conflict). The procedure of ad hoc conciliation commissions provided for in the Annex to the Convention becomes applicable in a rather late stage in the development of termination conflicts. Furthermore, the task of these commissions is mainly to help effect a substantive settlement of the dispute, and their competence to regulate the bargaining process outside of the conference room is not very clear. Even if the commissions assume such a competence, the convention does not specify any criteria for regulating the action-reaction process that usually characterizes termination controversies. It remains to be seen how this enormous task of both formulating general criteria and controlling particular conflicts can be achieved in practice by specially constituted ad hoc commissions. In addition, other important modifications, it has been pointed out, should be introduced into the convention's conciliation procedure before it can be effective in achieving substantive settlements of particular disputes. It should also be noted that the NLRB has worked well partly because there has been a court system over it

---

53. For a discussion of the dangers inherent in purposive interpretation when carried too far, see Fuller, "Positivism and Fidelity to Law—A Reply to Professor Hart," 71 *Harv. L. Rev.* 630, 671 (1957–58).

54. Smith, "The Evolution of the 'Duty to Bargain' Concept in American Law," 39 *Mich. L. Rev.* 1065, 1108 (1940–41).

that has been reviewing the standards set and practiced by the administrative organ.

Second, even if in the future some conflicts about termination might be settled within the conciliation commission or by adjudication or arbitration (an assumption that is by no means warranted), since the conflicts would be decided on their merits, there would usually be little point in consuming precious time with the more cumbersome bargaining process itself. These cases will therefore be of little use, if any, as precedents for the majority of other cases.

Third, because adjudication and arbitration in many cases are voluntary, and the commissions' reports themselves do not have the formal status of binding decision, it can be assumed that parties regarding these methods of settling a dispute desirable would not resort to the kind of tactics and practices that are sought to be regulated (at least not prior to the adjudicative or conciliatory decision.) Fourth, since third-party decision making usually brings up matters of relatively minor importance, the most difficult questions with regard to authorized strategies and practices would not arise in these cases. Threats, warnings, unilateral acts, moves while talks are taking place, preconditions, tie-ins, faits accomplis, etc., are used to a greater extent in critical conflicts, usually those related to treaties of power and security. These are so-called conflicts of "vital interest" which, as a rule, are not submitted to the judicial process. Yet these are the decisions the making of which involves a higher threat to minimum order. The conciliation commissions as currently conceived by the convention are inappropriately structured and insufficiently equipped to handle such crisis situations effectively. Since the regulation of bargaining on termination is not provided for in the Convention on the Law of Treaties, and since it can be predicted that it will not be substantially developed in the near future by the International Court, tribunals, or conciliation commissions, it will continue to be determined mainly by the actual practice of the parties.

We should not be overconcerned by this prospect. Even the per se violations and other authoritative requirements of the NLRB, for example, have actually been derived from common practice among the participants. The factual foundation of reciprocal dependence on which labor contracts and international agreements in general rest, supplies guidelines for rules that are generally lacking in private contracts where the contractors part permanently in a bitter litigational feud. Admittedly, while the NLRB, the United States courts, and the ILC (as the inclusion in the convention of the concept of "good faith" suggests) have sought guidelines for ideal bargaining, a great many norms to be extricated from current international reciprocal practices may be of a considerably different nature.

# 7   Unilateral Acts and Faits Accomplis

He that will believe all that they say, shall never be saved by
half that they do.

Shakespeare, *Anthony and Cleopatra*

We have seen that one reason why negotiation and adjudication
are not separated in Article 65 of the Convention on the Law of
Treaties is that its authors (and writers in general), preoccupied as
they were with the problem of abuse, did not wish to put much
stress on uninstitutionalized settlements. To do that would have
directly raised the involuntary question of termination by unilateral acts. If any conclusion may safely be drawn from Article
65, the accompanying ILC commentaries, and the debates in the
ILC and in the Vienna Conference, it is that while a standard
of conduct has not been advanced by them, the major emphasis
has been of a delimiting character. There seems to be complete
agreement on what the procedural provision would not do, but
not on what it would do. Article 65 does not authorize nonconsensual termination in case of a stalemate, nor does it require
that termination be effected only by a new agreement between
all parties.

At most the article indicates an intention to impose an indefinitely greater burden on the claimant party than on the
objecting side. The claimant is required to explain the grounds
upon which the claim is based, to submit a proposal, and to
specify a reasonable time for the reply of the other party or
parties. The objecting side is required only to raise an objection
within the specified time. Since the convention does not contain
policies relating to self-help enforcement measures and sanctions,
a party that has the power to bring about termination can content
itself with the convention. A party that has the power to force
compliance with the treaty can also justify the decision by the
convention. Both arguments will be equally well founded. Article

65 furnishes the parties with a convenient verbal justification for any decision, but not with policies to guide a decision.

## Various Acts in Termination

Obscurity in legal provisions is not always an anomaly that re-sults from mixed legislative motives or from analytical confusion. Some obscurity must inevitably exist in any legislation, since it aims to generalize policies. Furthermore, ambiguity may on occasion be a tactful and useful technique. What seems to be, in our case, a violation of the law of identity (an act cannot be both forbidden and authorized at the same time) is not necessarily a violation of the logic of life. A determination of whether "termination" should be authorized cannot be simply an affirma-tive or negative answer to the question in general; an appropriate response would involve broader considerations. A balance of the policies at stake should be made and related to a specific context. The context that must be taken into account is, of course, not merely or chiefly procedural but should include the whole setting of the problem. This context includes such components as the specific issues at stake, the validity of the claim, the power rela-tion of the parties, the time and crisis factors, and the ameliora-tion for the deprivatory effects of the decision.

To say that the "termination of agreements" is a variable con-cept, and that answers to the problem depend on a multitude of specific factors, is not to say that some level of generality in formulating the relevant policies can never be attained. After all, it is a minimum public-order policy that stability of expectations be maintained through authoritative principles. A rule-making behavior solely dependent on the context is not a rule at all. Contexts by definition vary. At the barest minimum one requires a statement of policy, a reference to the contexts, and a way of making these references empirical.[1] What may be required in the

1. The National Labor Relations Act, for example, addressing itself to a prob-lem the solution of which depends greatly on specific contexts, by requiring a "fair practice" has transferred the task of formulating particular rules from Con-gress to a more specialized agency. The complaint registered against the NLRB is not so much that its decisions are unfair, but that it has failed to develop gen-eral rules. The board in many decisions has addressed itself to the unique fea-tures of the individual situation, with the effect that attempts by parties to learn

articulation of formal principles and the clarification of common interests is not *the* rule or *the* answer to all situations, but answers more or less suitable to certain categories of decision.

This problem of good draftsmanship reveals, as no other problem can, the cooperative nature of the task of maintaining a public order. In international relations, national officials often assume the role of the competent decision makers in particular controversies, and if they are to discharge their responsibilities in this respect, the convention must not impose on them senseless and obscure tasks. The legislative draftsmen, in turn, must be able to anticipate rational and relatively stable modes of behavior and interpretation of their work, and cannot be preoccupied with the possibility of arbitrariness and abuse. This is only another aspect of the reciprocal dependence between what appear to be discrete decision functions.

The question of whether termination by unilateral acts should be expressly authorized is an embarrassing one for conscientious draftsmen. Their task is to formulate general policies, but a definite answer to this question depends so much on a complexity of particular contextual factors. However, whether clarity or open-ended vagueness is to be preferred in the language of a specific provision depends on the nature of the problem at hand. There are times when the relation between the activity in question and the legislative remedy is obvious. In commercial law, for example, requirements of fairness can take on definiteness of meaning from principles of conduct and commercial practice shared by a community of economic traders. The conduct required by law in certain other situations should be specified. In the regulation of treaty relations that concern matters of power and security, "fariness" assumes, if any, an altogether different meaning.

Good faith is not a substance or a discrete concept that one can find in a code or in behavior. In a most comprehensive sense it is a function of the expectations of effectiveness entertained about a process of decision. Insofar as parties believe that the

---

beforehand whether their case constitutes an unfair labor practice are not always successful. For this problem of good draftsmanship as related to the following discussion, see L. Fuller, *The Morality of Law* 63 (1964).

process—or a sector of it—is effective, they tend to take its formulated and unformulated norms seriously. Where expectations of effectiveness are low, good faith—broadly understood—is commensurately low. Hence the requirement of good faith of which jurists are so fond is the wrong place to begin to try to change behavior.

On the other hand, the frequent characterization of good faith as a state of mind is also distorted. In addition to the obvious psychological components, there are critical behavioral dimensions. In the process of reluctant negotiations, adversaries often stumble into perceptions of common interest, and the resulting agreements generate bona fides. From a policy standpoint it is important to remember that demands for negotiations in the most inauspicious circumstances can be manipulated and produce good faith.

In general, whenever the subject matter of a treaty requires a mutually profitable adjustment, as when cooperation is needed to achieve a greater production or wider distribution of the value concerned, no difficulties arise in this respect. The factual foundation of reciprocal dependence on which these treaties are based may provide definite and shared meaning to the concept of fairness, if referred to by authoritative provisions and studies. This is particularly true with regard to trade treaties. Authoritative studies in regard to such international agreements, however, are speciously clear. There seems to be the most complete agreement among authors in international law that treaties of commerce are subject to denunciation, withdrawal, or termination upon demand and reasonable notice, when they do not contain a provision regarding their duration or termination.[2]

Even regarding other types of treaties, the Convention on the Law of Treaties does not accord with the view (so fashionable among legal scholars during the 1930s) that they could lawfully be terminated only by a new agreement between the parties or following a declaration authorizing termination by an international tribunal. Nor does the convention support the opposite

2. McNair, *The Law of Treaties* 504 (1961). Waldock, (Sec.) *Report on the Law of Treaties*, [1963] 2 Y.B. Int'l L. Comm'n, at 36, 66(6), U.N. Doc. A/CN.4/SER.A/ 1963/Add.1. For the requirement of good faith in private law, see Kessler and Fine, *"Culpa In Contrahendo,* Bargaining In Good Faith, and Freedom of Contract: A Comparative Study," 77 *Harv. L. Rev.* 401 (1964).

view that it is unlawful for a party to enforce by unilateral sanctions treaty obligations whenever the other party claims that some legal grounds of termination or invalidity are applicable to the case. In other words, Article 65 does not force upon us the traditional either-or concept of unilateral termination. Such a notion, it has previously been observed, is unrealistic: it rests on assumptions that do not accord with modern conditions.

Perhaps the most important contribution of the convention to the enforcement and termination of treaties is that it does not refer at all to "unilateral termination." The convention is a clear authority for the terminable character of treaties, and for the view that something less than a new agreement between the parties or a decision of a tribunal is required for such a termination. Termination of an agreement, it may be recalled, can realistically be viewed only as a variable concept denoted by the list of interdependent subdecisions made by both parties in the course of a particular conflict. Indeed, in the similar situation of collective bargaining in the United States, the relevant legal provision has been developed by subsequent decisions into per se prohibitions of specific acts. The weakness of the convention is that it stops short of regulating at least some of the various acts that together constitute a conflict about termination (for example, the duty to negotiate, the topic for discussion, the problem of compensation, the lawfulness of certain unilateral acts, reprisals, retaliations).

## Notification After the Fact

That the authors of the convention, who could not agree on any specific measures in connection with termination and invalidity controversies, were intent at least on rejecting the traditional either-or distinction of unilateral and consensual termination, is evident from an examination of Article 65(5). This provision clearly treats unilateral termination as a temporary move, or a sequence of interdependent moves in the larger context of bargaining, and not as a final outcome.

### Article 65(5) of the Convention

Article 65(5) seems to provide for an exception to what is supposed to be a general rule that the claimant party should first notify the other parties, explaining the grounds upon which the claim is based, and should then wait at least three months for the other side's reply. Unlike the rest of Article 65, subsection 5 cannot be assailed on the ground that it is too vague to connote any definite idea. The exception is relatively clear, though it is at the same time broad enough to override the entire article and to give a definite, perhaps undesirable, meaning to the solution advanced by the convention. Subsection 5 is clear evidence that minimum order, strictly defined, was the sole consideration of the drafting of Article 65. It reads as follows:

> Without prejudice to article 45, the fact that a State has not previously made the notification prescribed in paragraph 1 shall not prevent it from making such notification in answer to another party claiming performance of the treaty or alleging its violation.[3]

This provision does not deal with noncompliance due to a special hardship or inconvenience, since cases of "special urgency" are explicitly dealt with in subsection 2. But to construe the above-quoted provision as applying to all situations and all kinds of agreements is to deplete Article 65 (1) altogether. To what situations, then, was the provision intended to apply? The phrases "party claiming performance of the treaty" and "alleging its violation" suggest that the primary reference is to *obligatory* treaty provisions rather than *executed* or territorial ones—to treaties not involving, for any of the parties, relatively consummated transactions like the conveyance of a territory, leases, and perhaps servitudes, and other agreements that have already been performed in whole or in part.[4]

Executed ("earned," "acquired," or "real") rights are species of property, and as usual in concepts of property law they rigorously draw upon black and white distinctions that would be out of place

---

3. Vienna Convention on the Law of Treaties, U.N. Doc. A/Conf.39/27 (1969) in 8 *Int'l L. Mat.* 679, 703 (1969).

4. The distinction between these two categories is one of degree, not of kind. Even the conveyance of territory projects some policies into the future, implying a pattern of conduct on the part of both parties with respect to the territory transferred. Like any distinction of degree, the executory-executed one is hard to maintain in some cases. Supra ch. 1, notes 37 and 40.

in most areas of law, including that of ordinary contract. The objection to the application of principles of termination such as the doctrine of rebus sic stantibus to executed treaty provisions [5] is based on policy consideration: to admit that consummated transactions can be affected by later changes in circumstances would expose territorial and other possessions to insecurity, and this insecurity would increase in direct proportion to the length of time in possession.

The executed international agreement has, however, an additional quality not shared by contracts and treaties in general. One difference between executed and obligatory rights relates to the way in which they are performed. Generally, compliance with the former is negative, consisting primarily of refraining from action. Once the agreement is performed, it does not require continuous positive action by the grantor state. Hence, the difference in the enforcement of these rights is that between deterrent and coercive diplomacy, with a mixture of deterring and compelling strategies in-between to suit treaty provisions of the mixed type and changing situations. By the same token, noncollaborative termination of the executed treaty provision can effectively be made only by an affirmative act of overt coercion.

Any termination of a treaty, when made against the will of the other party or parties, can be regarded as coercive, since it results in deprivation. But in the given situation, the coercion involved is far more excessive. In treaties that have already been performed, apart from the depriving effects of the termination, the means by which the decision can be carried out unilaterally necessarily involve a direct act of coercion, strictly defined. If the value preponderance is in the hands of one side, and the subject matter of the treaty is a strip of territory or a physical *res,* termination by means of self-help is usually limited to physical seizure. For the maintenance of peace, it is of course preferable not to encourage the party claiming termination to resort to coercive acts, physical or otherwise, and at any rate not before prior notification of the claim and the making of a proposal with the aim of reaching some sort of mutual understanding.

By the same token, Article 65 (5) seems to acquiesce in a fait

5. Ch. 1, notes 22 and 95 supra.

accompli, provided it is not made by an act of overt coercion. The provision does not state that in cases of obligatory treaty provisions a party need not comply with the requirements to make a prior notification justifying the claim and to submit a proposal, but only that noncompliance with these requirements would not have deprivational consequences on the claimant state. The difference, however, is only verbal, for the results are quite the same. If a party is allowed, after it has made a fait accompli, to invoke the grounds for termination in answer to a demand for performance or to a complaint alleging a violation, it is in fact allowed not only to bring about unilateral termination, but to do so without prior notification and the formal presentation of a claim.

While it may be conceded that, formally speaking, to "stop performance" is not exactly to "terminate" the treaty, in practice the effects of the two decisions (except in consummated transactions in which the decision involves a physical seizure or another coercive overt act) may be quite the same. It is true that after a fait accompli the parties are still bound to seek a solution through the pacific means indicated in Article 33 of the United Nations Charter, or may try to solve their dispute within a conciliation commission, so the decision could be formally regarded as one of suspension of the treaty rather than of final termination. However, a fait accompli of this sort changes the bargaining position of the parties and may decisively determine the final outcome of the dispute. Indeed, the phrase from Article 65(5) "in answer to another party alleging a violation of the treaty" suggests that a fait accompli, made before or during direct negotiation, is lawful if only the substantive grounds for termination of the treaty are later seriously invoked.

### The Fait Quasiment Accompli [6]

Since the Convention on the Law of Treaties does not really proscribe actual moves during bargaining on termination, even when they are not preceded by a notification, it is worthwhile to examine in this context some such instances.[7]

6. Where a party claims for its notification of a claim the presumably higher status of accomplished facts.

7. The main reasons that unilateral acts are inherent in conflicts about termina-

## Surprising the Opponent

Surprise is the most obvious advantage of a fait accompli, particularly when the timing is carefully calculated. The opponent may be found unprepared for immediate and decisive action. When the other side consists of a number of governments, as is common in treaties of power and security, they will usually need, before sharing a common front, to consult and to agree on the measures to be taken. This is by no means an easy task and may take quite some time at any rate. "Surprise" and "seizure of any opportunity" are usually (but not only) practiced by parties that are traditional opponents. To submit a prior notification of a demand for a change in the status quo in the context of traditionally adversarial parties, is clearly an invitation to warnings and threats from an adversary who may wish to stand firm against the demand. The best defense, of course, is to carry out the act before the threat is made, in which case there may be neither incentive nor commitment for retaliation.

Such were, for instance, the circumstances that led to the famous Declaration of London against the unilateral termination of international agreements discussed above. It was while taking advantage of the general preoccupation with the Franco-Prussian War of 1970 that Russia had begun to build a fleet in the Black Sea (contrary to some multilateral and bilateral treaty obligations). The official notification of the claim came only later. Forwarding a claim to termination instead of making the fait accompli could

---

tion have already been pointed out during the previous discussions of the mechanics of such conflicts (see chs. 4 and 5 supra). The present discussion deals only with the narrower problem of a party accomplishing, or pretending to have accomplished, facts before notifying the other side of its claim. The Soviet government, for instance, announced in 1918 through a radio proclamation "addressed to everybody" that the treaties of Brest-Litovsk were denounced. This announcement was regarded in 1925 by a German court as sufficient expression that the Soviet government regarded the treaty as abrogated and invalid. See S.E. v. G. and G. in Orfield and Re, *Cases and Materials on International Law* 83, 85 (1965). The Peace Treaties of Brest-Litovsk—by which Soviet Russia had to surrender a great part of the population and agricultural land of tsarist Russia— were forced upon the Bolsheviks by the German High Command (F. Iklé, *Every War Must End* 75 [1971]). A short time later Germany was forced to conclude peace with the Allies on similar terms. It was clear in 1925 that similar denunciations by Germany would have to be made in the near future.

have, under the circumstances, resulted in direct negotiations and, perhaps, in a new agreement among the parties. But an agreed solution, if not also the start of talks, could have been delayed until after the temporary crisis between two of the other signatory powers had ended. Prussia had no immediate interest in the neutralization of the Black Sea, and France, already engaged in a war in which she was eventually defeated, was not in a position to react militarily. The chances that Britain alone would attempt to enforce the treaty provisions were indeed nil. The time for the denunciation, then, was tactfully chosen. The British and French, not being then in a position to reverse the fait accompli, could only accept the decision, and, of course, reaffirm their confidence in the sanctity of treaties in regard to the future.[8]

### Dropping the Initiative

A fait accompli usually changes the roles the parties assume in bargaining situations. The purpose of the tactic may be to force the other side to make the initial claim or demand. Typically, there is a difference between when a party has to initiate a claim and when it has to contend with a counterclaim. The difference is in timing, in who has to make an offensive move, and in whose initiative is put to the test. Often, the purpose of unilateral acts is to maneuver into a new status quo position from which one can be dislodged only by an overt act precipitating mutual damage. By performing a fait accompli the party may condition its course of action on what the other side does. It may therefore transfer the actual decision to use violence to the other side, and evade the direct responsibility for escalating the conflict, making the outcome depend mainly on the opponent's decision. The objecting side is left with a narrow alternative decision: to acquiesce in the fait accompli, or to try to reverse it by means of some coercive action. It may benefit more by choosing the former.[9]

Furthermore, the side that put forward a claim is required, formally, and usually also by third-party pressure, to make an attempt at persuasion before committing a coercive act on the

8. See pp. 27 and 80 supra.

9. See T. Schelling, *The Strategy of Conflict* 137–38 (1963). For a discussion along these lines of the Cuban quarantine of 1962 and the erection of the Berlin Wall in 1961, see Lipson, "Castro on the Chessboard of the Cold War," in *Cuba and The United States* 178, 193 (Plank ed. 1967).

alleged violator of the treaty. Currently, the only claims for changes in the status quo that receive the serious consideration of the international community are those involving threats to peace. Procedures for effecting changes are generally considered in terms of such threats rather than in terms of the material needs of the particular states and the validity of their claims.[10] The pressures applied by third-party governments and international organizations to the parties to particular disputes are usually concerned with the immediate preservation of minimum order. They are, therefore, directed mainly at the party on whose initiative the outburst of violence appears to depend.

In 1947 Egypt brought its claim for the termination of the British military bases in the Suez Canal Zone before the United Nations Security Council (this was the first time a claim based on the principles of rebus sic stantibus and unequal treaties was put forward there). The British view was that the case did not involve any threat to international peace and security unless Egypt itself intended to break the peace, instead of accepting the provisions of the treaty which were binding on it. This view was widely accepted among the council's members and the issue was shelved.[11] Only after guerrilla warfare in the Canal Zone did the parties reach an explicit agreement on withdrawing the troops. A similar Tunisian complaint to the Security Council regarding the French military base at Bizerta was shelved in 1952, but in 1961, after violence had erupted, another complaint brought about a prompt General Assembly resolution favoring the Tunisian claim.[12]

Whether it is intended or otherwise, one gain of a party that performs a fait accompli is to shift the initiative for the resumption of direct talks or the resort to adjudication to the other side. The International Court has generally declined to decide treaty termination cases on various grounds unrelated to the merits of the disputes. The party in the position of countering a claim may expect, therefore, to win the dispute, or at least the judicial match, by

---

10. See F. Dunn, *Peaceful Change* 12 (1937).

11. Briggs, "Rebus Sic Stantibus Before the Security Council," 43 *Am. J. Int'l L.* 762, 764 (1949); p. 147 supra.

12. App. B, note 5 infra. R. Higgins, *The Development of International Law Through the Political Organs of U.N.* 344 (1963); Lester, "Bizerta and the Unequal Treaty Theory," 11 *Int'l & Comp. L. Q.* 847 (1962).

default of the court.[13] Besides, delays in answering correspondence before and during negotiations or adjudication, evasions in the form of negotiations about the desired procedure for settling the dispute (for example, whether to call the procedure "direct negotiations" or merely "discussions," whether to employ arbitration or a conciliation commission), and delays due to the conduct of talks about talks (the agenda, preconditions) usually operate to the disadvantage of the party initiating the claim. The longer the lapse of time from the alleged violation, the harder it is for the party demanding the performance of the treaty to justify a coercive act in the enforcement of the treaty.

Furthermore, during the interval the parties may have to go about their business as usual. Conditions may change and relationships, in general, may develop. Two years later an ad hoc conciliation commission may perhaps be established to review the past violation. After another year more or less, this commission may issue a report recommending, perhaps, that the parties restore the status quo ante. Will the commission's decision accomplish anything at this late date? The outcome previously achieved in the course of effective tacit bargaining is likely to be more viable than a legal document of dubious formal validity and addressed to a situation that is three or four years old.[14] Besides, at this late date the originally objecting party would still face the decision whether to commit resources and try to enforce the commission's report. By that time, however, the opponent would have to be asked to reverse what he has already accomplished instead of merely to stop the transgression in which he is engaged. The first is a more ambitious objective for coercive strategy and may require greater pressures to achieve.[15] The situation favors the party that is confronted with countering a claim, since it may win by default if the other party does not act immediately.

### The Tactic of the "Final Decision"

A maneuver into a fait accompli may supply a government with a commitment not to concede in negotiation. The aim may be to

13. Ch. 6 supra.

14. For a similar situation in collective bargaining see p. 180 supra.

15. A. George, D. Hall, and W. Simons, *The Limits of Coercive Diplomacy* 22–23 (1971).

make a seemingly irreversible maneuver, the effects of which are the reduction of the government's own freedom of choice and the renunciation of its own alternatives. Parties in international negotiations are not unitary decision makers. Other governments, domestic politics, internal governmental branches, bureaucratic differences within the executive branch, the public, personal motivations, and other factors alike, influence the parties' objectives and negotiating tactics. Since a government must continuously deal with these influences and obstacles, it must, if it can, arrange to make any retreat in negotiations dramatically visible. In this way the government places its reputation and effectiveness in jeopardy, and thereby becomes visibly incapable of serious concessions.

The conflict between the United States and France concerning the removal of American military bases and installations from French territory, along with NATO's council and headquarters, is instructive. The French demand was presented in the form of a fait accompli, but in this particular case it was impossible for France to make a fait accompli in any true sense. France, in the case of the bases, could not unilaterally and without previously submitting an official notification of the claim, fulfill its demand (i.e. territorial or executed rights). Such a decision would have required a forceful eviction of the bases, an act unthinkable in the case of friendly nations and dangerous in the case of hostile ones. The only way open to the French government was to forward to the United States a demand for the immediate removal of the bases and to NATO a demand to transfer its headquarters. Nevertheless, the French government managed to achieve the effect of a commitment not to reconsider and compromise, by presenting the notification not in the form of a claim to termination but in the form of a "decision" of termination. To support this appearance of finality, the French government refused to enter into negotiations on the question of termination. In other words, the French government, though it was the claimant party in the dispute, maneuvered itself by an act of *fait quasiment accompli* into the typical position of an objecting side.[16]

16. Sometimes negotiation cannot be dispensed with. In the Franco-American dispute, negotiation still had to be conducted, at least on incidental matters such as transportation of withdrawing troops, the gradual relocation of installations,

The fact that it is difficult for a government to change a decision that has already been made and supposedly implemented, may provide that government with an extra incentive to resist the opponent's pressures. The usual noisy reactions to denunciations, breaches, and violations of international agreements also assure the required publicity and incitement for such a commitment. Governments which, while ceasing to perform a treaty, still desire to leave the door open for a change in their initial position or a reversal of their decision following further bargaining or negotiation, may wish to cloak the repudiation in secrecy. This partly explains why it is common practice for parties to fail to forward an official notification of their decision to cease performance of a treaty to the other side. Often, the objecting side too, for similar considerations, does not forward an official demand for performance or an official complaint alleging a violation of the treaty obligations.

Bringing the controversy out into the open may commit the contending governments to irreversible positions and invite pressures upon them to expand the dispute by way of overt acts and reprisals. While the French demand for the removal of the bases and headquarters cannot be said to fall within the exception of Article 65(5), the same dispute involved the termination of other agreements that did fall within the exception and on which both parties at the time of the termination preferred to remain silent. Since this matter concerns the process by which termination controversies expand and include other treaty terminations, it will be discussed more fully in the following chapter. It suffices here to note that Article 65 (5) according to which the parties, in ceasing to fulfill an obligation, may dispense with a prior notification of their claim, may serve precisely this function of helping the parties to preserve the alternatives by not committing themselves in advance to too rigid a position.

---

and the storage of equipment that would be left behind. But the conduct of negotiation between the parties could undermine the French insistence that their decision was final. For two whole days the fifteen foreign ministers of NATO's nations were engaged unsuccessfullly in trying to resolve this problem. Another aspect of the same tactic is discussed at p. 123 supra.

# 8 Response to Violations

Once a claimant party undertakes to resolve a termination controversy, the enhanced probability we have seen is that the conflict will expand laterally and will include the termination of other agreements. Some of the difficulties in this respect might be reduced if these disputes were settled within an institutionalized framework. But the International Court, arbitration tribunals, and also the new procedure of conciliation commissions, as they are currently employed in international relations, are not conducive to the resolution of conflicts about termination. For similar and other reasons, the efforts of international organizations to influence the outcome of many of these conflicts have also been comparatively unsuccessful. The hopes for much-needed reforms in third-party resolution of termination controversies lie in the future; meanwhile the vast majority of these disputes will continue to be settled through bargaining. It is, therefore, increasingly important to consider the more immediate problem of how to keep the conduct of such conflicts within reasonable bounds.

## THE CONTAGIOUS SPREAD OF TREATY VIOLATIONS

Not only do conflicts about termination expand, but the spin-off process, for reasons discussed before, often progresses more by way of unilateral acts than by way of direct negotiations and formal agreements.[1] A number of similar practices took place before and after the 1966 French decision, discussed above, to withdraw from NATO's military organization and to demand the removal of American military bases from France. This dispute offers a good example of mixed talk-move negotiations. It is also of particular interest because of the parties' strong common interest and, consequently, their common desire to avoid uncovering the existence of a severe conflict of interests. No question of threats of violent action was involved, partly because the conflicting parties were politically and ideologically allied in an outer

1. Ch. 5 supra.

directed association, which came into being expressly as the result of an anticipated threat from a common external enemy. Moreover, there were no visible inhibitions on the conduct of direct talks, since NATO's council and other political and military departments of the organization are permanent organs in which both parties were represented and in which discussions were continuously taking place. Other members of the alliance had to be seriously taken into consideration by the parties, since they actively participated in the dispute or, alternatively, played the role of the mediator. Yet, despite the availability of an institutionalized communications system, attempts at formal agreement failed. The conflict was mainly resolved by unilateral moves and countermoves.

Faced with a 1962 unilateral decision which had replaced the American policy of "constant nuclear retaliation" with a new one of "flexible and controlled response," and which they had allegedly sought unsuccessfully to change for almost two years, the French resorted to unilateral decisions of their own. In 1964, French naval units were withdrawn from allied forces in the Atlantic and the English Channel. At the same time, French naval officers were recalled from NATO's integrated command. The French move hinged on a single issue, the United States' new strategic doctrine: "We have protested and we have withdrawn our forces from military maneuvers that were too obviously based on this new theory." [2]

The limitation of the French maneuver to naval forces was significant. A nuclear naval force is an all-important factor in a military strategy that is founded upon massive nuclear retaliation as a deterrent. A mobile system of retaliatory nuclear forces in general, and a fleet of atomic submarines in particular, is difficult to detect and hence provides a striking force that is less vulnerable to surprise attack. It therefore produces the maximum of deterrent effect, since the power of the attacked nation to strike back cannot be eliminated.[3] Indeed, the French government itself had had prior plans for the production of atomic-powered submarines

2. Statement of Premier Pompidou to the French National Assembly in *New York Times*, Apr. 21, 1966, p. 7, col. 1 (late city ed.). This was his answer to U.S. and internal opposition charges earlier in the debate that France had withdrawn from NATO without attempting to negotiate with the United States.

3. H. Kissinger, *The Necessity for Choice* 15, 24, 119 (1961).

equipped with intermediate range missiles. By withdrawing its naval forces from the integrated allied command, it emphasized a determination to pursue a separate and independent nuclear retaliatory strategy.

This French maneuver was followed by increased pressures, or rather what appear in retrospect to be punitive measures, on the part of the United States. In November 1964, the United States government refused to comply with a bilateral agreement, entered into in 1959, to provide France with enriched uranium [4] needed for the operation of a French submarine reactor. Even a cursory textual examination of this treaty reveals that the United States decision to cease performance could easily be justified as being lawful.[5] Yet, when pressed by French officials to give an explanation for the decision, United States officials refrained from stating specific grounds except for a vague and unofficial reference to "over-all developments" within NATO.[6] It seems that the objective sought by the United States was not the final termination of the agreement but to press the French government to acquiesce, without loss of face, in the new NATO strategy.[7]

4. Agreement with France for Cooperation on the Use of Atomic Energy for Mutual Defense Purposes, May 7, 1959, 10 *U.S. Treaties & Other Int'l Agreements*, V. 2, at 1279 (hereafter referred to as the *Uranium Agreement*). Up to November 1964, when performance under the agreement ceased, the United States had delivered about one-third of the quantity agreed upon.

5. Article 1 of the *Uranium Agreement* stated: "[T]he United States will transfer by sale to . . . France agreed amounts of [enriched uranium] . . . provided that the government of the United States determines that such transfers will promote, and will not constitute an unreasonable risk to, its defense and security." Article 4(c) stated: "The enriched uranium . . . shall be used by . . . France exclusively in the development and operation of a land based prototype submarine nuclear propulsion plant in the preparation or implementation of defense plans in the mutual interests of the two countries." The very fact that the United States government decided not to comply with the agreement meant that it considered the French plan as not being in the mutual interests of the two countries.

6. As alleged by the French government in a later phase of the dispute. *New York Times*, Apr. 17, 1966, p. 24, col. 6 (late city ed.). In order to justify its decision by the terms of the *Uranium Agreement,* the United States government had to invoke conflict of interests within the alliance, which constituted "unreasonable risk" to its defense (note 5 supra). But to make such an argument was to support France's claim that the then existing defense arrangements posed unreasonable risks both to the United States and to its European allies.

7. At the effective date of the *Uranium Agreement,* France had begun the construction of a separation plant to produce enriched uranium. In April 1966 (18 months after the breach of the agreement) the plant was still not completed.

The effects were quite the reverse. The supply of enriched uranium, and other items of military aid, were regarded in France as the quid pro quo for the land and other facilities made available for exclusive American military use in France.[8] It is probable that the demand for the removal of the bases would have been made anyway, though the timing might have been different if the United States had continued to honor its commitment. In fact, the French were the first to make public the refusal of the United States to comply with the Uranium Agreement, but only more than a year after the decision had been made, and when the crisis within NATO had already reached new heights.[9] The late disclosure of the incident, together with the demand for the termination of the agreements concerning the bases, was aimed at showing that faits accomplis in the form of noncompliance, repudiation, and termination of agreements were in fact mutually practiced, and that indeed the process had been initiated by the other side.

The accusations of outright repudiations of agreements and the resort to faits accomplis were, indeed, mutually made. Observe, for example, the following statement by Sulzberger in the *New York Times,* written in the midst of the conflict regarding the military bases in France and when the outcome of the dispute still seemed to be undetermined:

> France also contends it remains in NATO but is simply quitting its integrated military organization. American diplomats complain sourly: "De Gaulle is in NATO when it comes to making mischief and out of NATO when it comes to obligations."
>
> Legal problems aren't going to matter in the end because legal niceties have already been coldly disregarded by Paris. Thus, for example, on December 8, 1958, the U.S.A. signed with de Gaulle's Government a "System of Communications Agreement" valid for the duration of NATO unless both

8. See generally M. Ball, *NATO and the European Union Movement* 89–90 (1959); Ismay, *NATO, The First Five Years, 1949–1954,* 134–35 (1955).

9. The French government announced the United States' refusal to comply with the agreement in April 1966, after it had forwarded its claim for the removal of the American military bases. The announcement also stressed that there was no French request pending for United States fuel pursuant to the agreement. *New York Times,* supra note 6, p. 1, col. 4.

signatories desired modification or one gave a year's advance notice of a wish to change its terms. Such advance notice wasn't presented, but France unilaterally voided the agreement.[10]

It so happened, then, that each party was the alleged victim of the other's "mischief." And though—to use the wording of Article 65 of the Convention on the Law of Treaties—notifications of claims to termination were dispensed with, and "claims for performance" and "complaints on violation" had usually not been officially submitted, each party was delighted, when the appropriate time came, to indicate to the public how it was victimized by the other side's fait accompli. Indeed, a leak about an unknown treaty violation often gets more public attention than an open confrontation.

### Mitigating Damages from a Breach

#### Articles 42(2) and 60

The lateral expansion of conflicts about termination is a common phenomenon. The Franco-American dispute itself included several other terminations that have not been mentioned in the present discussion. So also, most of the other disputes discussed in this book have included more than the mere termination of the treaty initially at stake. Such action-reaction patterns that escalate conflicts of termination seem to run afoul of traditional international norms. For example, Article 42(2) of the Convention on the Law of Treaties states:

> The termination of a treaty, its denunciation or the withdrawal of a party, may take place only as a result of the application of the provisions of the treaty or of the present Convention. The same rule applies to suspension of the operation of a treaty.[11]

The first approximation in the convention to the process of mutual unilateral acts, reprisals, and retaliations is the principle

---

10. Sulzberger, "Foreign Affairs: Alliance Against Itself," *New York Times,* June, 8, 1966, p. 40, cols. 4–5 (late city ed.).

11. U.N. Doc. A/Conf.39/27 (1969), in 8 *Int'l Legal Mat.* 679, 696 (1969).

that a party may terminate or suspend the operation of a treaty as a consequence of *its* breach by the other side. Article 60 of the convention states:

1. A material breach of a bilateral treaty by one of the parties entitles the other to invoke the breach as a ground for terminating the treaty or suspending its operation in whole or in part.

2. A material breach of a multilateral treaty by one of the parties entitles:

(a) the other parties by unanimous agreement to suspend the operation of the treaty in whole or in part or to terminate it either:

(i) in the relations between themselves and the defaulting State, or

(ii) as between all the parties;

(b) a party specially affected by the breach to invoke it as a ground for suspending the operation of the treaty in whole or in part in the relations between itself and the defaulting State;

(c) any party other than the defaulting State to invoke the breach as a ground for suspending the operation of the treaty in whole or in part with respect to itself if the treaty is of such a character that a material breach of its provisions by one party radically changes the position of every party with respect to the further performance of its obligations under the treaty.

3. A material breach of a treaty, for the purposes of this article, consists in:

(a) a repudiation of the treaty not sanctioned by the present Convention; or

(b) the violation of a provision essential to the accomplishment of the object or purpose of the treaty.[12]

The combination of Article 42(2) and Article 60 is deceptively simple. According to the ILC Commentary to draft Article 60:

12. Id. at 701 (subsections 4 and 5 are omitted). See generally, B. Sinha, *Unilateral Denunciation of Treaty Because of Prior Violations of Obligations by Other Party* (1966); Bilder, "Breach of Treaty and Response Thereto," 1967 *Am.*

"A violation of a treaty obligation, as of any other obligation, may give rise to a right in the other party to take non-forcible reprisals, and these reprisals may properly relate to the defaulting party's rights under the treaty." [13] Despite this reference to reprisals, it seems more proper to regard Article 60 only as an instrument for mitigating one's damages in particular cases rather than as the authorization of strategic means for preserving treaties in general. To be sure, the right embodied in Article 60 may usually deter a party from committing some minor treaty violations. Most conflicts about termination occur, however, when the parties' interests in the given treaty's allocation of values are unbalanced, i.e. when the agreement operates to the clear disadvantage of the claimant party. This is a situation in which a party that repudiates some of the treaty provisions might still profit even though its opponent retaliates by terminating part or all of the same treaty. In such a case, a party's right to terminate the agreement because of the other side's repudiation, if considered in isolation from other possible steps, cannot deter the latter from committing a breach.

The provisions quoted above are therefore incomplete. They approach the problem as though the parties were lone passengers occupying one cabin for one voyage only. Effective answers to the problem described above are generally found in the arsenal of weapons available to the parties outside of the treaty in dispute. For the parties' common interest in a treaty usually embraces more than their interest in the immediate arrangement it contains. A particular breach, therefore, may generally not be worthwhile because it may engender serious reprisals in other bargains. Parties may often be willing to lose on a particular issue because they perceive that their gains from existing and future international cooperation are greater than the losses they suffer on a particular occasion.

---

Soc. Int'l L. 193. Schwelb, "Termination or Suspension of the Operation of a Treaty as a Consequence of its Breach," 7 Indian J. Int'l L. 309 (1967); Esgain, "The Spectrum of Responses to Treaty Violations," 26 Ohio St. L.J. 1 (1965).

13. [1966] 2 Y.B. Int'l L. Comm'n, at 253–54, U.N. Doc. A/CN. 4/SER.A/1966/ Add. 1. But see Briggs, "Unilateral Denunciation of Treaties, The Vienna Convention and the International Court of Justice," 68 Am. J. Int'l L. 51, 56 (1974).

In other words, conflict escalation is more likely to occur when the claimant party has more interest in the terms of a particular treaty than in certain other treaties with the same party or parties. Efforts to lessen the damage from conflict expansion should be designed to affect one or the other side of the scale. They should either develop some means of continuous appraisal and revision of treaties so that particular treaties in themselves have more to offer to both sides, or they should strengthen the procedural techniques of conflict resolution and stabilize the parties' choices during particular conflicts so as to make them less threatening to, and less disruptive of, general relations. The two objectives are complementary, and as we shall see, any criterion for connecting the response to a treaty violation other than that of the treaty itself, must have direct bearing on the revision or termination of the so-called unequal treaties.

It is doubtful whether this purpose of reducing the harmful effects of the expansion of conflicts can be achieved by outlawing all terminations that do not conform to the present articles on the law of treaties (Article 42[2]), while restricting the reprisals and retaliations against lawlessness to the "defaulting parties' rights under the treaty" (Article 60). This solution is unrealistic. It requires a party who is victimized by the other party's defiance of the code supposedly to retaliate by strictly adhering to the violated code. Suppose a party, on the ground of changes in circumstances, repudiates an agreement in clear violation of Article 62 of the convention (for example, termination of an executed provision). It may do so because direct enforcement of the agreement by the other side is impossible or too expensive, and retaliation within the same agreement is unfeasible. Why should the objecting side in these circumstances not retaliate and repudiate some other agreement in violation of Article 60? The violation of an obligation of a multilateral treaty on the law of treaties cannot be said to require a response different from the violation of any other treaty obligation.

Should the legal right of reprisals of low coercion be broadened to include the retaliatory repudiation of certain agreements other than the one initially at issue? Indeed, the authority for the broadening of this right may be found not only in the practice of states but also, as we shall soon see, in the writings of some well-reputed scholars. Even if this is rejected, for various policy reasons, as the basic tool for a normative theory (for instance, such a theory may erroneously be considered disadvantageous to small states), it is still of pragmatic importance in descriptive studies. And from a descriptive standpoint it makes little difference whether Article 60 is broadened or not. The problems inherent in this article permeate the fundamental problem of the relation between authority and control. The mutuality of benefits, reprisals, and retaliations are the fundamental empirical facts upon which, in the final analysis, important international norms must rest in order to be effective. A norm that ignores or purports to change these facts without coordinate changes in control allocation is simply not enforceable.

Although the current formulation of Articles 42(2) and 60 seemed to enjoy the support of most participants in the Vienna Conference, their commitment to observe these articles in particular interactions is just not credible. Some unenforceable commitments are credible and may reasonably be effective. Others are not. Commitments to make certain cooperative choices regardless of what the other side does lack credibility because a party would ordinarily expect an adversary to protect itself, or resort to compensatory retaliation, if faced with consistently competitive responses. Moreover, one should not expect a party to commit itself unconditionally to either cooperative or competitive choices, even if he intends to be consistently cooperative or competitive, for such a step will reduce the effectiveness of his strategy.[14]

### Broadening the Criteria for Authorization of Reprisals

The source of the gap between these normative directives and everyday wisdom lies quite obviously in a concentration of the norms on formal structure to the neglect of the purposive activity this structure is assumed to organize. This focus on the treaty itself rather than on some other criterion for the authorization of

14. See generally Radlow and Weidner, "Unenforced Commitments in 'Cooperative' and 'Noncooperative' Non-constant-sum Games," 10 *J. Conflict Resolution* 497, 498 (1966); R. Braithwaite, *Theory of Games as a Tool for the Moral Philosopher* 32 (1963).

reprisals and retaliations is arbitrary.[15] It is influenced by the simple and overplayed fact that the treaty initially in dispute usually provides the clearest point for expectations to converge.

The main problem in bargaining on termination is how to broaden the dispute while at the same time keeping it within reasonable limits. Any kind of general restraint on the conduct of conflicts requires some distinctive forms of restraint, i.e. conventional stopping places or dividing lines that can be easily recognized by both sides and will indicate to them what is within and what is out of bounds. The treaty in dispute is an obvious place to draw the line. There is, of course, no material or tactical reason to treat a reprisal "outside" the treaty differently from a reprisal "within" the treaty. Symbolically, however, there is a difference— not just one of degree but of kind.

Traditionally, people regard a reprisal outside the treaty as a new initiative and not as just more of the same activity. There is, therefore, some danger that once the parties depart from the treaty, the stopping places or the dividing lines will be lost. It will be up to each party to choose separately which congeries of events and objects should be considered as a unit for the purpose of working out what should essentially be implied exchange relationships.

15. Article 60 seems to entitle the innocent party to terminate or suspend the treaty in whole or in part, even though the subject matter of the terminated or denounced treaty is quite unrelated to the violated one. Similarly, Article 44 ("Separability of treaty provisions") does not require that responses to violations of multilateral treaties be restricted to those provisions affected by or reasonably related to the violation. Independent provisions relating to different subject matters may also serve as the basis for retaliation. With respect to this matter Article 60 conflicts with the opinions of other modern authorities on the subject (see Sinha, supra note 12, at 207, 208, 214–15). In a report to the Security Council on the Arab-Israeli armistice agreements of 1949, the Secretary-General of the United Nations states: "As a matter of course, each party considers its compliance with the stipulations of an Armistice Agreement as conditioned by compliance of the other party to the Agreement. Should such a stand be given the interpretation that any one infringement of the provisions of the Agreement by one party justifies reactions by the other party which, in their turn, are breaches of the Armistice Agreement, without any limitation as to the field within which reciprocity is considered to prevail, it would in fact mean that the armistice regime could be nullified by a single infringement by one of the parties. Although such an interpretation has never been given from responsible quarters, it appears to me that a lack of clarity has prevailed" (Doc. S/3596, U.N. SCOR, Supp., 723d Meeting, 11th year, 1956, p. 6; also quoted in Sinha, supra note 12, at 199).

Common criteria (other than the one already set by the contested treaty) for a legitimate *relation* between the reaction and the original action (for example, the subject matter of the treaty) are not amenable to a simple definition. Violations of the right to take some kind of reprisals outside the treaty, therefore, will not be easily discerned. Too broad a definition of the right to take reprisals, or the improper use of an inexact one—the argument may go—will in themselves trigger retaliations. The effects of such an explicit rule may be the opposite of what it is intended to achieve: it may contribute to the expansion of termination conflicts.

To this a number of responses should be made. Most importantly, since the present formulation of the rule is unrealistic, its effects may indeed be to promote exactly what it seeks to prevent. There are times when, though a party would like to conform to the formalities of the law of treaties and to avoid the unexpected, it has to abandon them, risk misunderstanding, and insist on other rules, because the convention is too restrictive in the choices it offers. Since departing from the treaty originally in dispute also means breaking the general principles of the law of treaties and the rules of a universal convention clearly applicable to the conflict situation, it becomes more dramatic. Indeed, governments that protest to the other side about violation of the rules frequently retaliate by repudiating *another* treaty, precisely because this can be clearly seen as a refusal to abide by the rules. The rules in this situation are not insignificant. Sometimes they become disproportionately conspicuous precisely because they are not observed. They serve as a symbol for the enlargement of the conflict situation. And since retaliation does in reality go beyond the scope of the treaty initially in dispute,[16] the only remaining question is how to make the dynamics of the ensuing conflict-escalation reasonably understood and therefore more predictable.

Unfortunately, legal writers who do allow for retaliations in other treaties do not agree on the exact nature of such a right. Moreover, none of the criteria suggested by them seems to fulfill

16. For a fascinating description relating to the contagious spread of violations of IATA's agreements and resolutions in response to violations initiated by one or few airlines, see K. Pillai, *The Air Net*, chs. 5–6 (1969).

the primary purpose for regulating reprisals and retaliations. According to one view, which is expressed by Vattel, the injured party "may, on the breach of one treaty by the other party, threaten him with a renunciation, on his own part, of all the other treaties by which they are united,—and may put his threats in execution if the other disregards them." [17] A different view is expressed by McNair, who maintains that the breach of one treaty gives rise to a right to abrogate another only in special circumstances, in which "it [is] possible to show that of two separate treaties each was the consideration for the other and that they were intended to be interdependent." [18] The former view, while adequate for the relatively limited international relations of Vattel's time, is too sweeping and disruptive of the currently more complicated and interdependent treaty relationships. The latter, modeled as it is on the English municipal doctrine of consideration, is perhaps suitable to isolated contractual relations between individuals, but is too restrictive for international relations, in which interdependence usually means something more than a single commercial transaction. Moreover, underlying this doctrine is the assumption that what was true yesterday will also be true tomorrow. Time as a factor is ignored, except for time past. For while it is possible that a particular bargain may be struck with a view of true and self-contained reciprocity, its termination

17. E. de Vattel, *The Law of Nations; or, the Principles of the Law of Nature* 214–15 (J. Chitty ed. 1854). This view is also expressed by writers, like Kelsen and Oppenheim, who maintain the traditional division of retaliations into retorsion and reprisals (ch. 9 infra).

18. A. McNair, *The Law of Treaties* 571 (1961). But see the case of the Russo-Dutch loan discussed id. at 557–65, in which the British government rejected attempts at the Commons to link two different subject matters even when contained in the same treaty. It is noteworthy that adherence by writers to the principle embodied in Article 60 of the convention does not necessarily mean that they exclude the possibility of lawful reprisal by the termination or denunciation of a separate treaty. The rule, as more precisely stated, is that an innocent party should not be compelled to perform its obligations under a treaty violated by the other party or parties (see, e.g., Sinha, supra note 12, at 40). Unlike McNair, most writers state this rule without any mention of the broader question of reprisals outside the treaty. Many writers seem to regard as lawful the termination of a treaty in reprisal for the violation or termination of another treaty, but discuss the matter under the general rubric relating to sanctions of international law. For the impact of such an approach, see ch. 9, infra. What makes the convention so restrictive is the combination of Articles 42(2) and 60.

or violation may later be sought precisely because changes in various conditions make such reciprocity unattainable, and a response in kind within the limits of the original bargain, impossible.

If a retaliatory reaction to the violation of a treaty is to be effective, it should exploit the broader reciprocal interests of the parties at the time of the breach. As will be further explained, room ought to be made in any strategy of this sort for the positive, or "carrot," aspect of reciprocity. Not only explicit offers, but also reciprocal acts conferring unilateral benefits may add a positive dimension to the usual behavior of negative quid pro quo. Even where the emphasis is put on negative reciprocity, it should not mean that any dispute about the validity of a particular treaty should necessarily endanger all treaties between the parties. Reciprocity between governments, even in time of war, usually assumes particular and concrete forms. It implies by definition the setting of self-imposed limitations on the parties' conflict behavior. Seldom, and perhaps only in matters of physical survival, do reciprocal punishments encompass all possible relations between the participants (for example, nuclear deterrent).

### CONTAINING THE FLAREUP THROUGH RETORSION

Reciprocal limitations are set by doing to the other side something analogous to what he had done himself. Accordingly, the test for the lawfulness of reprisals of low coercion should be whether a particular response—be it the termination of other provisions of the same treaty, or of the provisions of a separate one—is qualitatively and quantitatively identical to or approximates the alleged misdeed judged in terms of the particular benefits deprived or at stake.

There is much to be said in favor of connecting the repudiation of a new treaty to the treaty initially at stake. As Schelling states:

To relate the reaction to the original action, to impose a pattern on events, probably helps to set limits and bounds. It shows a willingness to accept limits and bounds. It avoids abruptness and novelty of a kind that might startle and excessively confuse an opponent. It maintains a sense of communication, of diplomatic contact, of a desire to be understood rather than misunderstood. It helps an opponent in understanding one's motive, and provides him a basis for judging what to expect as the consequences of his own actions. It helps the opponent to see that bad behavior is punished and good behavior is not, if that is what one wants him to see; unconnected actions, actions chosen at random, might not seem to follow a sequence of cause and effect. In case the opponent might think that one is avoiding the issue, turning aside and pretending not to notice, the direct connection between action and response helps to eliminate the possibility of sheer coincidence and makes the one appear the consequence of the other.[19]

These efforts at continuity become even more necessary whenever formal, recognized stopping points are being obliterated by the parties. When a party depreciates the value of the formal treaty, it must pay more attention to the creation of other recognizable stages and stopping points, lest the conflict overexpand.

The cases discussed throughout this study suggest an important point. Governments do feel obligated to embody coherence and pattern in their actions during the execution of termination conflicts and to explain their actions verbally in terms of such specific patterns. (This is a conservative requirement for establishing a customary international norm on a particular matter. The more liberal views require only what amounts to a discernible pattern of interaction.) They communicate by deeds rather than by words, by responding in similar language, and by keeping material things in the same medium of exchange. Coherence in this respect is not always the same thing as economic relevance; it is determined by the symbolic pattern of the set of actions that is formed and that goes simultaneously with the general and abstract cooperative or competitive relationship between the parties.

In the aforementioned Franco-American dispute, the French government was indeed making a connection, in other words, molding its reaction to suit the thing it was complaining against,

19. T. Schelling, *Arms and Influence* 149–150 (1966). He observes that such behavior amounts to observance of rules. See p. 263ff. infra for an analysis of legal criteria.

when it withdrew only its naval forces from integrated command arrangements that were allegedly based on the United States' new nuclear strategy. The United States was maintaining this connection when it suspended the performance of a treaty and stopped the supply of enriched uranium necessary for the operation of independent French nuclear naval forces. Nevertheless, the French demand for the termination of the agreements regarding the American bases in France expanded the subject matter in dispute from cooperation in nuclear deterrence to military cooperation in general. The French government sought to remain within bounds, however, by basing its claim on the argument that the American military bases in France had been established in pursuance of a particular nuclear strategy adopted by both parties in 1957, and repudiated unilaterally by the United States.

Claims and legal arguments narrow the issues in bargaining, emphasize the coherent pattern of events, and circumscribe the areas in which threats and unilateral acts can be made. The French legal argument drew a distinction between NATO's political organization and the adjoining military arrangements that had been developed later to accord with the changing political and military conditions. The French government was reinforcing its argument and the previous pattern of decisions when it reacted to the United States refusal to continue the supply of enriched uranium and to terminate the military bases in France, by repudiating a System of Communications Agreement, modifying the overflight rights to allied military aircraft, and abolishing various tax exemptions to American personnel in France (by "reinterpreting" some treaty provisions). The United States was keeping things in the same currency when it threatened to deny France the benefits of the European alarm system and the use of some nuclear warheads stored in Germany. France was still observing the limits when in retaliation it withdrew from Germany some of its air units.[20]

The United States disrupted this pattern of events when it rejected the French legal distinction between *military* and *political* arrangements and when it counterclaimed that the agreements

20. For some of these practices, see Stein and Carreau, "Law and Peaceful Change in a Subsystem: 'Withdrawal' of France from the North Atlantic Treaty Organization," 62 *Am. J. Int'l L.* 577, 584–87 (1968).

governing the bases were part of the general Atlantic alliance and therefore were to continue for the length of that alliance. This argument of a unitary and indivisible concept of the cooperation between the parties implied some drastic reprisals outside of the previously perceived limitations. In response to this argument, the French government maneuvered to convey a preference for political neutralism.[21] It is, perhaps, not a coincidence that at this point in the dispute both parties, as we have already seen, started for the first time revealing to the public the history of outright repudiation of agreements by the other side. Indeed, the tendency of governments in certain situations to debate continually with each other (even after the fact), to accuse one another, and to justify themselves by some criteria of coherence and connection between their responses and the other side's alleged provocation, reinforces the view that diplomacy itself is partly a form of legalistic adversary proceeding.[22] It is worth emphasizing that the lawyer in such a context may be performing a critical task: it may be compared to what Merton has called a latent social function.[23] The legal forms provide a flexible channel for continuing communications.

Legalistic reasoning, conventional neatness, tradition, and precedents make officials act in a coherent way; they narrow their range of choices and make their decisions come more naturally. By accusing each other and by justifying themselves (for example, why they were doing it and what they were not doing), the parties reiterate, separately but simultaneously, the dividing lines or modes of behavior that have been observed in the past. By doing that, they are also stating the plausible and expectable dividing lines, knowing that success on previous occasions may be essential for further understanding. The very fact that the parties continue to accuse each other in terms of their past performance usually indicates that there is no serious departure from routine. It is particularly interesting that this tendency to debate continually, to accuse and justify, is most common between countries that are hostile to each other, and each of them commonly insists on

21. See p. 101 supra.
22. Schelling, supra note 19, at 148.
23. Merton, *Social Theory and Social Structure* (1957).

scrupulous observance of all possible legal niceties. Such legalistic debates are so natural between traditional opponents that the unique functon they fulfill is hardly noticed. A remote but instructive example are campus radicals, especially when they put up candidates for office in student government or defend themselves by legal arguments before disciplinary tribunals (that may amount to "playing the game" or responding "within the system").

It is, therefore, not surprising that the parties in the Franco-American dispute started their mutual accusations and legalistic justifications at the point where they faced the decision of whether to depart from routine and drastically to enlarge the dispute. Paradoxically, "legalism" did matter from the very moment in which the diplomats of both countries started complaining to the public that "[l]egal problems aren't going to matter in the end because legal niceties have already been coldly disregarded by [the other side]." [24] Such a talk is, in itself, a departure from the routine of the generally cooperative context. These legalistic communications, therefore, symbolized to the parties not only the limits and bounds of the previous patterning of decisions, but also the new political context they would soon find themselves in if they departed from this pattern.

In the search for precedents on termination, reference should be made not to a collection of isolated cases but to the combined decisions to terminate as they were connected to each other. These cases should reflect the broadening of the disputes in question, the patterning of the parties' choices (not only what they did but also what they could but did not do), the way different decisions were associated, the symbolic relations between actions and reactions (tacit understanding, the particular cause and effect, etc.), in addition to the symbolic relations of the particular trends to the aggregate of interaction in the arena (general principles, etc.). It has been noted earlier that solutions to disputes about termination often lie in the connection of different issues, and that they are frequently solved more by tacit bargaining than by explicit negotiation and agreement. The central question is, how do the parties manage to maintain a *coherent* pattern of communication

24. Supra note 10, col. 5.

despite the interjection into the conflict situation of *different* disputes by unilateral acts pertaining to different subject matters.

Words and deeds are both relevant to this process of tacit bargaining. Unilateral acts are an integral part of the strategic situation of termination, and they are employed in conjunction with other diplomatic and propaganda maneuvers. Reprisals are usually employed when words alone cannot influence the other party's decision and make it discontinue what it is doing. They are subordinated to particular objectives and are used in limited, selective, exemplified, and incrementary ways. Reprisals should be distinguished from mere acts of vengeance or of destroying the opponent's capabilities. Rather, they are part of a political-diplomatic strategy for resolving and reconciling conflicting interests. As such, communicative signals are built into them. The success of a reprisal may be judged by whether it exerts the desired influence on the target, whether it stands by itself or is part of a credible threat to expand the conflict further, if necessary. An effective reprisal, therefore, while seeking to narrow some of the adversary's alternatives, should keep other alternatives open. This may be best achieved when retaliatory acts are understood to form part of a comprehensive strategy that combines negative sanctions with positive inducements.[25] A particular unilateral act, it has been pointed out in chapter 5, is often employed for both purposes: the stick is used to uncover a carrot. In such a case words may clarify the significance of the act and reinforce alternative positive patterns of reciprocity. Positive unilateral acts may be particularly called for in a crisis, as part of the moves that parties make on the way back from the "brink."

There can be no clear-cut rule appropriate to all situations as to when acts are preferable to words and vice versa. Both statements and actions might give confusing signals about objectives of demands, offers, threats, reprisals, and how a party will act further if the other side rejects them. Even in direct talks on important issues between countries with many ongoing relations, the signals may not always be clear. Each party has still to decide which words to believe since words usually come from different official sources,

25. For a strategy of unilateral acts leading to positive reciprocity, see generally C. Osgood, *An Alternative to War or Surrender* (1962).

are addressed to different audiences, and can be more easily contradicted or "withdrawn" by later verbal declarations. Actions, on the other hand, usually incur some cost or risk and they are therefore more credible. They are often used to reinforce the credibility of a statement. However, acts themselves may be misinterpreted and may require further verbal clarification.[26] Although actions may not always speak louder than words, they tend to communicate an either-or settlement rather than a more-or-less one. By portraying the distinguishing lines in black-and-white, they make the bargaining limits more distinct and therefore less amenable to an optimal solution.

Verbal communications (even after a fait accompli is made) contribute to creation of viable limits to the expansion of conflicts. The repeated discussions of possible (and previous) limitations create expectations and help the parties to perceive distinctions that might not have been recognized otherwise. Verbal activities are particularly important in situations where there are no empirical precedents, or where the parties face a serious decision whether or not to depart from routine, usage, or precedents. The natural instinct of a party in these situations is to do to the opponent what he thinks the opponent cannot do to him, or, at least, what he thinks the opponent "intends" to do to him, and do it first. The routine of legalistic adversary debates emphasizes to the parties in the latter case their direct responsibility for breaking the rules, and helps them realize that he who acts first does not necessarily act last. In the former case of asymmetrical capabilities, as we shall see in the following chapter, it also makes the parties realize the possible breakdown of any normative association between them, and in its place the institution of lawlessness and the destructive reign of arbitrary force.

26. See A. George, D. Hall, and W. Simons, *The Limits of Coercive Diplomacy* 30 (1971). The inability of the U.S. government to perceive the significance of the Chinese temporary withdrawal from battlefield contact during the Korean War is given as an example (id. at 13). For a study of signals in crisis situations, see R. Jervis, *The Logic of Images in International Relations* (1970).

# PART 4

# The Jurisprudential Frame

# 9  Reprisals and Retaliations

> The question was once put to him [Aristotle], what he had gained by philosophy; and the answer he made was this, "That I do without being commanded, what others do from fear of the laws."
>
> Diogenes Laertius

Almost all writers who have to face the issue of the legal equality of all states take to admonishing their readers about the necessity for a little bit of realism: "There is, of course, never complete equality, except in theory and as an ideal." Having restated the obvious and thus satisfied themselves—and perhaps their readers—that they are not naïve, writers in international law usually feel free to proceed and to cite all the familiar general principles, formal rules, universal declarations, and celebrated resolutions regarding equality. "Equality before the law, of course," they often hasten to add, as though this explains everything. The legal realists among this group even take the trouble to prove how shallow, in fact and in law, these principles of equality are.[1] The sum total of this effort is that one can twist Anatole France's famous saying: the law in its majestic equality forbids the great powers as well as the small and weak nations to denounce unilaterally their unequal and onerous obligations, and it authorizes them equally to enforce their rights by measures of self-help.

The legal methodology of analytical logic and concentration only on the formal significance of norms, of course, completely breaks with reality. Equals before the law are equal, if at all, only in the abstract relationships of rights and duties. In real life they are associated *inter se* in various dependent relationships: the

---

1. See, e.g., Corbett, "Social Basis of a Law of Nations," 85 *Recueil des Cours* 471, 511 (1954). For a constructive analysis showing, among other things, that rules of formal equality are actually discriminatory, see R. Arens and H. Lasswell, *In Defense of Public Order* (1961). Detter, "The Problem of Unequal Treaties," 15 *Int'l & Comp. L.Q.* 1069, 1072 (1966), points out the need for guarantees to protect young or small states.

shopkeeper and the big wholesaler, the ruined debtor and his creditor, the individual consumer and the mass producer, the satellite state and the big power, the government and the multinational corporation. All of these innumerable relationships of dependence-in-fact constitute part of the basis of normative arrangements and organizations, whereas for the purely normative theory it is as if they did not exist. A law that does not specifically take differences of individual capacities into consideration must necessarily be a law of inequality.

How does this discussion help establish some viable and constructive rules (based on both authoritative and effective power) for international behavior? It is usually enough for normative lawyers and legal realists alike to stop at this point of the analysis. If the latter went further they would become international lawyers, a term which supposedly does not agree with the "realism" of power as the motivating force in all international relations. States, it is often argued, are unequal by any measure, and the laws they prescribe and apply cannot treat them as other than what they essentially are. Legal realists and normative jurists, as we shall further see, share many assumptions. Both schools concentrate on unequal practices and coercive interaction. (Though the realist is intellectually more honest in that he brings his assumptions to the fore and does not cover them under the guise of jurisprudential logic, he may be even more naïve than the positivist.) These assumptions appear to be less a matter of descriptive observation than of their authors' preference for this mode of interaction.

### The Authoritarian-Expiative Syndrome of Conventional Internatioanl Law

What is interesting in statements about equality is the theory about law that underlies them. Terms like "equal before the law" imply an external authority that is to sit in judgment on its subjects. Though the Austin-Kelsen jurisprudential schools have recently fallen into disrepute, international law books still abound with principles, rules, and statements that are essentially based on the theories about law as a hierarchy of rules emanating from and enforced through force by a superior and commanding authority.

The word *command* which is, as Hart points out, commonly used only in military contexts, is chosen by the analytical jurists to characterize law because it "carries with it very strong implications that there is a relatively stable hierarchical organization of men" in which the commander occupies a position of preeminence.[2] Accordingly, Hart describes the more simplistic analytical concept of law (to which he does not subscribe) in the following terms:

> [T]here must, wherever there is a legal system, be some persons or body of persons issuing general orders backed by threats which are generally obeyed, and it must be generally believed that these threats are likely to be implemented in the event of disobedience. This person or body must be internally supreme and externally independent. If, following Austin, we call such a supreme independent person or body of persons the sovereign, the laws of any country will be the general orders backed by threats which are issued either by the sovereign or subordinates in obedience to the sovereign.[3]

Such authoritarian notions of law, which have been refined by Kelsen, are supposedly based on the observation that the validity of any rule of law rests on another rule that governs its creation, and that one ultimately arrives at a supreme or fundamental norm from which the validity of all the inferior norms is derived.[4]

Instead of totally rejecting this theory of law on the ground that it does not lend itself to any empirical observation in global interaction, international lawyers have usually sought only to modify

2. H. Hart, *The Concept of Law* 20 (1961).

3. Id. at 25. "Although Hart expresses dissatisfaction with the adequacy of existing positivist analyses (Austin's and Kelsen's in particular) he remains a willing member of the positivist tradition" (Hill, "Legal Validity and Legal Obligation," 80 *Yale L.J.* 47, 49 [1970]). For a discussion of vertical and horizontal models of law, see C. Murphy, Jr., "Some Reflections Upon Theories of International Law," 70 *Colum. L. Rev.* 447 (1970).

4. H. Kelsen, *General Theory of Law and State* 121–22, 190 (Wedberg trans. 1945). "A recurring characteristic of the analytical frame is extreme emphasis upon rules, to the exclusion of operations" (McDougal, Lasswell, and Reisman, "Theories About International Law: Prologue to a Configurative Jurisprudence," 8 *Va. J. Int'l L.* 188, 251 [1968]). Kelsen "does consider efficacy, but it too is a norm" (Id. at 252 n 198.).

the nature of this norm that supposedly constitutes the apex of the legal edifice.[5] The curious paradox is that those who call themselves positivists in international law are usually those who regard consensus as its primary basis. The theory that states can be bound by norms regulating their behavior only if they expressly consent to these norms or otherwise acknowledge their binding force, has been adopted because it has enabled international legal theorists to conform to the prevailing dogma that a state is a sovereign, i.e. "internally supreme and externally independent." However, the introduction at the very top of international law of a consensual element was not intended to affect its otherwise mandatory or hierarchical nature; theoretical consent has been fictitious in many applications. The overwhelming view, to cite only one example, has until very recently been that international law includes a positive rule that "agreements" which owe their existence to subtle forms of overt coercion are still binding legal obligations.[6]

The legal philosophy of supreme authority and hierarchical rules in international relations in many ways imply an obstacle to the development of meaningful notions of equality. The relation of a commander to the person he commands is one of obedience, unilateral respect, and expiation. Genuine reciprocity rarely exists between them. Generally speaking, even when the commander inflicts a reciprocal punishment for violation of his orders, the subject can hardly be expected to see in it something other than expiatory chastisement. Not only is there no possible

5. "The analytical or positivistic frame is comprised of a set of doctrines which probably enjoy more express adherence from contemporary international lawyers than any other articulate jurisprudence." McDougal, Lasswell, and Reisman, id. at 243. This is so despite the fact that analytical jurists often throw up their hands when thinking about the international arena: see J. Austin, *The Province of Jurisprudence Determined* 294–95 (H. Hart ed. 1954); Hart, supra note 2, at 208ff. For further discussion of positivistic rejection of international law and attempts at reconciliation, see Murphy, supra note 3. For Kelsen the fundamental postulate is not so much explicit consent as the patterns of effective power prevailing in a community at any moment (Kelsen, supra note 4, at 120ff.).

6. 1 L. Oppenheim-H. Lauterpacht, *International Law* 891–92 (1955). But Article 52 of the Vienna Convention on the Law of Treaties provides that "A treaty is void if its conclusion has been procured by the threat or use of force in violation of the principles of international law embodied in the Charter of the United Nations." U.N. Doc. A/Conf.39/27 [1969] in 8 *Int'l L. Mat.* 698 (1969).

equality between the authority and its subjects, but further, reciprocity among the subjects themselves cannot be produced to order. If anything, unilateral respect is of neutral content in relation to distributive justice among the subjects; a superior power can use the respect conferred upon it either to uphold equality and justice, to encourage reciprocal behavior and mutual respect among the subjects, or to impose rules contrary to these values. And reciprocal behavior that is imposed from without must necessarily remain subordinated to the ideas of external and superior authority which are its very negation. Such a theoretical relationship can hardly provide a realistic or desirable model for the international legal order.

The theory that rights and duties are always traced to some superior and external authority is historically incorrect and presents a distorted picture even of current interactions within states. It focuses only on official coercive regulation and overlooks the direct and indirect participation in the legal process of a host of nongovernmental decision makers, such as individuals, private organizations, corporations, political parties, and other pressure groups. Often, they influence the decision process even more than state officials do. The reason for overlooking nonofficial participation and characterizing it as being outside the legal process can be traced to the nineteenth century's philosophy of laissez-faire. Law as official commands backed by force is a form of regulation appropriate for the maintenance in the short run of minimum order and preservation of the status quo. Its net effect is to limit the interference of the state in the affairs of individuals. For the rising bourgeoisie the best law was minimum law, a law that protects only life and property and guarantees to business freedom from both legal regulation and notions of public welfare that might obstruct the so-called inherent laws of the market or political arena. Such a minimal law is inappropriate in the context of contemporary communities, which usually strive for higher goals. The latter cannot be achieved through prohibitive orders alone but must include positive sanctions, and require a wide redistribution of benefits, economic planning, and so on.

Not only does the authoritarian theory overlook nonofficial participation in the legal process and noncoercive legal techniques, but also it does not give account of the conflicting and common interests of state officials, and consequently overlooks the variety of reciprocal practices even between and within the departments of any governments. This, too, can be traced to the nineteenth century, when governments were relatively more coherent, representing the narrow and defined interests of a small class, and when the governmental decision-making machinery was relatively small and simple because of the minimal demands made on it.

In municipal societies the reciprocity out of which many lawful decisions arise, is not readily perceived since it traces subtle and obscure forms through the organized practices and governmental institutions of society.[7] In contrast, the reciprocal process from which international norms originate and through which they are enforced is much more visible. Since law in the world arena hardly rests on external and central authority, it also cannot appeal to the idea of expiative commands. There are, of course, less inclusive patterns of superordination and subordination, some fairly stable, some shifting with context. Nevertheless, in order to back up an authoritarian or mandatory rule, one needs to have, and occasionally to use, a most powerful and expiative method of coercion. In relatively uninstitutionalized arenas, in which it is up to the individual participant to enforce the rules, the commandlike law is therefore available only to those who command superior means of coercion.

Constraint, as the command of one person addressed to another and confirmed by force, therefore contradicts the basic condition precedent to lawful interaction in an unorganized arena. Superior constraint cannot be perceived in this situation as a social function, since it cannot come out as abstract and impersonal and as being effectuated in the interests of all those who take part in the legal interaction. Instead, since force is not applied by a central institution, the subordination to it signifies a

---

7. See L. Fuller, *The Morality of Law* 20 (1964). See generally G. Homans, *Social Behavior: Its Elementary Forms* (1961). For normative identity or diversity resulting from the operation of reciprocity in domestic and global arenas, see Lenhoff, "Reciprocity in Function: A Problem of Conflict of Laws, Constitutional Law, and International Law," 15 *U. Pitt. L. Rev.* 44 (1953–54). See also Lenhoff, "Reciprocity: the Legal Aspect of a Perennial Idea," 49 *Nw. U. L. Rev.* 619 and 752 (1954–55).

submission to the special interests and caprice of the particular party or parties from whom commands are issued.

Nevertheless, the authoritarian theories of international law, by making subordination to law and force as such indistinguishable,[8] enable the latter to assume the ideological appearance of an indispensable social function. By them, the coercive domination of one individual participant over another is effectuated as the authority of the law itself—that is to say, as the authority of an objective and impartial norm. Consequently, specific rules of enforcement of international normative arrangements that appeal to the idea of authoritarian expiation must necessarily be not only unequal but also ideologically deceptive. A concept of international law in which authority plays a proper role, as we shall further see, is not dependent on this positivistic preposterousness.

## EXPIATORY AND RECIPROCAL PUNISHMENTS

The questions involved in treaty sanctions and enforcements are similar in many ways to those pertaining to every relatively stable pattern of social activity. Whether our focus is the family, the school, the professional association, the municipality, the state, the region, or the globe, assurances of indulgence and threats of deprivation are integral to expectations about what is considered or demanded as appropriate behavior.[9] Deeply held expectations about rewards and penalties, inculcated in early childhood, influence thought and overt behavior. It may be useful here, therefore, before we proceed to discuss international norms and the

8. Although most activities of international law are not institutionalized and are made by state officials, positivist jurists often assume: (a) that it is not national officials as such but as representatives of the legal order or general community who issue the command; and (b) that their commands are subordinated to the general norm, which expresses once again the will of the general community. While the theory of *dedoublement functionnel* of national officials has merit in institutionalized interactions, as when state nationals hold positions in international organizations, it has none in regard to expiative commands in an unorganized arena. As will be further explained, commands addressed from one individual participant to another are the very negation of a community.

9. Sanctions are universally considered a requisite of a norm, and they are often treated by jurists as an essential part of lawful decisions. "Law which is not effective is a semantic exercise of minimum social significance" (Reisman, "Sanctions and Enforcement," 3 *The Future of the International Legal Order* 273, 275 (C. Black and R. Falk ed. [1971]).

practice of retaliations, to consider some of the more general conceptual differences with regard to methods of punishment which, in turn, are the product of differing predispositions about the desired or real nature of human relations.

The notion of expiation corresponds to that of heteronomy and duty pure and simple. It emphasizes the external and coercive authority of the behavior in question. Thus, rules of conduct are viewed as imposed from the *outside* by a superior power whose concern is to "compensate" for an offense by administering a proportionate amount of suffering. As Piaget observes, expiatory punishment is inherent in constraint relationships. A sufficiently powerful method of coercion should be applied to bring an individual back to his duty when he has transgressed a rule imposed upon his mind from without. And the only way to bring home his guilt to him is by means of painful punishment. What matters in expiation, therefore, is punishment as such: the sterner it is the better.

Thus expiation, as Piaget points out, involves a very simple mode of communication in the sense that the symbol chosen is "arbitrary in relation to the thing signified, that is to say, there is no relation between the content of the guilty act and the nature of its punishment." In the punishment of children, for example, it is "all one when a lie has been told whether you inflict corporal punishment on the transgressor, or take his toys away from him or condemn him to some school task." [10] Similarly, in the unilateral termination of an international concession agreement, for instance, it makes little difference whether one responds by inflicting military, economic, or diplomatic punishments. What does matter is only that a proportionate penalty as such should be felt by the transgressor. Thus expiative punishments are incoherent, inconsistent, and often insulting. The only message they convey is that one must submit to a superior force.[11]

10. J. Piaget, *The Moral Judgment of the Child* 205 (Gabain trans. 1965). The general distinction between expiatory and reciprocal punishments is developed on the basis of experiments made with children in ch. 3, id. The relevance to international relations of Piaget's thesis about the connection of the response to the provocation in content and form, and not merely in severity, was first noted by T. Shelling, *Arms and Influence* 148n. (1966).

11. Expiation may achieve submission in the short run; it backfires in the long run. Even when the target of expiation is a child, "if he has any self-respect he

This element of arbitrariness in obligatory expiation, and the reaction to it, will become more lucid when it is examined in the light of reciprocal methods of communicating punishment. The latter do not require that the parties have equal power at their disposal. They do require, however, that messages put emphasis on the basic idea: that the arrows in social interaction go in both directions. Verbal communications no longer sound like two monologues—one consisting of accusations and instructions, the other of denials and pleadings—but consist of an exchange and discussion. Actions are related to each other, so that transactions proceed in chains: each response is in turn a stimulus. In their elementary form reciprocal relations are bilateral and symmetrical (both sides understand that they can do the same to each other and that it is legitimate), not merely complementary (as when one lays down the rules and the other humbly receives them). Bilateralism, as we shall see, may develop in an aggregate community into pluralism.

The rules are viewed as governing relations *among* the participants and as means of cultivating communal bonds:

> Since the rule is no longer, as before, something imposed from without, something which the individual could dispense with, but on the contrary, constitutes a necessary relation between the individual and those around him, it suffices to make plain the consequences following upon the violation of this law in order to make the individual feel isolated and to make him long for a return to normal relations.[12]

---

must transgress again, to show to himself and to others that he is not a sissy" (H. Ginott, *Between Parent and Child* 53 [1965]). In a world in which many states have achieved formal independence, expectations rise, and demands for respect are made everywhere, international expiative punishments as such have become increasingly worse than useless. They ensure, as we shall see, that obnoxious acts will be repeated.

12. Piaget, supra note 10, at 206. Commenting on Duguit's theory about law, which maintains that the basis of legal obligations is the social fact of "solidarity" among men, Brierly states: "[S]olidarity is not the only natural fact; the struggle for existence, inequality of strength and skill, are also natural facts. Why may they not equally give rise to rules of conduct?" (J. Brierly, *The Basis of Obligation in International Law* 57 [1958]). Inequality in resources, of course, may be the sole underlying policy of particular rules of conduct, and the traditional balance of power's rule of reprisals, as will be further discussed, bears witness to that. Instead of trying to generalize about the "nature" or "basis of obligation" of

Reciprocal punishments are tied up with cooperation, interdependence, and notions of equality. The participants interact with each other, rather than simply act one upon the other. Responses are necessarily related to the misdeed not only in severity but also in both form and content.

Since the rules are deemed as norms governing the group as a whole, their violation appears as a breach of the communal or social bond itself. In maintaining a relation between a response and an alleged misdeed, the participants reiterate that though some relations or norms have been broken, other relations still exist and are being reinstated and restored in the reaction. Thus, to use again a remote example of expiative punishment given by Piaget, the father who discovers his son has been playing hookey can forbid him to go to the movies the next day or make him copy out a poem fifty times. A more direct form of punishment is simply to refuse to believe the boy the next time it is to his advantage to tell the truth (as when he gets a good mark at school). This would force the boy to feel the effects of his misdeed directly and thus make him realize that lying does away with mutual trust.

Something more than reciprocity in the traditional sense is involved in such punishments. They do not consist merely of symmetrical actions by mutual repetition of misdeeds. The penalty itself illustrates the desired behavior. (Contrast the previous example with the case of a father who hits his older boy, saying, "This will teach you not to hit someone smaller than you.") The more sophisticated type of reciprocal punishment is motivating and educational, and as such should be distinguished from that of the cruder type discussed below. The former preserves the self-respect of the transgressor as well as of the respondent. There are, of course, many other dynamic aspects that contribute to normative arrangements. For present purposes we shall continue to consider the critical aspect of communicating a relation between the response and the alleged misdeed.

---

all times and situations, it seems more useful to note the differences in particular applications between expiatory and reciprocal rules of conduct. As the following discussion demonstrates, the former are usually found where interdependence is low.

## An Eye for an Eye

The relations of cause to effect that enter into reciprocal punishments are of a rich variety. Some retaliations in international affairs are eye-catching and easily perceived as reciprocal acts. Others, especially in economic matters within generally cooperative and interdependent contexts, are more complicated and are disguised in other forms though still bearing on the intricacies of the activities involved. The former, commonly called "reciprocity proper," or "simple reciprocity," consists mainly in doing to the transgressor exactly what he has done himself (this idea is expressed in the term "to exact a punishment"). It is most commonly associated with violence and acts of irreparable destruction.

Returning evil for evil (or good for good) is human behavior in its most elementary form. It is prevalent among young children, and appears, for instance, as a rule of law in biblical society, where it was up to the next of kin to avenge the death of his relative. Such interested vengeance or self-help in disputes relating to affection or property, for example, is still commonplace in today's Middle Eastern and African communities, where it is considered just punishment and where customary rules come in and make precise the distinction between what is right and what is wrong in private reprisals.[13] Criminal law has been justified also in Western societies by saying, as Kant did, that a person who commits an unjust act affirms that it is right for all people, himself included, to be dealt with in the same way. "[T]he undeserved evil which anyone commits on another, is to be regarded as perpetuated on himself. Hence, it may be said: 'If you slander another, you slan-

13. Compare with the biblical rule: "thou shalt separate three cities for thee in the midst of thy land . . . he shall flee unto one of these cities and live; lest the avenger of blood pursue the manslayer, while his heart is hot, and overtake him, because the way is long, and smite him mortally; whereas he was not deserving of death, inasmuch as he hated him not in time past" (*Deuteronomy*, 19.2–6). The contemporaneity of this injunction is clouded by the archaic language in which it is expressed. Among the Dinka of the Sudan "[t]heft of cattle in self-help is more frequent but does not provoke the ordinary moral disapproval of ordinary theft. . . . Even the court does not entirely equate them. The ordinary rules governing theft and the sentence normally inflicted on thieves will only apply in cases where the circumstances of seizure are aggravating." (F. Deng, *Tradition and Modernization* 269–70 [1971]).

der yourself; . . . if you kill another, you kill yourself.' " [14] Kant
and other retributionists have made the right of retaliation (*jus
talionis*) the basis of criminal law. They reason that if retaliatory
punishment cannot always be literally effected, because it might be
intolerably vindictive and cruel or in some cases physically impossible, it should still be effected at least in the spirit of equality
—by exacting from the offender a punishment equivalent to the
offense.

Historically, private reprisals were regarded as only one aspect
in the pervasive struggle for existence and self-defense. Today,
they are widely associated with vengeance and are distinguished
from self-defense by the fact that the one injured does not respond
immediately to the attack but defers his response to a more convenient time. Only when legal equivalents, whether criminal or
civil, for individual retribution do exist and are rejected as shame-

14. I. Kant, *The Philosophy of Law* 194–96 (Hastie trans. 1887), reprinted in
*Freedom and Responsibility* 503–04 (H. Morris ed. 1961). The advocates of utility
in the administration of justice, on the other hand, reject the principle of retaliation as such and claim that punishment should serve the end of promoting
the common good. Its specific capacity for serving this end, according to utilitarian
theory, inheres in the punitive power to prevent, control, or correct socially undesirable behavior. Therefore, punishment must always be justified by the good
consequences it produces. In other words, the utilitarians' contribution to legal
history is the making of punishment to depend for its justification on something
other than itself. They are accused, not without some justification, of treating
people as means for an end, of permitting on occasion the "punishment" of the
innocent (e.g. punishing the relatives of those who have committed crimes since
this may deter potential criminals) and, therefore, of foregoing the principle of the
equality of all men. For an attempt to reconcile the retributive and utilitarian
theories in this respect, see Benn, "An Approach to the Problems of Punishment,"
33 *Philosophy* 325 (1958), reprinted in *Freedom and Responsibility*, id. at 517.

The analogous carry-over of municipal legal doctrines to international law is an
everyday phenomenon, and it would be surprising indeed if the dogmatic debate
between retributionists and utilitarians did not influence international law doctrines on the matter. Quantitative proportionality, as shall be further explained, between an alleged mischief and the punitive action it provokes, is also an important
requirement in international law. But, because of the material difference between
municipal and international conditions, there are and should be present, additional
qualitative criteria for international retaliatory punishments. And despite retribu-
tionist and utilitarian dogmatic assertions to the contrary, there is, as will be further
explained and illustrated, no inherent contradiction in basing punishment on retaliations that are authoritatively tested by the politically and socially desirable consequences they produce.

ful, and when personal vengeance as such is regarded as a sacred obligation, does the act of deferred action take on a new attribute of vengeance that it does not have when there is no such alternative. The idea of the *only* adequate means of retribution is part of it: the emphasis that blood spilled is the sole equivalent for the blood previously spilled.

It is at this point of the quest for legal equivalents that blood vengeance coincides with *jus talionis*—the principle of equal retribution, whereunder the vengeance taken by the person injured, or by his group, settles the account and eliminates the possibility of further vengeance. Customary laws of blood vengeance seem, in one way or another, already to express a growing measure of interdependence between hostile groups; they are motivated by the group's desire for self-preservation, which is being threatened by the destructive spread of clannish feuds. Blood vengeance that is not regulated by custom is of a different character. This vengeance forms a basis for new vengeance, and it is transmitted from one generation to another until the hostile clans are exterminated. Without the customary rules of equal retribution, revenge—even disinterested revenge—would rest only upon sympathy, or antipathy as the case may be, and thus would remain arbitrary. The individuals involved and the larger community would not have the feeling of punishing the guilty and defending the innocent, but simply of fighting an enemy and defending a friend.

The retributive practice of returning evil for evil in the last analysis is based on an unsophisticated notion of the principle of equality. The many variations of the same idea in common language indicate that it is still popular even in everyday affairs: "Do as you would be done by," "No cross, no crown," "Whoever hath, to him shall be given," "Fair exchange is no robbery," "Tit for tat," and "You scratch my back and I will scratch yours." The principle of an eye for an eye, of course, merely increases the number of blind people in society. Sheer reciprocity stands so high in the eyes of many people that they seek to apply it even when it seems to border on crude vengeance. The reason for this is that in certain circumstances the sheer feeling of equality with all its vindictive brutality still outweighs equity. Especially in the international arena, refined notions of value equivalencies are not yet formed everywhere. Punishments are still thought of by many in terms of self-defense.[15]

## TRANSNATIONAL SELF-HELP

The history of international law reflects the inability of one person, or group of persons, to attain the superiority in power necessary to command all other groups by threats of expiation. Already before the emergence of the modern sovereign state, reciprocal self-help measures were identified with the law of nations. Giovanni da Legnano, a legal scholar who lived in fourteenth-century Bologna, described the laws of reprisals in his time in the following words:

> In the early days of the supreme Pontiffs and the Roman Emperors, when all were in subjection both in law and in fact, there was no need of reprisals, since the complement of justice was administered by princes, with observance of the due order of law. But when the Empire began gradually to be exhausted, so that now there are some who in fact recognize no superior, and by them justice is neglected, the need arose for a subsidiary remedy, when the ordinary remedies fail, but which is on no account to be resorted to when they exist. But this extraordinary remedy had its origin in the law of nations . . . no positive law, canon or civil, ordains that reprisals should be declared. For both laws ordain a mode of obtaining the effects of justice. It is even forbidden to seize one's own property. . . . But this declaration of war belongs only to one who has no superior. For one who has a superior cannot violate the remedies of law on his own authority. Therefore only one who has no superior, both in law and in fact, may declare reprisals. Also he against whom they are declared should have no superior or, if he has, that superior should neglect to do justice.[16]

---

15. This identification of self-help with self-defense forces scholars to restrict all lawful coercion to self-defense, and also to widen the ambit of self-defense. See McDougal and Feliciano, note 20 infra; Halderman, "Regional Enforcement Measures and the United Nations," 52 *Geo. L.J.* 89 (1963). For a criticism of this view, see W. Reisman, *Nullity and Revision* 839, n. 6 (1971).

16. Giovanni da Legnano, *De Bello, de Repbresaliis et de Duello* 307–09 (T. Holland ed. 1964; notes omitted).

The fourteenth-century rules of reprisals, therefore, befitted the political conditions of their time. They were drawn on a clear distinction between situations in which the positive law of the land should be applied, and situations in which appropriate redress could be found only in the reciprocal relations among those who had no superiors. Accordingly, Legnano's book contains a network of rules whose aim was to prevent reprisals from disrupting the measure of interdependence and cooperation that already existed between the various independent jurisdictions of his time.[17] But the rules of reprisals and retaliations formulated by legal scholars during the eighteenth and nineteenth centuries gave expression more to ideas of superior authority and expiation than to the growing interdependence and reciprocity in the world arena. Historical, political, and economic conditions account for this development.

## *The Focus on Single Events*

A key difference between expiatory and reciprocal rules of conduct, as we have seen, is between judging an act and its response as arbitrarily isolated events, and viewing them as phases in a continuing relationship. In light of this observation, consider again the aforementioned rule about the right of a party to terminate or denounce a treaty because of prior alleged breach

17. Reprisals were restricted to property and were executed by private citizens against private citizens belonging to another jurisdiction. An individual who claimed reprisals needed to obtain from his jurisdictional authority a grant authorizing him to take the self-help measures. The granting authority conducted hearings in which anyone who had an interest in the case could appear, and issue a declaration of reprisal after it had been satisfied that the remedy had been sought and denied in the jurisdiction of the wrongdoer (id. at 310ff.). The high degree of regularity which characterized the enforcement of private reprisals in the thirteenth and fourteenth centuries was achieved not only through the development of relatively uniform local laws but also through the conclusion of treaties on the matter. During the fifteenth and sixteenth centuries, private reprisals were gradually abolished by treaties, and their ultimate disappearance was facilitated by the development of alternative practices. One of the most important of these was the development of legal proceedings based on notions of reciprocity and comity for the settlement of disputes in which foreigners were involved. But with the development of the practice of enforcing reprisals exclusively by official forces for public ends, there has been almost complete disappearance of well-understood and uniform regulation of methods of enforcement. To this day, official reprisals have remained almost completely free from formal regulation. E. Colbert, *Retaliation in International Law* 5, 12, 60 (1948).

of the *same* treaty by the other party. This focus on a single transaction to the exclusion of all other relationships between the parties can be justified only on historical grounds. The rule has allegedly been adopted by analogy drawn from private law,[18] where an innocent party may usually refuse to perform a contract following the other party's default, and/or seek redress in the form of equitable remedies such as indemnity and specific performance.

When this rule was originally adopted, there were perhaps good reasons to draw an analogy from private law. Until lately, governments were reluctant to enter into complex treaty arrangements of the type prevalent today. States were generally regarded as economically independent and self-sufficient units needing only few treaty relationships, mostly in matters of power and security. Even as late as the second part of the nineteenth century, by the very nature of this view, the conclusion of a treaty was regarded as an episode rather than as a regular occurrence. Treaties were therefore relatively self-contained; that is to say, they defined and regulated a single and unique international transaction between or among the parties. The enforcement of treaties was thought of in similar terms. The innocent party was confronted with a single alternative: to threaten the violator of the treaty provisions with terminating the whole treaty, or to try to enforce the treaty provisions by self-help measures, the declaration of war included (international law's so-called equivalents of specific performance and indemnity).

Treaties reflected the balance of power in the arena. This usually meant that in treaties between relatively equal states some proportionality was kept between burdens and benefits, and that in treaties between great powers and small states there was definite inequality between rights and obligations. The sanction of annulling a treaty if the other party infringes its terms may or may not be effective, depending on how far a state contemplating infraction would consider the continuance in force of the treaty beneficial to its interests. In the relations among the great powers, therefore, the threat of terminating a treaty in response to a vio-

18. Ch. 8 supra. B. Sinha, *Unilateral Denunciation of Treaty Because of Prior Violations of Obligations by Other Party* 58ff. (1966).

lation of its terms by the other side usually constituted a sanction of significant deterrent value. On the other hand, parties to treaties whose observance involved great burdens on the part of one state with little or no commensurate advantage to that state, were under continuing pressures to disregard their provisions. Changes in the power positions of parties to such unequal treaties, with the effect that they no longer reflected the real balance of power, were understood to justify their termination or revision.[19] Obviously, when the unequal power relationship between the parties had remained unchanged, it was not the option to have the same treaty annulled that deterred the party at a disadvantage from committing a material breach, but the probable application by the stronger power of various sanctions in a direct attempt to enforce the treaty.

Currently, war is not an acceptable method of enforcing treaty obligations. However, the whole gamut of self-help measures, short of the threat or the use of force against the political independence or territorial integrity of a state, is still considered authorized.[20] Following the alleged breach of particular treaty pro-

19. See, e.g., ch. 1, note 38 supra.
20. The earlier limitation of the employment of force for collecting contractual debts may be found in the Porter Convention. This convention restricts the lawful employment of military self-help in cases of debt enforcement to coercing the debtor state into arbitration and to enforcing the ensuing award. Convention (II) Respecting the Limitation of the Employment of Force for the Recovery of Contract Debts (1907), in J. Scott, *Reports to the Hague Conferences of 1899 and 1907*, 489 (1917). Article 2(4) of the U.N. Charter states: "All Members shall refrain in their international relations from the threat or use of force against the territorial integrity or political independence of any state, or in any other manner inconsistent with the Purposes of the United Nations." Under both explicit textual and contextual interpretations, this article is claimed either to exclude altogether or to tolerate in some measure armed reprisals. For doctrinal illumination of the former view, see: P. Jessup, *A Modern Law of Nations* 158–59 (1949); H. Kelsen, *The Law of the United Nations* 269 (1950); M. McDougal and F. Feliciano, *Law and Minimum World Public Order* 207 (1961); 2 L. Oppenheim-H. Lauterpacht, *International Law* 154 (1952); Waldock, "The Regulation of the Use of Force by Individual States in International Law," 81 *Recueil des Cours* 455, 492 (1952). Falk, "The Beirut Raid and the International Law of Retaliation," 63 *Am. J. Int'l L.* 415, 429 (1969), cites additional authorities in support of this view. For the opposite view, see 1 D. O'Connell, *International Law* 341 (1965); J. Stone, *Aggression and World Order* 95 (1958); Reisman, supra note 15, at 846–51. International practice, as Reisman shows, substantiates this construction of the charter. The *Corfu Channel* case (Merits) [1949] ICJ Rep. 4, censured the acquisition of

visions or other obligations, force is often used, diplomatic relations are ruptured, foreign assets are frozen, seized, or attached, shipment of surplus grain and other forms of foreign aid are discontinued,[21] an economic embargo is initiated, internal subversion is tacitly encouraged, and so on.

Sometimes the only discernible connection between these indirect self-help measures of enforcement and a particular treaty is that they are used against an alleged treaty-breaker and violator of international law. Insofar as these sanctions are not connected to the alleged misdeed in form and content, and do not promise to change the behavior pattern of the delinquent target, they have a strong expiatory-punishment complexion. At other times, such indirect methods of enforcement are used by way of reciprocity in its crudest and most destructive form. Not only do conflicts usually expand by unregulated reactions of this type, but the spin-off process occasionally destroys many others, and sometimes even general relations between the parties. Defining criteria for connections of retaliations to alleged misdeeds, therefore, does not merely concern the content of a particular rule of principle, but is also an important test of the general authority and effectiveness of international law.

## Traditional Reprisals and Retorsion

What are the accepted legal criteria for self-help measures? Retaliations of low coercion in international law are generally di-

---

evidence for international litigation by self-help measures but accepted the evidence and applied no deprivatory sanction upon the United Kingdom. United Nations practice has tolerated self-help even in extreme situations (Reisman, supra note 15, id. at 851). However, the British retaliatory bombing of the republic of Yemen was expiatory and was condemned by the U.N. (see note 56 infra). In one phase of the Anglo-Iranian Oil Company dispute, the use of military force was contemplated by Britain but was not carried out (A. Ford, *The Anglo-Iranian Oil Dispute of 1951–1952*, 58, 95, 124 [1953]). The 1956 Suez campaign has been widely regarded as an unlawful exercise of military force. (Reisman, supra note 15, at 851). See note 38 infra for an interpretation of Charter Article 2(4) that reconciles these cases and conforms to the main theme of this study.

21. The lawfulness of the manipulation of foreign aid as means of securing compliance with international law is controversial. This particular means of enforcement is available only to a few great capital-exporting states and is clearly an unequal strategy. Thus, Cuba claimed that the United States' termination of sugar agreements was a hostile act, tantamount to economic aggression and legitimizing

vided into two distinct categories, which are termed "retorsion" and "reprisals." "Retorsion is the technical term for retaliation for discourteous, or unkind, or unfair and inequitable acts by acts of the same or a similar kind." [22] Note that the act which calls for retorsion is not really illegal; on the contrary, retorsion is a specific form of retaliation which is prescribed only against acts that are within the competence of their authors. The rule about retorsion springs from the awareness that a state may commit many official acts which, though they are not internationally illegal, involve some injury, discourtesy, or unfriendliness to another state. Examples of such practices on behalf of a government are raising custom barriers for economic protectionism, flooding the market with a particular foreign currency stocked in its reserve, devaluating its own currency, or discriminating against foreign nationals who visit or reside in its territory. "Retorsion consists in retaliation for a noxious act by a noxious act. But a State, in making use of retorsion, is by no means confined to acts of the same kind as those complained of, acts of a similar kind being equally admissible provided they are not internationally illegal." [23] The reader will note the high degree of normative ambiguity implicit in the term "legal" in conventional definitions of retorsion.

The usual definition of reprisals is as follows: "Reprisals are acts which, although normally illegal, are exceptionally permitted as reaction of one state against a violation of its right by another

---

retaliatory nationalizations (Reisman, supra note 15, at 854–55, n. 52). See also the following text. For possible connection between the manipulation of foreign aid and the doctrine of unequal treaties, see E. Vattel, *The Law of Nations, or the Principles of the Law of Nature* 200 (J. Chitty ed. 1854).

22. 2 L. Oppenheim-H. Lauterpacht, *International Law* 134 (1952). See also Kelsen, infra note 24, at 25. For additional references see Colbert, supra, note 17, at 2, n. 1.

23. Oppenheim-Lauterpacht, supra note 22, at 135. Some states adhere to the notion of a "jurisdiction in retorsion" (e.g. Austria, Czechoslovakia, Italy, Canton Tessin, Yugoslavia, and Hungary). Their enacted laws provide that "where a foreign state has granted courts jurisdiction on grounds which by the *lex fori* do not constitute a basis for jurisdiction, the forum may retaliate by exercising jurisdiction against citizens of that foreign state on identical grounds." (Lenhoff, supra note 7, at 68–69 [notes omitted]). Retorsion of this type seems unconstitutional in the U.S. and was not practiced even against foreign citizens. For judicial cases in other matters based on the policy of retorsion in American conflict of laws, see Lenhoff, id. at 70–71.

state." [24] The nonfulfillment of treaty obligations, for example, is an international delinquency, and therefore can also be made into an act of reprisal. But a party, according to the traditional rule, does not necessarily have to respond to another state's violation of a treaty by the nonperformance of treaty obligations in relation to that state; nor should the nonperformance of treaty obligations necessarily come in response to another state's breach of treaty obligations. For, unlike retorsion, reprisals do not have to be confined to acts even similar in form to those complained of. They consist in retaliation for an illegal act by an otherwise illegal act, and, again according to the conventional view, it does not matter much of what particular nature the provocation or the response is, provided they are both of illegal character. Thus, a classical definition: "An act of reprisal may be performed against anything and everything that belongs to, or is due to, the delinquent State or its citizens. Ships sailing under its flag may be seized, treaties concluded with it may be suspended, a part of its territory may be militarily occupied, goods belonging to it, or to its citizens, may be seized, and the like." [25] In bringing examples of correct reprisals, writers often do not even mention the act which elicited them.[26] Attention is focused solely on single events. The violation of a particular right and the act of reprisal are each treated separately.

An example of such a reprisal is the case of the violation of the treaty of commerce of 1816 between the Two Sicilies and Great Britain, in which certain commercial advantages were secured to the latter. In 1838, the Neapolitan government granted a sulphur monopoly to a company of French and other foreign merchants. Following the violation of its treaty rights, Great Britain laid a successful embargo on Sicilian ships in the harbor of Malta and

24. H. Kelsen, *Principles of International Law* 23 (1952). See also Oppenheim-Lauterpacht, supra note 22, at 136.

25. Id. at 139 (note omitted).

26. "Thus in 1895 Great Britain ordered a fleet to land forces at Corinto, and to occupy the custom-house and other government buildings, as an act of reprisal against Nicaragua; again, in 1901 France ordered a fleet to seize the island of Mytilene, as an act of reprisal against Turkey; and in 1908 Holland ordered a squadron to seize two public Venezuelan vessels as an act of reprisal against Venezuela." Id. (note omitted).

ordered its fleet in the Mediterranean to seize Sicilian ships. The grant of the sulphur monopoly was withdrawn and the captured vessels were restored to their owners.[27] Similarly, when in 1908 Venezuela dismissed a Dutch minister resident at Caracas, Holland considered this step to be a "violation of her dignity" and captured, by way of reprisal, two Venezuelan vessels.[28] But when in 1740 Russia arrested without just cause a natural-born Russian subject who had become naturalized in Prussia, the latter country seized two Russian subjects and detained them until he was liberated. Prussia was not stronger than Russia militarily, and the reprisal, of course, was connected to the alleged provocation, both in content and in form.

This element of qualitative reciprocity has been ignored, however, and the case is cited as an example only for the rule that "[t]he persons of officials, and even of private citizens, of the delinquent State [not only its property] are possible objects of reprisals." [29] The general rule, as formulated by legal scholars, by way of hypothetical example, is that "a state would not be justified in arresting, by way of reprisal, thousands of foreign subjects living on its territory because their home state had denied justice to one of its subjects living abroad. But it would be justified in . . . ordering its fleet to seize several vessels sailing under the flag of that State, or in suspending a commercial treaty with it." [30] Thus, the only meaningful legal requirement in traditional reprisals is that they be in quantitative proportion to the offense to which they are responsive, and to the degree of coercion necessary to get reparation.[31] This anomaly should, if nothing else, at least raise ques-

27. Id. at 137; Colbert, supra note 17, at 66–67.

28. Oppenheim-Lauterpacht, supra note 22, at 139; Colbert, supra note 17, at 66.

29. Oppenheim-Lauterpacht, supra note 22, at 139.

30. Id. at 141. This statement was written before the conclusion in 1958 of the Convention on the Freedom of the High Seas, according to which such a seizure of ships is unlawful.

31. Id. Kelsen, supra note 24, at 24. Colbert, supra note 17, at 76ff., 201, also points out some operational limitations of the rule about quantitative proportionality. References are usually made to the arbitral decision in *The Naulilaa*, 8 *Recueil des Tribunaux Mixtes* 409. See also chapter 10 infra. Falk neither establishes nor sustains a distinction between retorsion and reprisal, and does not require that retaliation should be made in a similar subject matter and by parallel instrument of power. He puts forward, however, in addition to proportionality, numerous other requirements in order to reduce the possibility of arbitrariness

tions about the restriction upon acts of retorsion. Would dissimilarity alone make retorsion illegal?

While such statements tell us very little about the reciprocal relations among governments, they are all too common in the literature of international law. They do tell us a great deal, however, about the so-called rules of retaliations and the notions of punishment inherited from previous generations. The essence of the distinction between retorsion and reprisals is that punishments for mischievous acts that do *not* violate particular and formal international norms should be connected not only in severity but also in form and in substance to the misdeed, but that punishments for acts that violate such norms need *not* be so connected. In other words, according to this view, inequities short of defying legal rights should properly be punished by reciprocity, but the violation of particular international laws is punishable by expiation. This conclusion should not come as a surprise to us in view of the authoritarian philosophy about law that underlies it.

### Historical Origin of the Rules

There are, however, corrective forces at work. What is so baffling about the distinction between retorsion and reprisals, of course, is not why legal scholars provide for expiative punishments within the sphere of the law, but why they provide that punishments for acts committed outside the ordinary domain of legal regulation should always be reciprocal. In other words, why have they not drawn the distinction merely between legal and illegal acts and formulated the rule that a retaliation to the former should be confined to legal acts, while retaliation to the latter may include what would otherwise be illegal acts? Why have they added the

---

and abuse that retaliations entail. One of his requirements is that "the use of force amounts to a clear message of communication to the target government so that the contours of what constituted the unacceptable provocation are clearly conveyed" (Falk, supra note 20, at 441). Criteria of reciprocity and equality in armed retaliations for situations of low interdependence may differ somewhat from those involving a higher measure of interdependence. See the following discussion on the Arab-Israeli conflict. For a study of self-help measures to enforce international judgments and awards, see Reisman, supra note 15, at 836ff. It may be that different policies should apply in the case of nonperformance of a judgment or an award, since the dispute has already been dealt with in an institutionalized arena.

requirement that legal acts that respond to unfriendly legal acts should always be confined to acts of the same or similar kind as those complained of?

During the classical balance of power period (eighteenth, nineteenth, and beginning of the twentieth centuries), from which these rules have been derived, retorsion could usually be practiced only between states of roughly equal power. Weaker countries were not committing "legal but inequitable" acts when they raised their customs barriers, granted or refused a commercial monopoly, and denied justice to nationals of great powers. Rather, they were committing acts which were illegal in formal term; matters such as economic and commercial protectionism, and the degree of due process of law to be afforded alien residents and visiting merchants, were regulated as between the great powers and the weaker nations by the so-called unequal treaties and treaties of capitulation in which the great powers secured for themselves many unilateral advantages.[32] The violation of legal rights emanating from treaties was, of course, conceived as an international delinquency which called for reprisals. There was no thought of enforcing such treaties by reciprocity; within the treaties the benefits were overwhelmingly one-sided, and the general relationship outside a particular treaty was that of unilateral respect. Indeed, it often did not matter much whether the legal right whose violation was complained of originated in a formal legal instrument or not. The rule, it may be recalled, specifies that internationally illegal acts which call for reprisals include the violation of the "dignity" of a foreign state,[33] (as in the previous example of the 1908 reprisal by Holland).

On the other hand, relations among the roughly equal powers of Europe could not be other than reciprocal. Because of the nationalistic and economic theories of the time about the self-sufficiency of states—theories that could be supported in practice due to colonial expansion and the conclusion of unequal treaties with

32. Tseng Yu-Hao, *The Termination of Unequal Treaties in International Law* 6ff. (1931); B. Röling, *International Law in an Expanding World* 26ff. (1960); Detter, supra note 1, at 1073ff. For a discussion of the doctrine of unequal treaties see app. A infra.

33. Oppenheim-Lauterpacht, supra note 22, at 136–37; Colbert, supra note 17, at 68–69.

Asian countries—matters of economic interdependence were usually not subjected to inter-European agreements. Nevertheless, there were many domestic legislative, administrative, or judicial acts which, although not considered at the time to be internationally illegal, were injurious to other countries. Naturally, in the relations between equals, punishments for such injuries had to be reciprocal, that is, retaliations for unfriendly but legal acts had to be restricted to acts of the same or similar kind as those complained of.

Characteristic of balance of power rules, the distinction between retorsion and reprisals is based solely on minimum order considerations. In the relations among equals self-help measures usually provoke countermeasures, and the limiting of the ensuing conflict escalation usually requires some distinct forms of self-restraint. Responses therefore should be restricted to retaliation in similar subject matter and parallel legal form. But in expiatory relations, like those existing in the nineteenth century between the great powers and the relatively powerless states, conflict escalation through reciprocal exchanges is not possible. Expiation, by definition, means the inability of the inferior participant to match the responses of its superior. It was possible for the great powers to send their regular forces against powerless states that did not live up to their commercial, financial, or other obligations, because these measures of enforcement were not expected to incite serious resistance or counter-retaliation. Since the enforcement of unequal treaties did not usually pose dangers of conflict escalation, it was unnecessary to limit reprisals either in form or content.

Similarly, because of the prevailing laissez-faire theories of the time, treaties among the great powers in Europe dealt primarily with political matters relating merely to the maintenance of peace and security. The enforcement of these treaties, it may be recalled, was based on the clear-cut distinction between obligatory and territorial rights. The former were understood to terminate automatically when conditions materially changed; the latter were said to be terminable only by a new agreement between the parties, and their enforcement was viewed to depend on the so-called automatic threat of general war. And since punishment for treaty violations in Europe excluded the possibility of conflict escalation,[34] it became unnecessary to limit reprisals in form or in content.

## Modern Criteria

The rule that injurious "legal acts" should be punished by quantitatively as well as qualitatively proportionate acts, and that, beyond the quantitative requirement, punishments for formal illegal acts may include almost any conceivable illegal act in the world, is merely of historical significance. This rule should be rejected not only because of its obvious inequalitarian connotations, but also for a variety of other policy reasons. Most importantly, self-help in the currently interdependent world almost always invites retaliation, and it therefore poses danger of conflict escalation. It has been observed in the previous chapters that governments feel obligated to characterize their actions in terms of specified and coherent patterns of communications consisting of both deeds and words. This is currently becoming true whether the self-help measures are directed against big or small nations, whether they are taken between traditional allies or opponents, and whether they occur in diplomatic, economic, political, or military subject matters.

Such, for example, have been the practices discussed earlier between the United States and French governments concerning NATO's military strategy. In the aftermath of the Suez crisis, Western attachment of Egyptian funds was more than matched by Egyptian attachment of Western funds.[35] Similarly, in the context of the 1973 Arab-Israeli war, the Arab oil-producing countries initiated and successfully maintained an oil embargo against the United States and Western European countries, the declared purpose of which was to induce the implementation of a 1967 Security Council resolution relating to peace settlement in the Middle East. In the dispute over expropriations of American-owned property in Cuba, the latter in 1960 required American oil companies in Cuba to refine Russian crude oil. The oil companies refused. By

34. See the section on the balance of power period in chapter 1 supra.

35. "These measures of the Western countries followed the pattern of economic warfare as experienced through blocking of property in World War II." Domke, "American Protection Against Foreign Expropriation in Light of the Suez Canal Crisis," 105 *U. of Pa. L. Rev.* 1033, 1039 (1957).

a process of actions and reactions, the American oil refineries were seized, the United States in reprisal cut the Cuban sugar import quota by 95 percent, and Cuba in retaliation for this move (threatened in advance) began the nationalization of all United States property in Cuba.[36]

Consider another example. When, in August 1964, torpedo boats out of North Vietnamese ports allegedly launched two repeated attacks on an American destroyer thirty miles off their coast, aircraft from American carriers attacked naval installations in North Vietnamese ports, reportedly damaging about twenty-five torpedo boats and setting fire to a petroleum installation. Equivalent damage to other miltary or industrial facilities—North Vietnamese airports (because the torpedo boats had been proven ineffectual against the destroyer and the next attack was expected to come from airplanes), or its army (because its troops were fighting American forces in South Vietnam), or its military supply lines into Laos (from which the guerrillas in South Vietnam received supplies and reinforcement)—might have made more sense militarily, but the symbolism would have been different. Being an act of reprisal, the important factor, as Schelling points out, was not its success as a military operation but its symbolic connection to the particular provocation: "Equivalent damage . . . would not have carried the same meaning and would not have seemed nearly so fitting. What made it seem fitting was not its success as a military threat. It was as an act of reprisal—as a riposte, a warning, a demonstration—that the enterprise appealed so widely as appropriate." This connection in form and content was what distinguished the reprisal from other military hostilities between the United States and North Vietnam so that there could be no doubt "about precisely what military action was directly related to the attack on the destroyers."[37] And the message this action appeared

36. For a brief historical note of these developments see 1 A. Chayes, T. Erlich, and A. Lowenfeld, *International Legal Process* 28–30 (1968).

37. Schelling, supra note 10, at 145. As it was, however, the Tonkin Gulf reprisal, which marked the first American bombing of North Vietnam, considerably furthered the escalation of the armed conflict between the parties. The response was out of proportion to the alleged provocation. In addition, later hearings of the Senate Committee on Foreign Relations have revealed contradictions in the administration's account of the alleged provocations that had led to the reprisal.

to convey was unambiguous: the air raid on North Vietnamese territory was not intended to bring about a general escalation of the existing armed conflict unless similar provocations were repeated in the future.

Rules in simple interactions of single-transaction conflicts of the type prevalent in previous centuries are little more than a gesture, a parting shot; there are no further decisions to be made, so the signaling rule cannot much change the existing state of affairs. Rules can serve a constructive purpose, however, in modern interdependent interaction in which similar transactions are simultaneously and successively repeated, for they still influence the future choices of the same or other parties. They should not, however, be formulated in static terms that focus on single events, but in symbolic terms that reiterate the indispensable relations of causes and effects among the parties. Because retaliations should communicate to the other side why they are done and what they could further do—but in fact do not do—such principles cannot be viewed in terms of isolated gestures that signal to the parties,

---

Doubts concerned questions such as whether the alleged second attack on the destroyer (after an American note of protest and warning had been submitted to North Vietnam) had occurred at all, whether the destroyer had penetrated North Vietnam's claimed territorial limits before the alleged incidents, whether it was in the area for legitimate purposes, and whether the attacks were provoked. See "The Gulf of Tonkin, The 1964 Incidents," Hearings before the Committee on Foreign Relations, U.S. Senate, 90th Cong., 2d Sess. (Feb. 20, 1968). For a particularly indignant review of the facts, see I. F. Stone, "International Law and the Tonkin Bay Incidents," in *The Vietnam Reader* 307, 310ff. (M. Raskin and B. Fall eds. 1965).

That the alleged incidents perhaps did not take place, does not detract from the validity of the analysis in the text about the message that the "reprisal" was intended to convey, at least to the American public. The manifest connection of the "response" to the "provocation" weighed heavily in the making of the Senate Southeast Asia Resolution. The message of reciprocity and limited intention that the act seemed to contain helped mobilize the popular support that was required to push this resolution through the Senate. The administration later interpreted the resolution as a general authorization to step up the war effort in Vietnam, and to take up military action elsewhere when it deemed necessary. But the United States did not retaliate after the attack and capture by North Korea in 1968 of the intelligence ship *Pueblo*, allegedly in international waters; nor did the United States take any reprisal when a similar provocation occurred and an American intelligence plane was downed in 1969 by North Korean aircraft. Fears of the escalation of the conflict seem to have weighed heavily in these decisions not to react.

as in traditional reprisals, the end of any, and possibly every, normative association between them.

The first step, then, toward a more constructive management of conflict is to bring the formal rules of international law in line with the international practice, and thus to repudiate this historical distinction between retorsion and reprisals. All lawful retaliations should be required to follow coherent patterns and traditional criteria formerly reserved only for retorsion. So also, the formal distinction between illegal and legal (but still injurious) offenses may be dispensed with; no matter how valuable such a distinction may seem to be, it is suitable only to central authorities in institutionalized arenas that claim to punish expiatively for violations of their edicts, and to tolerate reciprocal relations only among the subjects, and with respect to injuries that are not specifically regulated by the official edicts. However, since international reciprocal practices are essentially sequential, each act depending on evaluations of intentions and effects of the previous deeds of others, regulation should focus on the particular injurious consequences attributed to certain acts, and not merely on the symbolic forms of these acts.[38]

### AUTHORITARIAN REGULATION OF EXCHANGE RELATIONSHIPS

The unilateral respect and sense of inequality upon which authoritarian notions of law and expiatory rules of enforcement

38. The requirement that reciprocal reprisals be connected in form and content to the alleged injury, necessarily implies that the violation of particular forms of legal arrangements should be answered by a violation of the same or similar form. The following is the interpretation that should be given to Charter Article 2(4) regarding armed reprisals (see note 20 supra): the threat or use of force is unauthorized only when directed "against the territorial integrity or political independence of any state, *or* in any other *manner* inconsistent with the *Purposes* of the United Nations" (emphasis added). This is precisely what the text so clearly demands. Among the most fundamental of United Nations purposes are those relating to the development of relations among nations based upon the principles of equality and dignity of all peoples and nations, large and small (U.N. Charter, Preamble, Arts. 1[2] and 2[1]. For additional resolutions and declarations supplementing the Charter's principles of equality, see Detter, supra note 1, at 1071). The Charter does not reject military self-help that is not directed against the territorial integrity or political independence of a state, if it is executed in a manner consistent with this notion of equality and reciprocity but is not expiatory. Other fundamental policies of the Charter may in particular

are founded usually result from a relative lack of interdependence. Some conflict situations in the world arena, being still conditioned by low interdependence, do not offer the parties enough options in making reprisals. Interaction between Arabs and Israelis, for example, consist mainly of exchanges of military blows. Hence, retaliations in this context are usually limited to mere expiation or crude reciprocity. They have all the ingredients that make for instructive cases: explicit normative arrangements, their violent breach, provoked punitive actions, counter-reactions, and even third-party decision-making machinery.

### The Arab-Israeli Armistice Agreement

For many years the relations between Israel and its neighboring states had been governed by the general armistice agreements of 1949. From the Arab perspective, recurring patterns of Israeli behavior were in manifest and intentional violation of the agreements. In addition to diplomatic protest, different Arab groups sought small-scale military remedies. From the Israeli perspective, armed infiltrators from Arab-controlled territories were continuously breaking fundamental clauses of these agreements,[39] causing death and destruction. Since protests could not induce the Arab governments to stop these incidents, the Israelis tried to make them do so by reprisals and retaliations. The breaches of the armistice agreements between Israel and the Arab states were, in the beginning, small in scale. Each of them involved only a few deaths, woundings, kidnappings, or slight destruction of property, and therefore they seemed not to justify the total denunciation of the agreements. But each punitive action carried behind it the full blast of accumulated fury and frustration. Thus there was an escalating dynamics. Small incidents, transborder crimes, retaliatory raids, counter-retaliations, and so on, built up stresses that were only partially dissipated by the open wars of 1956, 1967, and 1973.

---

contexts be, of course, equally relevant. The distinction between reciprocal and expiatory manners of enforcement is, it may be recalled, also based on the minimum order policy of limiting the expansion of conflicts. This interpretation of Charter Article 2(4) will be further illustrated infra.

39. See, e.g., Article 3(2),(3) of the Israel-Syrian General Armistice Agreement, 42 U.N.T.S. 327, 330; see generally N. Bar-Yaacov, *The Israel-Syrian Armistice: Problems of Implementation, 1949–1966* (1967).

The armistice agreements provided, among other things, for a United Nations Truce Supervision Organization (UNTSO) whose main task was to investigate incidents that violated the agreements. In addition, each armistice agreement provided that there should be Mixed Armistice Commissions to supervise the working of the agreement. The commissions were composed of an equal number of delegates from each party, presided over by the Chief of Staff of UNTSO as chairman, or by a senior U.N. observer whom he designated after consulting the parties. The commissions were instructed in the agreements to make particular decisions with a view to "equitable and mutually satisfactory settlement," in order that peace be ultimately restored to Palestine.[40]

The Mixed Armistice Commissions were not effective. Their conciliatory and recommendatory functions were usually ignored by everyone concerned. They degenerated into legalistic agencies in which delegates "were apt to wrangle like shyster lawyers, with the object of securing a condemnation of the other party in the strongest terms for subsequent political and propaganda use." [41] According to U.N. personnel, the commissions' failure to influence the parties' conflict behavior was partly due to the fact that they lacked power to impose physical sanctions for breaches of the armistice agreements.[42]

There is nothing really new in international relations about not having a central and mandatory power to impose sanctions. Nevertheless, the commissions' chairmen used their power to pronounce on violations of the agreements in the rather familiar way of expiation and superior authority. They were always addressing the proceedings and the resulting formal decisions to single events and incidents, even when these were clearly connected with other events (in themselves viewed as separate items in the long and never-ending list of the commissions' agenda). General Burns, former UNTSO Chief of Staff, justified this approach by saying that the armistice agreements allowed no exception to the clause that forbade acts against the other party: "There was no provision that reprisals were justifiable in any circumstances." So that when

40. Supra note 39, at Article 7(7), p. 338.
41. E. Burns, *Between Arab and Israeli* 27 (1962).
42. Id.

Israeli troops attacked an Arab military or police post, and the Arabs complained of it to the Security Council, "the Council had to condemn the Israelis' action." [43]

Not only did the commissions and the Security Council focus on separate episodes, but presumably in trying to be objective and external to the parties' viewpoints, the former occasionally went so far as to treat the single event as two different ones. Frequently, both sides submitted complaints regarding the same incident. The complaint that had been submitted first was discussed first in the meeting of the commission. The chairman voted for the complaint. Thereafter, the commission discussed the other side's complaint and its proposed resolution was also voted for by the chairman:

> It did often happen that the MACs adopted, by the Chairman's vote, two resolutions relating to the same incident, each side condemning the other for the breach of the GAA. There was nothing else the Chairman could do, *legally*. To fire across, or to cross, the ADL [the Armistice Demarcation Line] was a breach of the GAA, even if the other side had fired first, or crossed first. And there was hardly ever evidence as to who had fired first, or started the trouble.[44]

Note the word *legally*. If one could in the Arab-Israeli context depend on legality in the conventional and domestic sense, it would be a very neat world indeed. Central authorities have a keen interest in avoiding troubles regardless of who started them, and in condemning anyone who actively participated in them instead of trusting the police to do their job. In such circumstances, therefore, the authorities may try each participant separately in order to determine his individual guilt for breach of the peace. It is true that the armistice agreements did not specifically authorize reprisals, but nothing compelled this sweeping interpretation of the agreements excluding the possibility of any act of self-defense or reprisal, except for the quite irrelevant and authoritarian notion of legality.

To begin with, firing across the armistice demarcation line in

43. Id. at 63.
44. Id. at 152 (emphasis added).

immediate response to the other side's fire is not necessarily a retaliatory measure, and should occasionally be regarded as a legitimate act of self-defense. Second, according to general principles of international law, reprisals are lawful; and the reprisals between Arabs and Israelis could also be justified according to the relevant principles relating to the violation of international agreements, since they concerned the violation of particular treaty provisions in response to the violation of the same provisions by the other side.[45] Such literal interpretation of the armistice agreements, to the exclusion of generally recognized principles of international law on the matter, seems to have been partly influenced by the existence in this particular case of a third-party decision-making organization. Undoubtedly, the existence of such an external agency is an important mitigating factor in the conflict behavior of parties, and the commissions' decisions reflected this fact.[46] But since the commissions' chairmen themselves lacked the instruments of power necessary for coercive enforce-

45. "Any violation of armistices is prohibited, and, if ordered by the Governments concerned, constitutes an international delinquency. . . . Serious violations empower the other party to denounce the armistice, but not, as a rule, to recommence hostilities at once without notice. . . . But since the terms 'serious violation' and 'urgency' lack precise definition, the course to be taken is in practice left to the discretion of the injured party" (Oppenheim-Lauterpacht, supra note 22, at 555–56 [notes omitted]). This doctrine is formulated in either-or terms which do not accord with modern conditions. No matter how serious particular violations may look to the injured party, it may still consider total denunciation of the armistice agreement and commencement of general hostilities as too drastic a remedy. The injured party therefore should always seek to limit its response to local incidents. For additional discussion and references to the view that compliance with the cease-fire provisions of an armistice agreement is conditioned by similar compliance by the other party, see ch. 8, note 15 supra. But some writers assert the extreme view that according to Charter Article 2(4) any armed reprisal is unlawful, regardless of any wrongs that provoke it, and that despite the unavailability of collective relief, the injured party may still have to submit indefinitely to the continuance of these wrongs. For this and different views, see notes 20 and 38 supra. Partly because of this extreme doctrine, which is absolutely and unconditionally adhered to by governments only in the case of armed reprisals by others, Israel often justified its reprisals on grounds of self-defense. See the following text. See also Bowett, infra note 47, at 2ff.; Blum, infra note 51.

46. The immediate reestablishment of a broken cease-fire, regardless of who had started the trouble, was one such mitigating factor. In addition, consider the following passage by Commander Hutchison, former chairman of the Israel-Jordan Mixed Armistice Commission: "Actually, my job was to determine guilt according to facts brought out by the investigation. If conclusive evidence could not be uncovered, then it was my duty to ask for further investigation. If this were im-

ment, they should have addressed their decisions to the immediate causes and effects of particular events rather than have proscribed reprisals altogether.[47]

It seems that the objections of the U.N. observers to Israel's official policy of retaliation did not arise only from authoritarian notions of legality. General Burns himself readily concedes that from the viewpoint of morality one could not condemn the parties for taking reprisals. But he questions the efficacy of the reprisals taken. He traces the origin of the Israeli doctrine of retaliation to identical practices the British had pursued in Palestine earlier. The British forces had conducted punitive operations against rebellious Arab villages in Palestine, and for many years before that on the northwest frontiers of India and elsewhere. General Burns holds that the same technique should not have been applied in the Arab-Israeli context:

> [T]he position of Israel vis-à-vis its Arab neighbors and that of the British Empire vis-à-vis the Mahsuds and Afridis was very different. To *punish,* one must have such power that the culprit cannot return the punishment. The Israelis were trying to punish Arab states that were potentially, though not actually, more powerful than themselves. . . . The Israelis were not in the position of the British Empire versus isolated Arab villages, or barbarous tribesmen, but sometimes they behaved and talked as if they were. And, in the end, the British themselves found that reprisals would only keep lawless villages and tribes quiescent for a time. No problem was or could be finally settled by them.[48]

---

possible then I would have to abstain. One international news writer suggested that for political expediency I should condemn Jordan. [He lacked, in his opinion, enough evidence to implicate Jordan in the murderous ambush of the Scorpion Pass bus incident.] Had I done so, the consequences might have been tragic, since there would have been excuse for another bloody retaliation." E. Hutchinson, *Violent Truce* 49 (1956).

47. The commissions' decisions in this respect followed the Security Council resolutions on some of the Israeli reprisals. See the following text. Bowett, "Reprisals Involving Recourse to Armed Force," 66 *Am. J. Int'l L.* 1 (1972).

48. Burns, supra note 41, at 62. The analogy between the two practices is, of course, not misleading simply because, unlike many of the British punishments, the Israeli retaliations fall within the category of operations between independent entities.

It is clear that this passage refers to punishment by expiation as distinguished from punishment by reciprocity.

Indeed, the evidence by which General Burns supports his argument about the nature of the Israeli policy of reprisals leads him to the conclusion that Israeli actions were in fact something more than simple reprisals for enforcing adherence to the provisions of the armistice agreements. According to statements that he quotes from Israeli officials, reprisals in the Israeli view were necessary because the outcome of any retaliatory battle was interpreted by Arab governments as a measure of Israel's strength: "If the Egyptians did not declare war after the Gaza clash, or the Jordanians after Nahhalin, it is an indication that they and the other Arab countries were unable to defeat Israel." [49] According to this Israeli view, the purpose of the official punitive actions was to make the Arab governments see themselves as helpless to counter the drastic Israeli military operations, thus forcing upon them the realization of being militarily inferior to Israel. This extra-dimension in the Israeli reprisals, according to General Burns, is what made them inadmissible:

> The wrongness of the policy was not that it sought to make the Arabs stop sending marauders into Israel, but that it was a slightly indirect method of using military power to force the Arab states (primarily Egypt) to accept the Israeli terms of peace. That is to say, it was an attempt to settle an international dispute by military force, in complete disregard of Israel's engagements as a member of the United Nations.[50]

This is considered by many sources as a telling and valid point against the way Israeli retaliations were conducted. One can only wish it had had a different influence on the commissions' decisions. The commissions had, undoubtedly, to condemn these so-called reprisals, since their expiatory dimension ran afoul of the commissions' efforts in the area. Not only were expiative measures

49. A reported statement of General Dayan, the then Israeli Chief of Staff, to Army officers as quoted in Burns, id. at 63. The majority of the newly established state consisted at that time of refugees who had just arrived in the country from different countries. It seems that these so-called reprisals were also deemed necessary in order to bolster Israeli morale.

50. Burns, id. at 64.

not conducive to reaching a peaceful solution of the dispute between the parties, but they further threatened the tenuous ceasefire arrangements between them. Indeed, even "reprisals" that were successful from a military point of view failed to check the marauding; in fact, they were usually followed by worse attacks. The chain of events led, through provocations, retaliations, and attempted counter-retaliations, straight to the open war in October 1956.

However, to say that the commissions should not have tolerated expiatory punishments is a far cry from saying that they had to ignore the fact that some actions came in response to the other side's provocation, on the grounds that "legality" means that all responses to the violations of the armistice agreements, expiative as well as genuinely reciprocal, were unacceptable. This expiative mode of third-party decision-making, which in itself was motivated by the desire to check on similar conduct, could only lead to opposite results. For one thing, the U.N. chairmen were not in the position of municipal judges but sometimes behaved and talked as if they were. For another, the provocations were always there, and to condemn the responses to them separately and on equal footing with the violent incidents that had led to them, was to encourage further violations of the armistice agreements. And since the decisions were based on the argument that all reprisals as such were proscribed, they could not be influential in putting pressure on the Israeli government to modify its policy of retaliations.

This is particularly true for the many Security Council resolutions which, as a rule of thumb, signaled out an Israeli military action without any condemnation or even mention of the provocatory acts against which it was allegedly made. Though the council repeatedly threatened Israel with material sanctions if such actions were not stopped, no such measures of enforcement were ever taken, the ultimate sanction upon which the resolutions rested having been public opinion. Paradoxically, while the purpose of particular Israeli retaliations may have been to force on the Arabs a realization of their helplessness in the face of Israeli military superiority, Israel's foreign policy aimed to show the world the country's potential inferiority. This is because Israel depends, for achieving superiority in power, on governmental and private foreign assistance, for which the image of a small country threatened with extinction by numerous, big, or hostile countries is sometimes more appropriate.

Had the Security Council resolutions, therefore, addressed and condemned both the provocations and the responses, justifying the condemnations of reprisals on the grounds that they were expiatory and even more provocative than the alleged provocations, while according to international law reprisals should be reciprocal, they might have influenced the Israeli policy. The authoritarian elements in the Israeli retaliations could, to a large extent, go on unchecked because of the authoritarian-expiative notions of law on which the Security Council resolutions were based. As it was, these resolutions, which invariably focused on a single event of an Israeli "action" without mention of the acts to which they were allegedly a reaction, were conspicuously one-sided. They reinforced in the minds of many people the realization that Israel was not only inferior to the Arab countries in resources, but was also politically isolated in the world. Indeed, the rigid pattern of votes in the Security Council in matters relating to the Arab-Israeli conflict indicates that the one-sided formulation of particular resolutions on reprisals had been influenced more by considerations of special interests based on political alignments than on a genuine desire to solve particular problems.[51]

### The Beirut Reprisal

Let us examine more closely one of the most famous and controversial of these Israeli reprisals. In July 1968, four armed men, for the first time in the Arab-Israeli context, forcibly seized control of an Israeli commercial jetliner in midair enroute from Rome to Tel Aviv, and ordered it to fly to Algiers. In an official statement issued from its headquarters in Beirut, a Palestinian Arab guerrilla organization claimed responsibility for the act.[52] Officials of the organization acknowledged that the hijacking was

51. See Falk, supra note 20, at 435–37; Blum, "The Beirut Raid and the International Law of Double Standard," 64 *Am. J. Int'l L.* 3, 98–104 (1970); Bowett, supra note 47, at 22–23.

52. *New York Times*, July 24, 1968, p. 16, col. 3 (late city ed.).

a new and different kind of guerrilla activity, but justified the departure from tradition by claiming that Israel's civil aviation had been used for military purposes. Furthermore, the guerrillas' spokesman in Beirut forecasted "more of the sort," that is to say, some additional acts of violence that would also sharply depart from prior restraint. The Israeli government, too, emphasized the novelty of the activity, pointing out that if the attack went without response, it would be repeated either in the air or at sea. Nevertheless, because the crew and male passengers were being held as hostages in Algiers, the response was limited to putting indirect diplomatic and economic pressures on the Algerian government to release them. These pressures produced an indirect agreement between the two governments by which Israel released a handful of Palestinian Arab prisoners in return for the release of the kidnapped airliner, its crew, and male passengers.[53] At the same time the Israeli government declared that any further action against Israel's civil aviation abroad would be met by reprisals.

The next incident occurred only three months later. The same guerrilla organization sent its men to Athens Airport to machine-gun and hand-grenade an Israeli commercial airliner, killing one passenger, wounding others, and damaging the plane. The enterprise proved that the Palestinian organization was still after Israeli planes outside Israel, and that both its objectives and its means were unlimited indeed. The diplomatic efforts in connection with the hijacking to Algiers had evidently produced nothing but the aforementioned ad hoc agreement between Israel and Algeria. Moreover, this agreement itself had compromised a number of fundamental principles: the neutrality of third-party states from which or through which the flights moved, the right of free and safe passage through the air, the security of international communications and commerce, in addition to the cease-fire agreements between Israel and the Arab states. After the Athens raid, it became clear that some action must be taken lest these principles be completely ignored by Arabs and Israelis.

But what kind of action? While punitive actions are necessary in order to assert and reestablish violated principles, they must be

53. *New York Times*, Sept. 1, 1968, p. 1, col. 7 (late city ed.); *New York Times*, Sept. 4, 1968, p. 36, col. 8 (late city ed.).

carefully tooled, or miss their objective and obliterate them completely. The difference is between carefully aiming a gun at a particular and well-defined point in the target and aiming with a cannon, on the assumption that while a bullet is more economical and may hit its point of destination, an explosion is surely not going to miss. Since the airliners' raiders had no fixed base, the Israeli policy was to strike at their host countries in the hope that they would find their hospitality too costly. Several Arab countries could qualify for retaliation, since they invariably supported the same guerrilla organization (for example, Jordan tolerated training activities and overt military presence while Syria supplied arms and gave an official backing. But in connecting the response to the provocation, appearances are important; a clearly discerned causation is sometimes even more relevant than a more substantive but less evident one. Accordingly, the Israeli government sent its regular forces into Lebanon, from which the attackers came and their organization declared responsibility for the raid, and destroyed thirteen Arab civilian aircraft at Beirut International Airport.

## Security Council's Condemnation

Both Israel and Lebanon asked for an emergency meeting of the Security Council in connection with this incident. The resulting Security Council resolution mentions only the attack at Beirut:

> *Observing* that the military action by the armed forces of Israel against the civil International Airport of Beirut was premeditated and of a large scale and carefully planned nature,
>
> *Gravely concerned* about the deteriorating situation resulting from this violation of the Security Council resolutions,
>
> *And deeply concerned* about the need to assure free uninterrupted international civil air traffic,
>
> 1. *Condemns* Israel for its premeditated military action in violation of its obligations under the Charter and the cease-fire resolutions;
>
> 2. *Considers* that such premeditated acts of violence endanger the maintenance of the peace;

3. *Issues* a solemn warning to Israel that if such acts were to be repeated, the Council would have to consider further steps to give effect to its decisions;

4. *Considers* that Lebanon is entitled to appropriate redress for the destruction it suffered, responsibility for which has been acknowledged by Israel.[54]

This resolution, of course, is a political compromise, and in its compounded form embodies the full demands of none of its formulators. Nevertheless, its formulation, its style, and its choice of evocative symbols is revelatory of the authoritarian-expiative syndrome described above. Hence it requires close analysis. The resolution is not intended to state a general principle, but it is supposedly a concrete decision addressed to a single act made by a particular participant.

Yet, with the exception of a few ambiguous and pejorative utterances, the resolution does not make clear what, exactly, the rules or principles were whose violation brought down on the accused the anger of the authority.[55] No one had disputed that the

54. U.N. Doc. S/RES/262 (1968), adopted unanimously by the Security Council on Dec. 31, 1968; reprinted in 63 *Am. J. Int'l L.* 681–82 (1969).

55. The terms "premeditated" and "of carefully planned nature" are ascriptive, not descriptive; their primary function is not to describe things, events, or anything else, but quite literally to ascribe responsibility for the action in question. They originate in the well-known maxim in criminal law, *actus non est reus nisi mens sit rea,* "which has tempted jurists (and less often judges) to offer a general theory of 'the mental element' in crime (*mens rea*) of a type which is logically inappropriate just because the concepts involved are defeasible and are distorted by this form of definition" H. L. A. Hart, "Ascription of Responsibility and Rights," 49 *Proceedings of the Aristotelian Society* 171 [1949] in *Freedom and Responsibility* 143, 144 [H. Morris ed. 1961]). Hart points out that in order to determine what this mental element is ("foresight," "voluntariness") and how its presence or absence is established, it is always necessary to refer back to the various admitted defenses that eliminate or reduce responsibility (e.g. mistaken facts, provocation, accident, insanity). It is inconceivable that any governmental operation such as the Beirut retaliation could be carried out without some prior planning. One can also imagine the disastrous consequences to the civil airport and its occupants if the operation had not been of a "carefully planned nature." The nonsensical term "premeditated" (based as it is on a double fiction: that a state can be viewed as a person to whom the fictitious dichotomy between the body and the mind may be applied) does not denote a description of an occurrence according to some criteria of illegality, but merely ascribes guilt to the target state. The material question is, of course, whether the defenses of provocation, self-

precipitating event was an act of coercion in a sequence of violence. The entire question was whether that act, in context, was lawful. The resolution simply does not address itself to this crucial point, and the impression gained is that the act is unlawful because the authority says so.[56] And the authority is not to be questioned, for it commands the subject to cease and desist instantly from "such acts," again without telling the convicted party what it is, precisely, that he is ordered to refrain from doing. But though the "external" authority is composed of various interested parties, the majority of which are traditional opponents of the accused, and though it purports at one and the same time to legislate, apply, and solemnly execute its commands by threats, it is still to be considered a benevolent authority, since it is interested in distributive justice among its subjects. One may even think upon reading the text of the resolution, that all the Lebanese representative to the United Nations had to do after the decision, was to catch the first plane (preferably not an Arab or Israeli one) to Switzerland in order to pick up the awaiting Israeli compensatory check.

The resolution was obviously an exercise in political futility, a

---

defense, reprisal, etc., are applicable to the case. The term "in violation of its obligations under the Charter" is not helpful in this respect. Neither the resolution nor the debates preceding the resolution go beyond the mere assertion about the illegality of the act in question. The term "in violation of the cease-fire resolutions" simply begs the central question, since each party considers its compliance with these resolutions as conditioned by the compliance of the other side. Israel claimed to have violated these resolutions precisely because of alleged similar violations by Lebanon. The question is whether these alleged violations by Lebanon justified the particular reaction by Israel. The point is that without any explicit, or at least tacit, reference to the alleged provocation, there is no way by which the ascription of lawlessness could have been reasonably explained in the resolution.

56. But see Falk, supra note 20, at 429 where reference is made to the Security Council's condemnation (April 9, 1964) of Britain's bombing of the Yemeni town of Harib on March 28, 1964, in retaliation for alleged Yemeni support of the anti-colonial struggle in Aden (U.N. Doc. S/RES/188 [1964]). This resolution, unlike the Beirut one, widens the context and establishes a corresponding reciprocal obligation on the part of Yemen. The British retaliation was not connected to the alleged provocation either in form or in content, and was carried out in an expiatory manner reminiscent of the reprisals prevalent in the nineteenth century. As such, it was clearly incompatible with the purposes and principles of the U.N. Charter. See note 38 supra.

classic *brutum fulmen*. Everyone knew it would not be obeyed; every Israeli also felt with a sense of deep indignation that it should not be obeyed. In terms of the analysis developed above, the structure and expressed language of the resolution announced its own futility. The phrase "issues a solemn warning" is only figuratively used. It is a ritualistic symbol by which the competent authority claims a mandatory and authoritarian status for its decision, and not a real commitment to punish. In the context, the warning lacked credibility because this very same, supposedly threatening, formula had already been included in almost all the many resolutions on "such acts" between Israelis and Arabs, and though such acts had always been repeated, the warning had never been made good.

The potential effectiveness of the resolution was further eroded by its authoritarian character. No criteria were given for the decision, hence it struck one as arbitrary. And indeed, there is a moral hypocrisy in it because nothing is offered in the text of the resolution to help answer the many questions that it persistently raises: was it not inconsistent and hypocritical under prevailing international conditions to condemn and threaten a country with collective punishment only because it helped itself? And had not the U.S., whose vote was the determining factor in adopting this resolution itself under similar circumstances, resorted in 1964 to a reprisal against North Vietnam? [57] But the central defect of the resolution was its stubborn and obtuse one-

---

57. The United States representative in the council justified the apparent inconsistency of his government in supporting the resolution, by the need to put the United Nations in the "forefront of efforts to perfect new rules of international law" that make it clear that "no pretext whatsoever justified interference with international civil aviation" (6 *U.N. Monthly Chronicle*, No. 1, at 17 [Jan. 1969]). But before the Bay of Tonkin incident, the U.S. stated in the Security Council in connection with the British retaliation against the Yemini town of Harib, its disapproval " 'of retaliatory raids, wherever they occur and by whomever they are committed' " (Stone, supra note 37, at 307). But in 1972 the United States vetoed a proposed Security Council resolution condemning Israel for retaliatory air raids against Lebanon and Syria on the ground that it did not mention the provoking terrorist act. "[O]ne-sided resolutions of the type which the Security Council had so frequently adopted in recent times did not contribute to the goal of peace" 9 *U.N. Monthly Chronicle*, No. 9, at 5 [Oct., 1972]). For a similar retaliation by France against Tunisia in 1958, see Stone, supra note 33, at 307.

sidedness: why did the resolution only condemn the attack at Beirut and not mention the similar attack at Athens?

## The Binding Force of International Law

When a decision must be urgently made and its text preferably short, explanations cannot be elaborated upon and may therefore be condensed into terms that symbolize the principles upon which the decision is based (such as "equality," "reciprocity"). But explanations about equality and reciprocity lessen and qualify what should otherwise be regarded as absolute command. International lawyers are the ones who draft or recommend the language of these Security Council resolutions, and they, of course, see to it that the resolutions appear more as binding legal obligations in the positivistic sense than as just or equal. Such an extreme authoritarian formulation of decrees is not commonplace even in municipal decisions, whose binding or otherwise punishable nature, unlike international law's decisions, is taken for granted. But many professionally insecure international lawyers feel a constant need to quiet criticism about their craft not being law proper, and they do so by formulating rules and decisions in the most positivist language possible.

This is particularly true in the Security Council resolutions, whose binding force is a subject of heated controversy within the legal profession itself. When the United Nations organization was established, it was primarily thought of in terms of a collective security, international political system. The theory of collective security, it was noted, is characterized by a high degree of minimum-order orientation. Accordingly, the competence of the Security Council to make enforceable decisions was specifically limited to threats or breaches of peace. Substantive decisions of the council in this respect require the concurring votes of the great powers.[58] The underlying assumption in such a system is that the overwhelming force of the great powers should be an effective instrument in maintaining or restoring minimum order, and that in

58. Charter Articles 24, 27. For a discussion of collective security on which the present discussion is based, see chs. 1 and 2 supra. The strict interpretation often given to Charter Article 2(4) (note 20 supra) seems to have been influenced by an assumption, so common immediately after World War II, of collective armed measures (Reisman, supra note 15, at 848).

crisis situations the urgency of the problem and the extreme threat to peace involved may facilitate the reaching of unanimous agreement between the major powers on the action to be taken.

In extreme crisis situations, such as when hostilities are already taking place, the members must issue orders and back them up by the threat of superior force without any underlying sympathies they may have for claims of frustrated justice enunciated by the disturbers of the peace. Decisions of the council in such situations, therefore, should preferably be drafted in the greatest authoritarian terms and focus on the relatively infrequent and isolated event of an extreme crisis. But during the years the council has had to make decisions that do not immediately concern the cessation of ongoing hostilities or a threat to the political independence or territorial integrity of a state. To situations such as the Beirut reprisal, which do not call for immediate coercive enforcement, the expiatory and unegalitarian competence of the council is irrelevant.[59]

### The Reciprocities of Economic Interdependence

This focus, away from the real interplay of sanctions in interdependent situations, caused the Beirut reprisal resolution to have no bearing whatsoever on how and who actually pays the costs of the kind of activities condemned; it is addressed to an isolated transaction between Israel and Lebanon, overlooking all other consequential transactions. Here are samples of these transactions. The Lebanese, and also the Americans and French who owned shares in destroyed Arab aircraft, picked up the checks for their losses in London, where they had insured their business enterprise. British insurers had to pay about twenty million dollars. Part of the cost was absorbed by the usual reinsurance mechanisms—part,

59. For the authority of Security Council resolutions in matters that do not involve provisional or collective measures in order to deal with acts of aggression, other breaches of peace, or threats to peace, compare Falk, supra, note 20 at 435 with J. Halderman, *The United Nations and the Rule of Law* 86 (1966); Halderman, "Some International Constitutional Aspects of the Palestine Case," in *The Middle East Crisis: Test of International Law* 78, 83–85 (J. Halderman ed. 1969); Halderman, "Some Legal Aspects of Sanctions in the Rhodesian Case," 17 *Int'l & Comp. L. Quart.* 672, 700 (1968). For the effects of inequality in international organizations, see Oliver, "Unmet Challenges of Inequality in the World Community," 118 *U. Pa. L. Rev.* 1003, 1006 (1970).

according to reportedly cheerful London market gossip, falling on an Israeli company.[60] It took a televised appeal from the president of the United States to the American airline companies to make them lend their Lebanese counterparts several aircraft so that they could continue with their business activities without a long interruption. This is because owners were reluctant to fill the gap when they knew their jets were in danger of being destroyed on the ground while they wore Arab or Israeli colors. And, despite interested groups' assertions to the contrary, the attacks must have affected the willingness of ordinary air passengers to trust themselves to airlines based in these troubled countries. In addition, insurance rates for Arab and Israeli passenger planes were reviewed, and insurance rates for cargo transportation to the Middle East were generally raised. The implications of all these things for economic interdependence, international communications, and the national budgets and foreign exchange earnings of the countries immediately affected are obvious.

Attacks on civil aviation, therefore, whether done in foreign or local airports, are different from other armed attacks between Arabs and Israelis. They immediately affect the whole world's web of economic and communicational interdependencies and cannot be viewed as just another insignificant violation of cease-fire arrangements between several states. Moreover, because of this interdependence, any attack on commercial aircraft must directly affect not only the country against which the raid is directed but also the country from which the attackers come. Calculated in dollars and cents, Israel paid for the Beirut reprisal not less, and perhaps more, than Lebanon did. To put it differently, no matter what the general power relations between Israel and Lebanon, the relation was equal as far as armed attacks on civil aviation were concerned. To be successful, therefore, any act against civil aviation in response to the other side's departure from tradition should have exploited and communicated this aspect of genuine reciprocity and equality.

Lebanon in 1968 had the largest tourist industry among the Arab countries of the Middle East, and the largest civil aviation industry that served all Arab countries. There were less expensive,

60. *The Economist,* Jan. 4, 1969, at 43.

less destructive, and less arrogant ways of delivering the message that Lebanon was as vulnerable in this critical industry as was Israel, and that Lebanon's interest in policing violations would have to be as great as Israel's. In an unexpressed way, Lebanon already understood that. It is one of the weakest and most commercially oriented countries in the world. Its government had always tried to stay clear of the continuing Arab-Israeli hit-and-run operations. The Lebanese government at the time of the Beirut incident already had an open understanding with the Palestinian guerrilla organizations (as a condition for Lebanese toleration of the guerrilla's political, recruitment, and training activities in the country) that they might not attack Israel's territory from Lebanon. This agreement had for the most part been complied with, and relations between Israel and Lebanon had been relatively stable. Israeli reciprocal pressures could have induced the Lebanese government to extend this arrangement to attacks abroad that were not border crossings in the literal meaning of the term.

### Humiliating the Weak

Thus, the Israeli retaliation at Beirut airport was ill-devised. The Israeli raiders did the damage they set out to do with textbook precision. The attack was short and bloodless, designed for maximum disruption and destruction of empty aircraft. The action was less lethal than the Arab attack on the packed Israeli jetliner in Athens, which killed one passenger and could easily have killed the lot—less lethal than normal Arab-Israeli actions and reactions. If one were, therefore, to apply to this reaction the traditionally only substantive legal criterion of quantitative proportionality, it would have undoubtedly been regarded as a proper reprisal. But by landing regular troops in the heart of Lebanon and in three hours wiping out half of the country's commercial aviation, Israel committed an act of war, as opposed to acts of sabotage across frontiers, which could be regarded more in light of border incidents. It was clear to everybody that this reprisal was possible only because of the enormous power difference between Israel and Lebanon. Worse, the elegance and sharpness of the operation, instead of being understood as self-restraint and limited intention on the part of the attackers, only symbolized this disparity in power. That the Israeli forces were able to do the damage they set out to do without hurting themselves or anybody else, reinforced in the minds of Arabs and Israelis alike the notion of a mighty force punishing and imposing its superior will on an inferior one.

In other words, the Beirut reprisal was generally taken to be expiatory in character and not reciprocal. It brought home to the Lebanese feelings of inequality, shame, and the humiliation of being unable to defend their country against a superior force. No matter how necessary the principle of the security of civil aviation seemed to many people in Lebanon, in the wake of the Beirut attack they instinctively regarded it as something imposed by force from without, and not as a reciprocal and indispensable relation. Furthermore, it was the humiliating defeat in the Arab-Israeli war of 1967 that had brought the military into bad repute in the Arab world, and enhanced the popularity of the guerrillas. Lebanon had not taken part in that war, and it was only after the Beirut reprisal that its public's support of the guerrillas reached its peak. The attack raised a huge public uproar in Lebanon, the moderate government had to resign, recruitment for the guerrillas more than doubled, and the group responsible for the raids on Israeli airliners issued an additional statement saying that from then on it would "specialize" in airliners.

## Perceptions of No-Alternative

The wrongness of the Beirut attack, therefore, was not that it was a punishment for a similar attack, or that it sought to make the Arab governments stop sending or harboring people who terrorized commercial airliners. The wrongness of the raid was that it did not draw a distinction between terror against civil aviation and other military operations between Arabs and Israelis. Indeed, the Israeli representatives in the Security Council did not justify the Beirut attack on grounds of reciprocity and equality in matters of civil aviation but primarily on the ground of the right of self-defense:[61]

61. 6 *U.N. Monthly Chronicle*, No. 1, at 6 (Jan. 1969), alluding to Soviet and Lebanese arguments that the raid at Athens was not an international delinquency

Any attack against an Israeli civil aircraft, wherever it might be, was as much a violation of the cease-fire as an attack on Israeli territory and entitled the Israeli Government to exercise its right of self-defense . . . the attempt to blow up the aeroplane at a neutral airport was of the *same character* as other acts of Arab terrorism. . . . For 20 years there had been Arab warfare by terror. For 20 years there had been Israeli self-defense counter-measures. *The only way to avert this chain-reaction was to terminate the Arab warfare.* Mr. Tekoah [the Israeli representative] said he had returned from Israel only a short time before, and that the people were prepared to defend itself, *regardless of how warfare against itself was waged or how it was defined.*[62]

In other words, the Israeli government did not distinguish between rungs of escalation in the Arab-Israeli conflict. The only alternative it saw to avert the chain reaction of the Athens-Beirut kind was to terminate the Arab general warfare. The Beirut "reprisal" can only be understood in light of this larger objective. It was a military operation whose immediate target for destruction happened to be Arab civil aviation, because the "Arabs" had turned to the civil aviation front as a new target of operations. Its political objective, however, was to terminate Arab warfare in general by impressing upon the Arabs that the superior force of Israel remained unchanged. As such, the operation was clearly expiatory.

Unfortunately, the authoritarian element in the Israeli retaliation, as we have seen, was matched by the authoritarian and static formulation of the Security Council resolution on the matter. And just as the symbolism of a reprisal was lost in the act, what was lost in this resolution was the signal for a need to preserve some rules and relations in the chaos that had resulted from the defiance of all indispensable relations. Had the resolution been drafted in reciprocal and not in authoritarian terms, focusing on all the relevant events, and therefore pointing out that the broadening of this

---

since it took place in the territory of a sovereign state. The Soviet representative stated that, according to "modern international law," reprisals in response to actions taken by individuals are "absolutely inadmissible," "because the acts of individuals cannot be taken as violations of international law" (id. at 15).

62. Id., at 6 and 14 (emphasis added).

particular conflict could be prevented only by the reciprocal efforts of all the parties concerned, Israel would still have been condemned for its act, but the symbolism of that condemnation, and the message from the United Nations as to future events, would have been different. As it was, the Israeli action reinforced Palestinian incentive to mount further attacks on commercial aviation; and the Security Council response, condemning only Israel for its "attack" without any meaningful reference to the raids to which it was supposedly a direct response, supplanted the official encouragement for such raids.

The next attack on an Israeli airliner came about two months later at Zurich airport. This time, however, a battle ensued between the attackers and Israeli guards. Paradoxically, the arming of civil aircraft so that they could return fire whenever attacked, reinforced in many governments the realization that attacks on civil aviation cannot be seen as simply Arab-Israeli military operations. The response at Zurich could not be arbitrarily separated from the provocation, and there were reasons aplenty for everyone to be immediately concerned about what happened there. As the *Economist* put it immediately after the raid: "[W]hen Arabs and Israelis are seen shooting it out in, of all places, neutral Switzerland, with machine guns, grenades and sticks of plastic explosive by them, the time has come to stop believing that the Arab guerillas are a species of desert boy scout. In Zurich, they acted as a bloody menace to everyone." [63] After the Zurich and other attacks on civil aviation that followed the Beirut raid, the Israelis did not move again to prove that the Arabs are merely a species of cub scout, and that they are the boy scouts. Instead, the Israeli government tried to restore safety to civil aviation through diplomatic and organizational channels. By then, however, not only Israeli or Arab airliners were being attacked, but also American, British, Austrian, German, and Swiss airliners, and violence spread to other neutral airports.[64] Not only did the immediate conflict ex-

---

63. *The Economist*, Feb. 22, 1969, p. 14, cols. 1–2.

64. Other such incidents included hijacking and destruction of American, British, and Japanese jetliners at Damascus, Cairo, and Benghazi airports and in the Jordan desert in 1968, 1970, and 1973; explosions in midair of Austrian, Israeli, and Swiss jetliners in 1970 and 1971; attacks with machine guns and hand grenades against passengers of Israeli, French, and American airliners at Munich,

pand in form and content, but also in the number of parties directly involved.

## SUMMARY OF TRENDS

In the previous discussions a distinction was noted between two contradictory types of enforcement measures. Each category implies a different value choice regarding the international sanctioning system. Sanctions can be arbitrarily employed in an authoritarian fashion that stresses unilateral respect and expiation in the rules avenged. Conversely, they can be reciprocally administered, communicating consistency, delimited objectives, and desirable social consequences to all parties in a dispute.

Among legal theorists, some describe law in explicit authoritarian terms that in effect focus on the hierarchy of power in a given arena (Austin, Kelsen). Others focus on the reciprocal practices of governments and people (Vattel, McDougal, Fuller, Falk). Many jurists either sidetrack the real issues by begging knotty questions, or pay lip service to so-called principles of equality while adhering in practice to principles of expiative enforcement. With the growth of interaction and interdependence during the last decades, the invariably simplistic command theories have been falling into disrepute. This change in philosophy of law, however, has been only partly followed by corresponding changes in the formulation of particular norms. Though the Vienna Convention on the Law of Treaties reflects some of the recent developments (for example, Article 52 invalidates treaties that have been concluded through substantial coercion), its termination provisions are either expiative or insufficiently reciprocal. In this respect, as well as in others, these norms reflect the historical balance of power period that produced them.

Recent trends of decision, both in collaborative and competitive contexts, have been toward reciprocal methods of enforcement and

---

Athens, Tel Aviv, and Rome airports in 1970, 1972, and 1973; attacks against Israeli athletes in 1972 at the Munich Olympics, and against Israeli airline offices and American, Belgian, and Israeli diplomats abroad during 1971–73. Also, the downing in 1973 by Israeli aircraft of a Libyan jetliner that had strayed over Israeli-controlled territory, and in 1973 the rerouting by Israeli aircraft of an Iraqi airliner over Lebanese territory and forcing it to land and submit to search in Israel.

coherent principles of behavior. More often than not, it has been observed, decisions communicate a pattern of collaborative interaction, both in form and in content. Less and less are self-help measures designed to intimidate and humiliate the target nation rather than to secure reciprocal conformity to particular norms. The United Nations Charter contains among its fundamental objectives notions of equality and human worth. And Article 2(4) of the Charter is explicit in rejecting armed reprisals that are taken in a *manner* which is inconsistent with these objectives, even if they are of minor intensity and are not directed against the territorial integrity and political independence of the target state.

That the Charter rejects authoritarian measures of self-help, of course, does not necessarily mean that this requirement will be adhered to in practice. It is one thing to suggest the guidelines that ought to govern decisions so that they will not be disruptive of basic human values, and quite another to suppose that these guidelines will be adhered to in operation. Some of the earliest writings in international law recommended principles of genuine reciprocity, but lacking the necessary conditions of interdependence, these norms were frequently not followed in the practice of states, and for the most part have remained a matter of juristic doctrine.

Where interaction is meager and relations are limited to a bare minimum, the options available to parties in conflicts are limited. The parties tend to stress conflict alone and to overlook whatever measure of common interest may exist in any conflict. Furthermore, in interaction that consists mainly of exchange of military blows (as between Arabs and Israelis), or in dependent relationships (as between colonial and non-European nations up to the present era), the parties tend to draw generalization from particular power relations to other value sectors. Since the superior power cannot be deterred by possible expansion of conflicts, reactions to alleged violations of the "norms" cover any possible relation. Furthermore, power is regarded as the single most important factor in interaction, and other values that do not directly make for military strength are discarded. Human dignity, peoples' worth, their cultures and social patterns are not respected.[65] Law is iden-

65. This, for example, was reflected in the so-called capitulation treaties, and in the habit of characterizing non-European nations as "uncivilized" (ch. 10 infra).

tified solely with hierarchial commands, and elementary normative behavior with coercion.

A growth in interaction enlarges the alternatives in particular disputes.[66] In multiple value relationships, parties more readily perceive in conflicts measures of common interests. Attempts to keep particular disputes from expanding to other relations, even between unequal powers, as noted, must necessarily involve reciprocal norms and practices.

The explanations commonly given by both officials and commentators of the reason why international agreements should not be violated illustrate the historical trend. The answers usually fall into four categories: (1) promises are "sacred" (the "sanctity of treaties"); (2) violations are "forbidden," they are contrary to the rules (pacta sunt servanda); (3) violations make cooperation impossible, you cannot make agreements anymore (the "security of treaties"); (4) violations (or unlawful enforcement) are contrary to reciprocity and equality (the evolving rules of retaliations and the doctrine of "unequal treaties").[67]

Though all these explanations are still invariably found in present inconsistent writings, they reflect the historical periods that produced them. The first answer can be traced to the Middle Ages, when interdependence was relatively rare. Agreements were "sacred" because the monarch had sworn to fulfill them. The monarch's honor and status depended on keeping his word, and he owed the duty primarily to himself and to God. The second answer accords with the political arrangements in the eighteenth and nineteenth centuries. During this period, in which unilateral respect and forceful constraint predominated, a rule was identified with coercive enforcement: agreements were still considered sacred but their violation was forbidden by public order and was

---

66. Interaction between two particular states is not only a function of transactions between them, but also of transactions between each of them and corresponding third parties. In other words, the range of choices in a dispute between countries A and B may depend upon ties of A to country C, B to country D, and corresponding transactions between A-D, B-C, C-D, and so on. As shown by Thomas Lawrie, Jr., "Third Party Functioning Relations Within a Subsystem: A Case Study of Pakistan" (unpublished paper), such third-party interdependency is particularly important in disputes between countries which maintain minimal level of direct interaction between them.

67. App. A infra.

suppressed by force.[68] The third and fourth answers reflect the growing interdependence and cooperation of the present century, during which international norms have become more of a direct emanation from the emergence of a more pluralistic world community. Violations of international agreements and the reactions thereto are more and more condemned (and justified) for reasons that appeal to these very notions of pluralistic cooperation and the resulting egalitarianism.

68. While by the second half of the nineteenth century the notion of international law as hierarchy of commands did prevail, rules based on reciprocity among the participants were also gaining foot. The rules during the classical balance of power period were intended to apply both to relations among the great powers and to those between great powers and small states. Jurists, therefore, had to provide for both simple reciprocity and expiation in the rules they formulated. (See, for example, the rules discussed above regarding lawful responses to treaty violations).

The industrial and technological revolutions of the nineteenth century had affected these two sets of rules in different ways. With improvements in military technology and in the means of transporting violence, the number of unequal treaties with remote countries mushroomed. At the same time, but in regard to intra-European relations the previous crude concepts of the law of simple reciprocity, whose essential element was direct punitive action, were gradually giving way to more refined notions of reciprocity. One manifestation of this development was the so-called invisible hand theory, discussed in ch. 1 supra. The growing interdependence meant that the ultimate punishment was not dependent solely on the decisions of those who were directly involved in a particular dispute, but also on reactions by the larger community.

# 10 From Balance of Power to World Community

> India likes gods.
> And Englishmen like posing as gods.
>
> E. M. Forster, *A Passage to India*

The origin of most of our conventional legal thinking, it has repeatedly been demonstrated, is traceable to the eighteenth and nineteenth centuries. It was then that familiar notions about what is good or bad, community, law, obligation, breach, and punishment, acquired many of their current traditional meanings. It was also then that the seeds of present developments and changing perspectives were sown, and the sprouts of modern interdependence initially appeared. Nietzsche, a contemporary of the later part of the classical balance of power period, observed:

> The concept of good and evil has a dual prehistory; *first,* in the soul of the ruling tribes and castes. Whoever has the power to repay good with good, evil with evil, and also actually repays, thus being grateful and vengeful, is called good; whoever is powerless and unable to repay is considered bad. As one who is good, one belongs to the "good," a community that possesses communal feeling because all individuals are knit together by the sense of repayment. As one who is bad, one belongs to the "bad," a group of subjected, impotent human beings who have no communal feeling.[1]

This may equally describe international affairs in the nineteenth century, and also in the first half of the twentieth century. The good or "civilized" (as they liked to call themselves) [2] were a caste, the few major actors in the balance of power political system; the bad or "uncivilized," the mass. Good and bad were at that time the same as noble and low, master and slave. But the oppo-

---

1. F. Nietzsche, *On the Genealogy of Morals* 167 (W. Kaufman & R. J. Hollingdale trans. 1969).
2. Röling, *International Law in an Expanding World*, ch. 4 (1960).

nent in the balance of power system is not considered bad or evil. He is good, an "essential" participant in the system, since he can repay.[3] The participant that does one harm is not considered bad or uncivilized but, rather, the contemptible participant. "In the community of the good, good is inherited; it is impossible that a bad person should grow out of such good soil. If one of the good nevertheless does something unworthy of the good, then one has recourse to excuses." [4] One blames a "hidden," or "invisible hand," for example, saying that "unforeseen circumstances" outside anybody's control (rebus sic stantibus) have caused one not to repay his obligations or not to react to others' breaches.[5]

Characteristically, the Law of Nations in the classical balance of power period—conceived as it was in terms of cautious trade and hostile balancing—was meaningfully applied only among the so-called civilized nations, those that were approximately equally powerful. Only where there was no clearly recognizable predominance and where acts of war would have meant inconclusive mutual damage did the idea dominate that one might come to an understanding and negotiate one's claim. Each essential actor repaid the other in proportion to what he received. Particular legal arrangements, too, were initially perceived to be based on an exchange, a contract between participants of more or less equal power.[6] The laissez-faire political theories of the time gave expression to these arrangements. Law was merely the application of a like scale.

Similarly, the initial character of retorsion [7] was also that of trade. Each essential participant repaid the other for injuries caused to himself in the same or similar coin. Retaliations to violations of norms and reactive actions to alleged injuries were made in the same value and in parallel modality of power. Thus retorsion is repayment and exchange on the assumption of an approximately equal power position. Retorsion is conceived as doing justice, as achieving fairness and restoring equality. Figuratively, re-

3. Ch. 1 supra.

4. Nietzsche, supra note 1, at 167.

5. See pp. 23–24 supra.

6. See pp. 4 and 12 supra.

7. For a discussion of the conventional principle about retorsion and reprisals, see chapter 9 supra.

torsion in this sense is the scale of justice, the instrument of trade, balancing the wrongdoing with the punishment. The offense is regarded as a special variety of turnover in which the exchange is established involuntarily.

The distinction between retorsion and reprisals originated without any regard to good or bad, civilized or uncivilized, or any other unworthy characteristics attributed to nations outside of Europe. These were convenient adjectives to describe those who did not have sufficient power to repay and participate in the community of traders; for retorsion originated above all to preserve a community. Because of the growing interdependence in Europe during the nineteenth century and the beginning of this century, many activities within states started having repercussions on the activities within other states. This meant that despite the rigorous and formal distinction between internal and international matters, Europe was growing into a community knitted together by a sense of reciprocal repayments and common interests in constantly increasing transnational transactions. The harmful impact of internal activties—whether legislative, administrative, or judicial—on domestic economies of other states could not be ignored. They called for reactions by the injured states.

But among those who are tied together by many transactions, or those who are approximately equally powerful, self-help measures [8] usually provoked countermeasures. The limiting of the ensuing conflict expansion so that it would not disrupt all possible relations between the parties required some distinct forms of self-restraint in both actions and reactions. Punishments for alleged misdeeds or injuries had, therefore, to be reciprocal: doing to the offender what he had allegedly done himself. The important element in these punishments was that the offender directly realize for himself that common interest, interdependence, communal bonds and relations were all involved in such injurious acts. Reactions therefore consisted not merely of repayment but of restitution and reinstatement of the communal bonds themselves. Con-

8. Because of the laissez-faire philosophy of the time, such matters as economic injuries were not supposed to be regulated by formal law, and therefore were usually not dealt with in treaties. They were supposed to be adjusted and settled by themselves in the open arena of self-help measures.

necting the response to the provocation in form and content manifested that though some relations, communal bonds, or rules had
been broken, others still existed and were, in fact, being maintained and reinforced in the act of retorsion.

In relations between European and non-European nations, it
may be recalled, "reprisals" were practiced, not retorsion. Unlike
retorsion, these so-called reprisals did not originally belong in the
domain of justice. Justice as expressed in retorsion derived from
prudent concern with self-preservation. Retorsion was motivated
by the consideration that in retaliating for an alleged wrongdoing
one could further harm oneself and perhaps not attain one's goal
anyway. It was a reactive action held in check and modified by
the idea that every injury has its equivalent and can actually be
paid back in the same currency. Retorsion belonged to the domain of determining and measuring values—that is, of building
a community. In relations between predominantly unequal parties,
on the other hand, nothing had value, not even one's human
dignity and worth. The less powerful participants could not bargain, exchange, trade, or repay; they did not belong to the community, they were simply considered unworthy or "uncivilized."
Reactions to alleged misdeeds, therefore, did not have to preserve
any communal bonds. There was no fear on the part of the powerful ones that conflicts would escalate and destroy whatever measure
of interdependence might possibly have existed. The relations
were those of dependency, unilateral respect, and blind obedience
to given orders.

Punishment for disobedience was rendered in any form conceivable to the more powerful participants. The responses were
completely arbitrary and were not related to the alleged provocations in any form or content. Reprisals for violations of unequal
treaty obligations relating to wealth, respect, and rectitude consisted of unleashing foreign mercenaries against local populations,
bombardments of port towns, and executions. The desire for vengeance—the exalting feeling of being allowed to vent one's power
freely upon one who is powerless—was turned loose in these so-
called punishments. Reprisals consisted in a warranty for and title
to severity, cruelty, and pain, reserved in "social contract" philos-
ophies of the time for those who lived "outside" of a community
in the savage and outlaw state of affairs.

No values were set in reprisals, only the pain and destruction inflicted on the offender were somehow measured. As jurists stated the principle, lawful reprisals only required that some quantitative proportionality be kept between the punishment and the alleged violation. This idea that every violation of a contract has its equivalent or price in bodily injuries and torture, and that it can actually be paid back merely through the measured physical pain of the culprit, has its roots in the oldest and most primitive personal relationships:

> To inspire trust in his promise to repay, to provide a guarantee of the seriousness and sanctity of his promise, to impress repayment as a duty, an obligation upon his own conscience, the debtor made a contract with the creditor and pledged that if he should fail to repay he would substitute something else that he "possessed," something he had control over; for example, his body, his wife, his freedom, or even his life. . . . Above all, however, the creditor could inflict every kind of indignity and torture upon the body of the debtor; for example, cut from it as much as seemed commensurate with the size of the debt—and everywhere and from early times one had exact evaluations, *legal* evaluations, of the individual limbs and parts of the body from this point of view, some of them going into horrible and minute detail. I consider it as an advance, as evidence of a freer, more generous, *more Roman* conception of law when the Twelve Tables of Rome decreed it a matter of indifference how much or how little the creditor cut off in such cases: *"si plus minusve secuerunt, ne fraude esto."* [9]

In the criminal law of antiquity, damage caused to property and damage caused to personality were equalized *inter se:* in ancient Roman law, while the delinquent debtor made a settlement with parts of his body, one guilty of mutilation answered out of his property. The concept of "state responsibility" in international law, which grew alongside the rule about reprisals, reflected a similar stage of development.

So much for the origin of the distinction between retorsion and reprisals and for the conventional so-called principle that

9. Nietzsche, supra note 1, at 64.

lawful reprisals and retaliations need only be in quantative proportionality to the alleged violation. It seems too obvious that
such policies are outmoded and no longer accord with modern
conditions in the world arena. Since the end of World War II
these conditions have worked to enlarge participation in international decision making and are bringing about the growth of a
truly world community. One expression of this development is
that the concept of "peace-loving nations" has come to replace the
former one of "civilized nations" to characterize participation in
international decision processes.[10]

Characterizing participants as peace-loving implies that, whatever the power relations may be in particular disputes, each participant can still disrupt, upset, and disorganize general relations,
and thus considerably spoil for others the values won in particular
conflicts. But the term also reflects attempts by some participants
to exclude others from world interaction by nonrecognition, political and economic containment, and the like. These are situations
in which interdependence is relatively meager, interaction is minimal, and common interests are peripheral to the conflicting ones.
But as a whole, current trends, as has earlier been demonstrated,
support and enable reciprocal modes of enforcement and coherent
principles of behavior. Decisions usually contain a communicative
signal: they are connected in form and in content to the alleged
wrongdoings so as not merely to vent one's power on another, to
intimidate and humiliate the target nation, but to secure reciprocal conformity to particular norms and relations.

It is a matter of common observation that interdependence will
continue to grow in the world arena. Punishments by reciprocity
are not only gradually supplanting punishments by expiation but
in some cases even end by being considered useless and harmful.
In the final analysis, what use is it to a party that the other suffers
damage after he has suffered on the other's account? For even in
reciprocal retaliations, instead of concentrating on oneself one
usually begins to think about one's opponent, looking for ways to
hurt him the most, and not to protect oneself against further harm
or to mitigate the damage that has already been caused. What
should matter is a restoration, not retorsion in itself, and this

10. Röling, supra note 2, at ch. 5.

usually cannot be effected through threats and warnings to cause equivalent or greater harms. Threats of retaliation can perhaps deter a party from initiating some undesired action, but once he has anticipated the costs involved in particular violations and deemed them worthwhile, they usually cannot compel him to act in restoration of the status quo ante. Instead, by a process of actions and reactions, other relations are also broken, or substantially altered, between the parties.

What seems so disturbing in nonperformance of international agreements is often not the redistribution of material values, but the precedent that is created by it for future interaction and general interdependence. At stake are not so much the immediate physical issues but the principle involved. For the treaty-breaker is above all a lawbreaker—a breaker not only of his word and his agreement with the other party but also of general trust and cooperation in regard to the community as a whole. By his act he seems to undermine and threaten the "sanctity" and "security of treaties," the interdependent foundation upon which most benefits and advantages of modern communal life rest. Without some expectations of stability, parties do not commit resources over time, aggregate production and sharing fall, and everyone loses. It is this stability of expectation which is critical to any system of order, and sanctions are applied precisely to police this fundamental aspect of social life. The ultimate test of the lawfulness of a sanction, be its form institutional or self-help, is thus the extent to which its response to a deviation from a specific treaty provision increases or decreases general stability of expectation.[11] For this purpose, both the precipitating breach as well as the range of alternative responses must be viewed equally.

The logic of punishments by reciprocity is that the lawbreaker is not only henceforth deprived of advantages and benefits similar to those he himself has negated, but that he is also reminded of what these benefits are really worth. Hence also, the explicit or tacit approval and the general understanding with which the reciprocal termination of treaties in retaliation for a breach of another or other treaties is met by third parties and the general public.

11. W. Reisman, *Nullity and Revision* ch. 8 (1971).

Retaliations, however, even when they are modified and held in check by refined notions of equality and reciprocity, are at bottom merely a further devlopment of the feeling of being aggrieved. They belong to the realm of reactive feelings, and because of this it is usually most difficult for those involved in them to remain objective, impartial, cool-headed, or fair. It is conceivable that, as the world's interaction increases and interdependence continues to grow, aggrieved parties may prefer not to avenge the offense themselves but to refer the dispute to community decision-making organs. This may happen because of the ever-increasing costs and mutual harm involved in retaliations, because retaliations mainly intend to harm the opponent and only provide for so-called negative equivalences in place of literal compensation for an injury, or because the violation of a particular treaty together with the ensuing lateral expansion of conflicts and the terminations of many other treaties that usually follow, could no longer be regarded as local and bilateral affairs. Self-help in this situation does not only mean that law is effectuated by each participant at his own risk, but also at the risk of the whole community. Reciprocal and bilateral punishments may put limits on the expansions of conflicts, but they cannot eliminate them. The latter may require some third-party judicial organization that will isolate disputes and embody the mutual guarantees that parties to agreements seek to give to each other.

It is possible that the growth in interdependence will increase the power of international institutions to achieve final settlements and even to issue expiative decisions. Of the two superpowers and few great powers effecting exchanges in the world arena, no one can emerge as the dominant regulator of the exchange relationships even with less powerful states; nor can any one afford to break general relationships over a particular and bilateral agreement. The community—the whole web of simultaneity and interdependence—will become more powerful than parties in particular conflicts. Constraint will originate from some abstract, universal arrangements, and will become institutionalized in the interests of all those having a part in community.

It is also possible, however, that as interaction increases and interdependence continues to grow, the power and self-confidence of the general world community as such will also increase, so that it may cease to take particular violations of international agreements so seriously. Such violations may no longer be considered dangerous and destructive to the whole world, as they are now. On the contrary, the world may even set out to protect the transgressor and itself against the retaliations of those he has directly harmed, in an effort to localize the affair and to prevent it from causing any further, let alone general, disturbance. The buds of such a development can already be seen in the recent Convention on the Law of Treaties which, while not unauthorizing unilateral termination (Article 65), seeks to contain and limit retaliations to the treaty originally in dispute (Articles 42[2] and 60), and directs the parties to negotiate their grievances within the organized framework of the conciliation commission (Article 66 and the Annex).

How many particular violations the world community can endure without suffering from them is the actual measure of interaction and interdependence. What are a few violations, the common reasoning in the future may go, for the security of so many treaties pertaining to such a great variety of commonly vital matters? Do a few spectacular breaches in themselves make international law not law? As interdependence continues to grow and the power and self-confidence of the world community increases, it may also be predicted, the law of treaties will become more and more moderate, and the common and substantive policies and principles of termination more and more liberal. It is a remote possibility, but not an unthinkable one, that the world community might attain such a measure of interdependence, consciousness of power, and self-confidence, that it could allow itself the luxury of letting those who seem to undermine the security of treaties in particular instances go unpunished.

A systematic development of the principle of protecting the community would require, not a mere tabulation of breaches and violations (with which the quantitative and qualitative measurement of punishment is associated), but an analysis of the conditions that are socially dangerous and an elaboration of the methods that must be applied in each given case in order to make the community secure.[12] A country can be made by equivalent measures

12. It is interesting to note here the thesis of the purged Russian legal philosopher Pashukanis. His analysis points to the relationship between law and ex-

to settle accounts for its government's conduct, but there is no sense in making it pay for the fact that the community recognizes it as dangerous. Authoritative decision would then concern itself not with punishment but with rehabilitation. Power would be used not to destroy but to heal and to build. The termination of international agreements would be deemed lawful on demand and would not represent the last word.

---

change, from which follows, according to him, that the juridic element in social relationships attains complete definiteness only in bourgeois society. Thus, he predicts, law will die out when this form of the equivalent relationship is ended. Pashukanis, "The General Theory of Law and Marxism," in *Soviet Legal Philosophy* 111 (Babb & Hazard ed. 1951). Of course, the so-called temporary Soviet state and government, like so many other structures pertaining to the subject of this book, seem in the meantime to have become permanent.

# APPENDIX A

# The Doctrine of Unequal Treaties

The question of the legal validity of the so-called unequal treaties has up to the beginning of this century received little attention. The term is of old origin: it was already defined by Vattel (1714–67), but later writers of the balance of power period found little use for it. During the last fifty years, "unequal treaties" has again become an attractive subject. The phrase has frequently appeared in governmental documents, which usually came out after recoveries from defeats in war, social revolutions, or colonial emancipations, and has consequently been expounded even by some Western European and American scholars.

The Convention on the Law of Treaties does not list inequality as a separate ground of termination or invalidity. Yet governments frequently express an extended view of other distinct principles, such as sovereign equality, coercion, and changing conditions, so as to apply them to unequal agreements.[1] Articles 53 and 64 on the effect of peremptory norms of international law, together with the Declaration on the Prohibition of Military, Political, or Economic Coercion in the Conclusion of Treaties (annexed to the Convention), may also support such interpretations.

Although governments and commentators often state that an agreement tainted with inequality is void, they never specify which factors may lawfully bring about this result. Some general and inconsistent criteria for inequality are implied from these statements, and they are all based on positivistic notions about international law (i.e. narrow focus on the single event of a given treaty). This, it may be recalled,

1. Detter, "The Problem of Unequal Treaties," 15 *Int'l & Comp. L. Q.* 1069, 1085 (1966); Lester, "Bizerta and the Unequal Treaty Theory," 11 *Int'l & Comp. L. Q.* 847 (1962); Buell, "The Termination of Unequal Treaties," 1927 *Proc. Am. Soc. Int'l L.* 90; Putney, "The Termination of Unequal Treaties," id. at 87. Haraszti, "Main Tendencies of Development in the Law of Treaties," 13 *Acta Juridica Academiae Scientiarum Hungaricae* 307, 321–22 (1971). For historical discussion see C. Alexandrowicz, *An Introduction to the History of the Law of Nations in the East Indies* ch. 7 (1967).

must lead in particular applications to results that not only are un-realistic but also negate the very sense of equality the doctrine is said to protect.

While a full exploration of this rich subject cannot be made here, a more limited treatment, corresponding to discussions in previous chapters, is still in order. It suggests an innovative interpretation of the term "unequal treaty," providing, however, for a principle of treaty termination rather than of initial invalidity.

## EXISTING CRITERIA

Since inequality in power relation is an everyday phenomenon, it cannot by itself be considered a sufficient cause for invalidating treaties. Hence it has been suggested that a treaty becomes unequal only when its provisions are extremely advantageous to the great power and burdensome or "enslaving" to the small state. So stated, the principle of unequal treaties is often regarded as international law's equivalent of doctrines of unilateral contract, or naked promise, in domestic laws. To prevent innocent and helpless individuals from being exploited, unilateral transactions of such persons, even though they have full legal power to make contracts, may still have no binding force. Similarly, unequal international agreements are claimed to be those

> by which "the things promised are neither the same nor equally proportioned" between the contracting parties. They "are more properly applied to treaties where promises are made only by one party, without any corresponding engagements, either equal or unequal, by the other." They create unilateral obligations, lacking reciprocity and principles of *quid pro quo* which, according to Vattel and Phillmore, are "requisite for treaty between states." [2]

Private law doctrines of unilateral contract deal with single and isolated transactions between individuals. Hence such principles cannot be analogously applied to treaties which usually form only a small part of a host of ongoing relationships between the parties. Although the terms of a particular treaty may be unbalanced, the seemingly dis-advantaged party may still be deriving benefits for the transaction from other transactions between the parties.

Difficulties may still exist, however, even with a doctrinal formula-

2. Tseng Yu-Hao, *The Termination of Unequal Treaties in International Law* 9–10 (1931; note omitted). The author quotes from Halleck, *Elements of International Law* 106 (1866), and R. Phillmore, 2 *Commentaries Upon International Law* 71 (1917).

tion that requires, before any conclusion regarding the inequality of a treaty can be reached, a broader contextual evaluation of its provisions. In most such controversies the values to be compared are not merely tangible. They include high feelings of national pride and demands for mutual respect. The complaints against these treaties are not merely that they do not provide for an exchange of benefits, but that their larger context is expiatory, not reciprocal.[3] In response to this very problem, Vattel draws a distinction between equal treaties and equal alliances:

> When people speak of equal treaties, they have commonly in their minds a double idea of equality, viz. equality in the engagements, and equality in the dignity of the contracting parties. It becomes therefore necessary to remove all ambiguity; and for that purpose, we may make a distinction between *equal treaties* and *equal alliances*. . . .
>
> *Unequal treaties* are those in which the allies do not reciprocally promise to each other the same things, or things equivalent; and an *alliance* is *unequal* when it makes a difference in the dignity of the contracting parties. It is true, that most commonly an unequal treaty will be at the same time an unequal alliance; as great potentates are seldom accustomed to give or to promise more than is given or promised to them, unless such concessions be fully compensated in the article of honour and glory; and, on the other

3. Tseng Yu-Hao's survey of unequal treaties in the thirties reveals that among their characteristics is "an element of a command in the language of some of these treaties—a command in the tone of a superior to an inferior, lacking the etiquette of mutual respect and friendly courtesy" (Tseng Yu-Hao, supra note 2, at 19–20). An illustration is the so-called Capitulation Treaties that were concluded by the middle of the last century between European powers and countries such as China, Turkey, Persia, and Egypt. These treaties provided full jurisdiction over their subjects to foreign consuls in Afro-Asian countries.

They contained intimidating clauses which protected the "superiority" and "dignity" of the consuls. It was contended by European jurists that unequal treaties were needed in countries where institutions were inferior or different from the civilization of most European and American States and Japan (1 L. Oppenheim, *International Law* 148 [1905]). These treaties were usually entered into for an indefinite period, and their beneficiaries continued to reject, even in this century, the many attempts at their revision. A great many of them were finally terminated by the deprived parties, and the doctrinal debates regarding the lawfulness of these "unilateral" terminations still preoccupy modern scholars (see Detter, supra note 1, at 1087). Most treaty provisions currently in effect satisfy formal requirements of verbal equality and mutual respect. The formal language used, however, is only symptomatic of the real problem.

hand, a weak state does not submit to burdensome conditions without being obliged also to acknowledge the superiority of her ally. . . .

Treaties *in which the inequality prevails on the side of the inferior power*—that is to say, those which impose on the weaker party more extensive obligations or greater burdens, or bind him down to oppressive or disagreeable conditions—these unequal treaties, I say, are always at the same time unequal alliances; for, the weaker party never submits to burdensome conditions, without being obliged also to acknowledge the superiority of his ally. These conditions are commonly imposed by the conqueror, or dictated by necessity, which obliges a weak state to seek the protection or assistance of another more powerful; and by this very step, the weaker state acknowledges her own inferiority. Besides, this forced inequality in a treaty of alliance is a disparagement to her, and lowers her dignity, at the same time that it exalts that of her more powerful ally. Sometimes also, the weaker state not being in a condition to promise the same succours as the more powerful one, it becomes necessary that she should compensate for her inability in this point, by engagements which degrade her below her ally, and often even subject her, in various respects, to his will.[4]

Vattel concludes that it is not unequal treaties per se which ought to be considered invalid, but unequal "alliances" (i.e. relations, communal bonds, norms) in which the greater obligations fall upon the weaker state. He warns that one can either maintain that it is not lawful to conclude unequal treaties based on unequal alliances or that parties are entirely free from the obligations of law. In other words, the debate about the legal validity of unequal treaty relations concerns the very question of whether international relations are or should be governed by some law, and is not a debatable matter concerning the content of a particular rule or doctrine.

## Modern Criteria

It is easy to see why Vattel's view is correct. The problem of the legal validity of unequal treaties and the more general problem of the methods appropriate to lawful enforcement of treaties are quite the same. They combine so readily that it is inescapable to think of them

4. E. de Vattel, *The Law of Nations; or, the Principles of the Law of Nature* 199–201 (J. Chitty ed. 1854).

as two sides of the same coin. This is because the main characteristic of a treaty which provides for a contextual inequality of burdens and benefits is that it is not amenable to enforcement by reciprocal means, but only by expiation. The essential element in reciprocal enforcement, it has been noted, is formal and substantive connection between the response and the alleged breach of the treaty. However, a contextual inequality by definition means the inability of the objecting side, who is on the upper side of the inequality, to confine his retaliation to the alleged treaty violation in the same or similar subject matter and in a parallel instrument of decision. There are in this situation no similar treaty relations by which, as far as burdens and benefits are concerned, the bargaining positions of the parties can be reversed. The only way to enforce such an unequal treaty is for the objecting side to resort to some punitive action in matters far removed from the subject matter of the given dispute. And when the benefits which are derived by the objecting side from an unequal treaty clearly exceed and overshadow all its other relations with the claimant party, the only enforcement measures that are likely to succeed are the threat or actual use of force.

Since the effect of unequal treaties depends on the expiatory nature of the measures taken in order to enforce them, the contemporary trends of decision toward reciprocal ways of enforcement may have a direct bearing on the question of their legal validity. A customary international principle to the effect that responses to alleged treaty violations should always be confined to reprisals in the same or similar subject matter and in a parallel form of decision, is equivalent to one stating that unequal treaties (i.e. situations in which such a symbolic connection is not possible) cannot be lawfully enforced. This is, of course, not really different from saying that such an unequal treaty can be lawfully terminated by the deprived and humiliated party.

Thus stated, the principle can be categorized as one of treaty enforcement. It purports to answer what is a lawful response to the violation of an international agreement. At the same time, these policies about treaty enforcement clarify the substantive grounds of termination. In other words, according to the suggested criteria, the two traditionally separate questions of when the termination of a treaty is authorized, and of how the other side should respond to an unlawful termination or violation of a treaty are tied together and receive one and the same answer.[5]

5. For the relation between legal duties, voluntary agreements, exchange, the bond of reciprocity, and equality, see L. Fuller, *The Morality of Law* 23 (1964). Note that the approach in the text enables us to bridge some of international

law's traditional gap between substantive and procedural rules. The distinction might be useful in highly institutionalized arenas where a great number of important decisions are settled in courts. It is obvious that in the contemporary decentralized world arena, the terms "substantive" grounds of termination and "procedures" of termination assume an altogether different meaning. These so-called procedures are for the most part, nothing but reciprocal strategies and tactics for implementing decisions. The present difficulties in the Convention on the Law of Treaties have arisen partly because foes of lawful terminations have managed to write into law some procedural provisions which are at cross-purposes with the substantive ones. This was done on the pretext that, in the absence of effective judicial machinery, the policies of termination are a weapon subject to gross abuse (supra, ch. 6, note 39). But no smoke screen of irrelevant legal categories can be allowed to obscure the need for the termination from time to time of some treaties in situations that lack judicial organs. In these situations, enforcement powers are subject to equal, or sometimes even grosser, abuse than the authority to terminate or invalidate treaties. Combining termination and enforcement in one principle will eliminate the double standard traditionally accorded to them.

# APPENDIX B

# Unequal Military Bases

The inequality of some treaties is nowhere more vividly demonstrated than in military bases, a problem cluster which, however, because it may involve military hostilities, must be distinguished from all other types of treaty termination. Treaties establishing military bases, thus, may perhaps require an additional set of policies.[1]

## THE PREVAILING DOGMAS

The termination of agreements concerning military bases abroad is currently subject to two diametrically opposed views. According to one view, being territorial or executed treaties, their termination should be considered a political and not a legal matter; in this context this is a euphemism for naked power. To such treaties, the argument goes, regular principles of termination cannot or should not apply. Rather, termination should be effected only by a new and explicit agreement. This view is usually not explained by any sophisticated consideration of policies. It is supposedly the logical result of some mechanical application of normative propositions,[2] and it must inevitably lead to absurd results that negate the policies relevant to this matter. It precludes, for example, the termination of executed treaties even by judicial or semijudicial organs.[3] Furthermore, it is incompatible with the universally accepted principle that treaties of alliance, not concluded for a specified period only, can be lawfully terminated on demand.[4] There is an obvious irony here: military bases abroad are currently concluded as part of a political alliance, and as such they represent even heavier commitments. The same policy that is applied

1. Conflicts about termination of military bases have been discussed throughout the previous chapters along with other types of conflicts. The following discussion is concerned with only one additional aspect of these conflicts.

2. Supra ch. 1, note 22.

3. Id. See also supra ch. 6, note 39.

4. See p. 33, note 50, supra. For the origin of the policy of flexibility of alignment and its relation to the philosophy of laissez-faire politics, see ch. 1 supra. A similar rule is applied to treaties of commerce.

to the latter should at least be applied to the first. And quite apart from all that, the exclusion of military base treaties from the application of legal principles is based on assumptions and leads to results that flout the most fundamental modern notions of equality and reciprocity.

This brings us to the other view on the matter, according to which treaties establishing military bases, not concluded for a specified short period only, are of no legal validity: "[S]uch agreements and treaties are based upon an inequality of rights and inequality of obligations. They have an invalid basis in international law and are incompatible with its norms and therefore void." [5] The deprived parties, it is argued, are entitled simply to disregard them.

While this view may, in certain cases, be jurisprudentially correct, it totally ignores the realities of power in conflicts relating to military bases. There can be no quarrel with the loud condemnation at the United Nations of unequal and other degrading practices. Such hippodrome gestures, however, require only a mimeograph machine. To describe a treaty as invalid does not by itself make it so, and authoritative pronouncements to this effect would run the risk not only of inviting acts of violence to dislodge a base, but also of not being able to influence the development of the conflict once such acts were initiated.

For this reason, the General Assembly's resolutions on unequal military bases usually sidestep doctrinal questions such as whether a given treaty is ipso facto invalid. They merely uphold the claimant case, if at all, and require the parties to enter into direct talks on termination.[6] Another step requires not only that legal principles help

5. As argued during the U.N. debate on the Bizerta dispute, quoted in Lester, supra. app. 1, note 1, at 850.

6. The resolution regarding the French military base in Bizerta (GA Resolution 1672 [S-III], GAOR, Third Special Session, Supp. 1 [A/4860] p. 2 [1962]) states that the General Assembly:

2. *Recognises* the sovereign right of Tunisia to call for the withdrawal of all French armed forces present on its territory without its consent;

3. *Calls* upon the Governments of France and Tunisia to enter into immediate negotiations to devise peaceful and agreed measures in accordance with the principles of the Charter for the withdrawal of all French armed forces from the Tunisian territory.

While this resolution clearly recognizes the validity of the Tunisian claim to termination, it requires that the complete evacuation of foreign troops be achieved by negotiated measures. Since resistance to direct talks and agenda formation are key problems in conflicts about termination, any authoritative pronouncement on these matters might influence the way they develop. Furthermore, characterizing

initiate the negotiative process through which a desired outcome may result, but also that they influence the negotiators to arrive at certain outcomes.[7]

## COMPONENTS OF A MORE REALISTIC PRINCIPLE

The simplest solution is to put a time limit on the duration of all foreign military bases. Such a rule may have several advantages. First, the period chosen may be more widely accepted than current doctrines, since it represents a compromise between the "never" and "always" dogmas. Second, a quantitative measure may satisfy the demand for clarity and involuntary application of the rule during bargaining under conditions of inequality of power (for example, the Soviet Union ardently supports the doctrine of unequal military bases but denies its relevancy to bases in the Warsaw Pact countries). It cannot be made a subject of open-ended arguments and doctrinal debates, and will therefore help not to yield one's lawful claim.

The appropriate measure in this case is one of a number of years representing some symbolic significance which may therefore be exploited in order to influence behavior. Indeed, for a commital strategy the period chosen may be arbitrary, or its policy relevance—if any—purely coincidental, so long as it conveys some symbolic message bearing on the case.[8] Such a technique of absorbing into rules quantitative measures whose legitimacy derives from what they symbolize, is quite familiar in legal history. It has been frequently used, along with many

---

the topic for negotiation as "termination" or as the "withdrawal of *all* foreign forces," considerably changes the bargaining positions of the parties in favor of the claimant (ch. 4 supra).

7. There are in this context inherent limitations on the power of General Assembly resolutions. Britain, for instance, simply disregarded a similar resolution calling for negotiations on Gibraltar (ch. 4 supra). It is also possible for a reluctant party to go through the formal appearances of compliance while stalling on an agreement. Further, the claimant government itself, being at a gross military or economic disadvantage, might be forced to accept a new agreement that in effect perpetuates the existing state of affairs. After all, the very notion of unequal treaty means that it cannot be bargained for in a regularly reciprocal manner. It is therefore often not sufficient merely to require the parties to negotiate on the termination of the treaty, especially since the Convention on the Law of Treaties does not provide for the regulation of the moves and countermoves the parties make during these negotiations.

8. For the relevancy of symbols to the bargaining process, see ch. 4 supra. In certain cultures numerical formulations may carry intense emotive tones. Thirteen, for example, is considered unlucky. Seven and eleven in certain subcultures are considered lucky. The number eighteen has a powerful connotation in Jewish theology since it means, when translated to Hebrew characters, "life."

other techniques available to courts (governments and legal scholars as well), to solve the dilemma of how to assume legislative functions while stirring a minimum of public controversy. The Common Law Rule against Perpetuities, for example, was originally expressed in flexible judicial terms of a "reasonable" period. It slowly evolved from an instrument of contextual investigation to a stable quantitative measure:

> The original formulation was characteristically vague; the final formulation, "lives in being plus twenty-one years," for all its irrationalities, is in theory capable of "mathematical" accuracy in application. The twenty-one-year period is not measured by anybody's minority, although the choice was not entirely accidental. It has *some* rational relationship to the period of minority, but it was powerfully influenced by the fact that twenty-one years was an available *number* with preexisting legal significance, so that it could be adopted and embodied within a rule of law without transgressing the bounds of judicial legitimacy.[9]

Similar manipulations of symbols, to achieve both authority and effective power for a rule, have also been used with regard to customary international law. In 1702, Bynkershoek laid down the principle that a state's sovereignty extends as far out to the sea as a cannon-shot will reach, understood at that time to be three miles. The strength of the principle was in what it symbolized and not in any material security it offered to litoral states. The three-mile rule was gaining acceptance during periods in which a cannon range exceeded this limit, although echoes of the cannon-shot rationale were still to be found in diplomatic documents.[10] Obviously, what matters in a rule-creating strategy of this sort is the symbolic quality of the number chosen as such, and not any direct policy relevance that it may or may not have.

### THE PRINCIPLE PROPOSED HERE

The number 18 seems to qualify best for a symbolic measure of the lawful duration of military bases. The legitimacy of an eighteen-year-limit principle derives from the content of the very claims and arguments that give rise to controversies about foreign military bases. A recurrent argument against their indefinite or prolonged continuation

9. L. Friedman, "Legal Rules and the Process of Social Change," 19 *Stan. L. Rev.* 786, 825 (1967; notes omitted).

10. J. Brierly, *The Law of Nations* 202ff. (1963); Kent, "Historical Origins of the Three-Mile Limit," 48 *Am. J. Int'l L.* 537 (1954).

is that one generation should not tie up succeeding generations with physical military commitments. Temporary decision makers, it is often contended, should be somehow restricted in making commitments for future generations on critical questions such as whether to go to war or to stay neutral, with whom to side and against whom to fight.[11] Certainly, those who have to fight wars should be given a say in deciding whether they ought to be fought. The argument is valid for people on both sides of the military commitment.

In most countries men are subjected to compulsory military service at the age of eighteen. A period of eighteen years, therefore, is capable of universally being considered a "generation" for purposes of military commitment. The commitment should be renegotiated at least at the conclusion of this period.

The fact that most eighteen-year-olds do not actively participate in the making of major decisions, or that in some countries the voting age may be higher, is immaterial. What matters is that the number 18 is capable of serving as a highly evocative and abstract symbol. It is a shorthand, it can evoke from people more than can usually be verbally condensed into any other alternative rule about the invalidity or termination of treaties establishing military bases.

Admittedly, eighteen years may often be too long a period for modern military planning. There is no reason, however, to be over-concerned in this case with the partial sacrifice of policy for effectiveness's sake. Most modern agreements of military bases that pursue genuine military alignment, and that are based on true planning, already contain provisions limiting their duration or otherwise specifying the time and procedures for their revision or termination. The general principle is necessary only for the minority of treaties which have been concluded for an indefinite or very long time. For the duration of such treaties, a time limit of eighteen years constitutes a significant improvement.[12]

11. Overseas bases have, of course, a variety of less important purposes. The expenditures connected with their construction and operation, for example, are a form of economic aid. When Britain in 1967 announced plans to withdraw two-thirds of its forces stationed in Malta, the latter responded by denouncing the defense agreement under which British bases had been established. The conflict developed into the regular action-reaction pattern. Britain threatened not to provide Malta with financial and economic aid over the following ten years promised under a 1964 financial agreement if Malta did not honor the defense agreement. *New York Times,* Jan. 28, 1967, p. 5, col. 1. (city ed.).

12. The application of the proposed principle is "automatic" in the sense that treaties of military bases will be considered as terminated ipso facto after a dura-

tion of eighteen years. This period is usually sufficiently long to justify foregoing any negotiations on compensation for the alleged deprivatory effects of termination. Bargaining may, however, still take place on the question of whether the foreign forces should continue to be stationed under a formally new treaty. Pressures can, of course, be applied on the terminating party to renew the treaty. But the proposed principle is symbolically strong enough to provide a willing party with a commitment not to yield to such a demand.

The proposed eighteen-year argument, if repeatedly invoked by parties through Article 56 of the Convention on the Law of Treaties, may be developed into an effective principle. Article 56 recognizes the validity of principles allowing for termination upon demand of specific types of treaties, without indicating which principles or noting precisely which types of treaties.

# Index